War Dead

D1554924

War Dead

Western Societies and the Casualties of War

Luc Capdevila and Danièle Voldman

Translated by Richard Veasey

Edinburgh University Press

© Éditions Payot et Rivages, 2006

Copyright in this translation © Richard Veasey

First published 2002, Éditions Payot et Rivages
106 boulevard Saint-Germain
75006 Paris
France

Edinburgh University Press Ltd
22 George Square, Edinburgh

Typeset in 11/13 Century SchoolBook and Neue Helvetica by
TechBooks, India, and
printed and bound in Great Britain by The Cromwell Press, Trowbridge, Wilts

A CIP record for this book is available from the British Library

ISBN-10 0 7486 2297 7 (hardback)
ISBN-13 978 0 7486 2297 9 (hardback)
ISBN-10 0 7486 2298 5 (paperback)
ISBN-13 978 0 7486 2298 6 (paperback)

The right of Luc Capdevila and Danièle Voldman to be
identified as authors of this work has been asserted in
accordance with the Copyright, Designs and Patents Act 1988.

Ouvrage publié avec le concours du Ministère français
chargé de la culture – Centre national du livre.

Published with the assistance of the French Ministry of
Culture – National Book Centre.

Published with the support of the Edinburgh University Scholarly
Publishing Initiatives Fund.

Contents

Foreword

This book is part of the affective turn in historical studies. In the 1960s, much social history followed social scientific paradigms. Some studies were quantitative; others were concerned with social conflict in general and class conflict in particular. It took time for scholars to abandon these approaches to social history. Quantification produced some interesting results, in particular in demographic history, but the interpretive gains rarely matched the enormous effort it took to register them. And much of labour history was 'Marxisant' in character. Again it took time for these practitioners to abandon the view that we could read political activity out of social position. By the 1980s both of these pillars of social history were gone.

In their place a new kind of social history arose which was centrally concerned with social practices and the language by which men and women in the past tried to understand their world. Here was a bridge which enabled a new generation of historians – including Capdevila and Voldman – to cross over from social history into its stepsister cultural history. Never fully separate, these two subdisciplines have merged to produce a rich literature on many subjects, including the cultural history of warfare and its aftermath.

Cultural history is a house of many mansions, but at its core are two subjects. The first is the social history of representations, of the images and notions through which we understand the world. The second is the study of signifying practices, those social activities which perform these representations in the light of day. This book is a fine example of both.

One way to understand their book is to see it as a twenty-first-century version of Freud's *Thoughts for the Time on War and Death*. What interests them is Freud's insight that in order to understand life we need to understand death. And in the twentieth century very few societies had the good fortune of giving their citizens the choice of dying one at a time. Mass death became a central element of social and cultural life, and there it has remained.

Among the most powerful signifying practices are those dealing with the commemoration of the victims of war in the twentieth century. These efforts have been studied in many different ways. Initially the emphasis was on State agencies of 'laughter and forgetting', as Milan Kundera felicitously put it. The approach used by the authors of this book is different. It is very much bottom-up and comparative, reaching from Chile and Argentina, to the United States and France.

The authors of this book offer us a striking chronology. What Capdevila and Voldman show is how deeply the shadow of the First World War is cast on our own generation. These two people are both historians of the Second World War, but locate their research within a longer time frame. They show that it was in the Great War that representations of war emerged which have endured. The first such notion is that war is not about nobility, but primarily and overwhelmingly about suffering and killing. It is not that many of those who died in war were in any sense ignoble; there was honour and dignity abundant among the men in uniform in all the wars of the twentieth century. But nobility has shrivelled as the statistics of mass death have grown and grown since 1914. What the Great War did in Europe, much more than in America, was to give the term 'the glorious dead' a taste as of ashes. This difference between representations of war derived from the 1914–18 conflict has endured and helps explain the vast distance which separates American from European perceptions of war both before and after 11 September 2001.

One of the innovations of this study is how it places the Holocaust in a continuum. We now see those who survive war primarily as victims. And the Jews of Europe were undoubtedly victims. But that understanding of victimhood antedated the Nazi plan to exterminate the Jews. It was in the 1914–18 War that images of bodies piled up like logs emerged, and it was then that industrialised slaughter took the lives of 9 million men. In a way, the conclusion is unavoidable: no Verdun, no Auschwitz. It is in this framework that we should appreciate the contribution of this book.

This shift in perceptions of war and death emerged most clearly around the question of how to find, enumerate, bury, and commemorate the dead. The first three decisions were military and political in character, but the fourth – commemoration – became a focus more for civil society than for the State. To be sure, political leaders tried to manipulate commemoration of war dead for their own purposes, but this matter was so explosive – and so full of affect – that it could not be contained. Small groups of people at every level of society developed their own ways of honouring and remembering the dead. These people brought their own feelings, ideas and beliefs to bear on this matter, and whether they were concerned to commemorate Vietnam, or the 'disappeared' of Argentina, or the victims of Pinochet's regime in Chile, they acted on the basis of representations of victimhood emerging largely from the First World War, representations which became universal after Auschwitz and Hiroshima.

Representations which endure are those which trigger emotion. The affective turn has brought us closer to the bedrock of emotions shared by millions of people over the last century of industrialised warfare, both wars fought against internal 'enemies' and against enemies of a different nationality. These emotions are at the core of our contemporary fascination with memory.

At the end of this study of loss and mourning, what emerges most clearly is not only a sense of the way war betrays the dignity of ordinary men and women. What they do after the wrenching knowledge of loss, irretrievable loss, is also arresting. Very often they re-gather their humanity and reaffirm life. This stubborn refusal of men and women to accept mass death passively, to let the names of the dead fade away, and their power to shape the ways we understand war and loss of life in it, leaves me with a sense of uplift, of affirmation at the end of this study of the transcendence of war.

Jay Winter
Yale University

Preface

'Our dead': from wooden crosses to the crematoria of Auschwitz, from shadows imprinted on stone at Hiroshima to the smoking ruins of the World Trade Center, from Algerians swallowed up in the dark waters of the Seine on the night of 17 October 1961 to the mass graves of Srebrenica; those killed in war haunt the collective memory of the living and disturb their peace. For, much more than ordinary death, death in war is special. It is at once heroic and appalling, dreaded and expected, unjust and accepted, and in no way resembles what was imagined before battle.

From the latter half of the nineteenth century, Western societies have been confronted with death on a mass scale produced by wars in an industrial age, and in particular with the millions of young men decimated during the First World War and then with the tens of millions of men and women of all ages wiped out in the Second. What did those who escaped do with all these human remains as they struggled for their own survival? Did the brutality, the suddenness, the sheer numbers of those killed change the relationship with death in the West?

If death itself does not permit indifference, death on a mass scale marks for ever the lives of generations who remain. Doctor Hachiya, who was in charge of a small hospital in Hiroshima and who survived the atomic explosion, wrote of one of his patients incinerated on 12 August 1945: 'Try to imagine the huge number of victims! Burying the dead in accordance with customary rites would have been an impossible luxury. But even taking into account the circumstances, it pained me that no priest was present to recite the prayer for the dead.'[1]

Death in war plunges those who mourn into an abyss because they do not have the bodies of those they have lost. 'We have a large photo of him on the wall,' said the young widow of a Soviet combatant killed on Afghan soil. 'My daughter says to me: "Take Daddy down. I want to play with him..." She surrounds his picture with toys and talks to him... I take her to nursery school,.... she cries... "Where is my Daddy?"... I am worn out with crying every day... If you could only come back for a moment... See how your daughter has grown!'[2]

The war dead are also a burden because countless bodies are a source of exasperation to those who are left behind, especially when unforeseen circumstances surround the tragedy of loss. 'We had to drag his body, his kitbag, his bullet-proof jacket, his helmet. He did not feel sorry for us', grumbled a Soviet veteran of the war in Afghanistan, criticising a fellow soldier who had committed suicide during their operation: 'He knew quite well that we carry the bodies of our men with us, that we do not leave them where they are.'[3]

The evolution of our relationship with death has a long history. The first signs of the simplification of funeral rites became apparent in the second half of the nineteenth century though there was considerable variation from place to place.[4] Historians and anthropologists of death have spoken of a break occurring in funeral practices in the West around the time of the First World War.[5] Amongst the most striking manifestations of new forms of behaviour, they noticed a decline in the observance of mourning, a lessening in the social expression of grief resulting from loss and a disaffection with large bourgeois ceremonies in which the dead body became a rallying point for the living. This 'totally new way of dying', for which Philippe Ariès coined the phrase 'inverted death', initiated a 'pornography of death',[6] the expression used by the English ethnographer, Geoffrey Gorer. He was one of the first to observe during the 1950s the tendency for Western societies to create a taboo around death – and more particularly around corpses – just as they had done with sex.[7] He saw the 1914–18 War, if not as the crucible, at least as an important factor in accelerating the process of change in behaviour. From his childhood memories of around 1917–18 in England where he was born, he recalled that the wearing of mourning clothes had become rare, whereas it had been widespread at the beginning of the conflict.[8] In his view, the weakening of the social practice of mourning, which became much more marked during the inter-war period, was a consequence of mass death, which made strict observance of old rituals untenable, though their role was to lessen the pain. The fact that this had become impossible only deepened the acute distress felt by the bereaved confronted with the pain of their loss.

Geoffrey Gorer's intuitions remained mere hypotheses, as Philippe Ariès and Michel Vovelle did not include the study of death in war in the work that they did, given their legitimate feeling that it was a whole new subject. Why study those killed in war, since war involves killing? Especially since studying how a society and its survivors reacted to the masses of bodies which confronted them is a disturbing, difficult and dreadfully complex issue. Yet it offers an essential perspective for an understanding of the dynamics of warfare and for grasping the mechanisms by which war remains a legitimate human institution, both from the point of view of public opinion and from that of the organisation of international relations by the community of nations.

Though it is an obvious issue, historians of the contemporary period have not dealt with the relationship between war and death as a whole and over a period of time. But, because it is linked to current questions arising from the increase in the number of bloody conflicts throughout the world, recent research has begun to cast light upon it. For the most part focused on the First World War,[9] this research approaches the subject from the point of view of mourning, remembrance and commemoration.[10] We are concerned, in this essay, with the fate of those killed in war, through what happens to their remains (bodies, fragments of bodies, bits, ashes, the absence of any remains), as well as with the attitudes of survivors and their feelings in the face of tragic events.

As two historians of the Second World War, our knowledge of French archives of this period provided us with the basic reference material for our study. But instead of it being an empirical study of a particular conflict, we wanted to reflect upon war and death today, when bodies are no longer included in the public discourse about contemporary conflicts. We are thinking, of course, of the way in which the information systems of the United States' army[11] and of the French, Israeli and Iraqi armies have dealt with the issue during the last decades of the twentieth century. We call to mind as well the screening of the attacks of 11 September 2001 by the North American networks which, whilst broadcasting loops of film showing the World Trade Center on fire, exhibited a collective reflex in banning from their screens scenes of people jumping out of windows, and in not showing any bodies or human remains.[12] It was an enigmatic moment... The war dead and the violence of their death fill this void sanctioned by the powers that be, invading television, computer and cinema screens through fiction, eyewitness accounts and documentaries.

The particular relationships which Western societies have developed with those killed in war go back to the end of the eighteenth and the beginning of the nineteenth centuries, a time when a feeling of nationhood began to assert itself. As a consequence, the individual and collective sense of sharing a destiny has been reinforced by international wars and by the death of those who were thought to have laid down their life so that the nation might continue to exist. But the shift towards conflict in the industrial age in the second half of the nineteenth century as well as the evolution of Western societies towards democratisation and individualisation, have progressively transformed their attitudes towards war and death.

The interactions resulting from conflict within the West, from alliances and negotiations between allies and enemies, created links and models which gave that Western world a cultural unity so far as the history of those killed in war was concerned. From the first military cemeteries which appeared around 1850 in the United States following the war with Mexico, to the tombs of the unknown soldiers who were buried simultaneously on 11 November 1920 in Westminster Abbey in London and at the Arc de Triomphe in Paris, a particular way of dealing with the war dead and of creating a collective memory has developed over a century and a half in Europe and on the continent of America. To have gone beyond the Western sphere would have led us to work on cultural areas (Africa, the Middle East, Asia) where the relationship with the individual and with death is fundamentally different. As we decided to analyse what took place within a civilisation, a shared culture was imperative. So, because of the dynamic processes which affected this particular sphere, within which the echoes of key events resonate (the trenches of 1914–18, the massacres in Spain, the Holocaust, Hiroshima, the violence in Algeria, the 'disappeared' in Argentina, etc.), our work is based on those wars which the West has witnessed since the nineteenth century. It draws upon three geographical areas which have suffered a great deal and in which practical experience of death in war and the rituals accompanying it have been so marked, thus enabling us to establish connections. The three areas are Western Europe, North America and the Southern Cone, that part of South American where the most bloody wars in the region have taken place since the end of the nineteenth century.

Our essay, whilst offering a history of death which has occurred on the countless battlefields of industrialised warfare, opens with a question that is more complex than it might seem: how does one define a person killed in war? That is because the definition of war dead, and therefore the possibility of identifying and counting them, has varied according to the period and the society concerned. Dying in war is a dated concept! Just as the way in which heroes and common soldiers, enemies and friends have been mourned has evolved, so the treatment of the bodies of the dead and the practice of funeral rites have undergone, sometimes unexpected, twists and turns. Does war, a collective activity borne and undertaken by the individual, express the ultimate meaning of society? In whatever way it has been expressed, the grief of loss which it causes, whether silent or deafeningly loud, public or private, at least defines its contours.

Notes

1. Michiko Hachiya, *Le Journal d'Hiroshima. 6 août–30 septembre 1945* (Paris: Albin Michel, 1956), p. 73.
2. Svetlana Alexievitch, *Les Cercueils de zinc* (Paris: Christian Bourgois, 1991), p. 76.
3. Ibid. p. 156.
4. Philippe Ariès, *L'Homme devant la mort* (Paris: Seuil, 1977); Michel Vovelle, *La mort en Occident de 1300 à nos jours* (Paris: Gallimard, 1983); more recently, a monograph by Robert V. Wells, *Facing the 'King of Terrors'. Death and Society in an American Community. 1750–1990* (Cambridge: Cambridge University Press, 2000).
5. By way of example, Arnold Van Gennep, *Le Folklore français. Du berceau à la tombe* (Paris, Robert Laffont, 1998 [1st edn 1943]).
6. Ariès, *L'Homme devant la mort*, p. 554.
7. Geoffrey Gorer, *Ni pleurs ni couronnes* (Paris: EPEL, 1995). The work opens with the French translation of 'Pornography of death', published in *Encounter* in October 1955, a text recognised as groundbreaking by historians and sociologists of death such as Philippe Ariès, Michel Vovelle, Louis-Vincent Thomas, etc.
8. Ibid. pp. 36–7.
9. Thierry Hardier and Jean-François Jagielski, *Combattre et mourir pendant la Grande Guerre (1914–1925)* (Paris: Imago, 2001).
10. Carine Trevisan, *Les Fables du deuil. La Grande Guerre: mort et écriture* (Paris: PUF, 2001); Stéphane Audoin-Rouzeau, *Cinq deuils de guerre, 1914–1918* (Paris: Noêsis, 2001); Jay Winter, *Sites of Memory, Sites of Mourning. The Great War in European Cultural History* (Cambridge: Cambridge University Press, 1995); G. Kurt Piehler, *Remembering War. The*

American Way (Washington & London: Smithsonian Institution Press, 1995).

11. We use the term 'United States' to refer to the United States of America and the adjective 'American' in relation to the whole continent.

12. Michel Guerrin, 'Les morts sans visage du World Trade Centre', *Le Monde*, 21 September 2001, p. 14; Daniel Psenny, 'Polémique autour de la "censure" des images', *Le Monde*, Media supplement, 23 September 2001, p. 6.

Acknowledgements

Writing jointly when one person lives in Paris and the other in Rennes, covering a vast geographical area moreover, requires financial resources which our institutions have generously granted us. We thank the Centre for Historical Research on West European Societies and Cultures (CRHISCO) and the Institute for the Study of Present-Day History (IHTP).

We were warmly welcomed by the office of the Secretary of State for War Veterans (the sections concerned with citations and heritage); the Historical Service of the Army (SHAT); the Historical Service of the Air Force (SHAA); the library of the Military Museum of the Invalides; the departmental archives of the Bouches-du-Rhône, Finistère, Ille-et-Vilaine, the Seine and the Somme; the archives of the Prefecture of Police in Paris; the State Financial Institution for Deposit and Consignment; the municipal archives of Laurens (Hérault), Rennes (Ille-et-Vilaine), Trélazé (Maine-et-Loire); the archives of the Red Cross in Paris and Geneva; those at the Andrès Barbero Museum in Asunción; the archives of the Military Museum; the archives of the Ministry of Defence; the National Archives and those of the Bibliothèque nationale.

Jean Astruc, Jacques Barcelo, Raphaëlle Branche, Florent Brayard, Catherine Brice, Claudia Castro, Renan Donnerh, Jean-Marc Dreyfus, Vincent Joly, Dominique Kalifa, Françoise Le Brenn, Gabrielle Muc, Denis Pelletier, Adelina and Carlos Pusineri, Bernard Rocaboy, Guido Rodriguez Alcalá, Ramon Rolandi, Denis Rolland, Jacqueline Sainclivier, Sylvie Schweitzer, Baya Sekhraoui, and

Jean-Yves Thévenin have been friendly and attentive readers and we have profited from their knowledge, their experience and the interest they have shown.

We would especially like to thank Michel Dreyfus and Fabrice Virgili who have unstintingly given of their time.

Finally, this book would not have appeared without the support of our editor, Christophe Guias, who believed in the project and encouraged us to complete it.

1 War dead

Death is the ultimate possibility for soldiers. When a combatant goes to war, the prospect of victory, achieved alive rather than dead, helps him to overcome his fear of death. In other words, if he accepts that he may lose his life, it is in the firm hope that he will not do so. But many more people than soldiers, who have not set off in search of glory, also die in war. And the circumstances as well as the manner in which they disappear have some bearing on the way in which their remains are treated. Amongst combatants, regular and irregular troops are rarely considered in the same way. Those wearing uniform are shown more respect than those who do not, who are readily identified as spies, bandits or terrorists and to whom states generally refuse to apply the conventions of war.

As for non-combatants, those amongst the civilian population who are afflicted by disease, who suffer from malnutrition, as well as hostages and the victims of suffering caused by military operations (fires, pillaging and assorted massacres), all those who die elsewhere than on the battlefield itself, are perceived in a variety of ways, depending upon the whole cultural and political context of the conflict and the actual circumstances of their death.

The nature of war has evolved since the middle of the nineteenth century. Until then, it was above all a military affair, even though civilian populations by no means remained unscathed. In the actual course of the fighting, as in the way it was conceived, civilians were sidelined. Their suffering, the horrors of warfare throughout the ages emblematically represented in the engravings of Jacques

Callot, were – in the phrase popularised much later, at the
time of the Gulf War in 1991 – merely 'collateral damage' in
a conflict the targets of which lay elsewhere. Of course, because of disruption in the country, many people have died
during conflicts from famine and disease as well as acts
of violence by the military. Sometimes they make up the
anonymous mass of the war dead. Of the 620,000 North
Americans who died during the American Civil War, more
than 400,000 died as a result of hardship and opportunistic
illnesses. During the Franco-Prussian War of 1870–1, epidemics of typhus, typhoid fever, dysentery and the harsh
winter weather accounted for more victims than the battles themselves, even amongst the soldiers. On the French
side, apart from the loss of departments in the east, the loss
of life caused by the conflict amounted to 600,000 men and
women set against the 139,000 brave souls who were killed
or who disappeared in the fighting. Nevertheless, the civilian population caught up in events as they unfolded were
neither targeted nor included in the military plans. These
distinctions gradually became blurred, as one kind of warfare gave way to another. One of the consequences of this
has been a change in the way death is envisaged and managed by armies, states and individuals alike.

In describing the different kinds of death which have occurred in war from the middle of the nineteenth century
to the 1970s, we shall draw attention to the way things
have evolved or abruptly changed as a consequence of each
particular event. But we should not lose sight of the fact
that ideas and cultural questions, systems of representation, evolved at a slower pace than political, geopolitical
and strategic organisations. We shall thus present broad
trends, which historiography has, moreover, taken into account in various ways, trying to preserve a balance between
huge changes and more ambiguous continuities.

Death in combat

Between the middle of the nineteenth century and the second third of the twentieth, the Western world (Europe and

the Americas) has experienced periods of warfare of different kinds. Whether they occurred between old powers or new nations, were colonial wars, wars of independence, territorial, racial or ideological conflicts – and they always shared several of these features – they have in common the fact that they transformed classic warfare and ushered in the age of industrialised warfare. This has had profound consequences for the behaviour of those caught up in them. Amongst the bloody episodes one might mention, Russia confronted the Ottoman Empire together with France and Great Britain in the Crimean War (1853–6); the American Civil War, which brought turmoil to the United States between 1861 and 1865, completed the birth of a nation; the war between Austria and Prussia (1866) set in train the unity of Germany; the Franco-Prussian War of 1870–1 firmly established the idea of the hereditary enmity of the two nations; the war of the Triple Alliance (1866–70) between Paraguay, on the one hand, which lost around 80 per cent of the total male population, and Brazil, Uruguay and Argentina on the other was savage; the Mexican Revolution ushered in the last century and brought about the death of hundreds of thousands of people, a million of whom died between 1914 and 1919 alone[1]. To this list can be added wars of independence (the Cubans against Spain in 1868–78 and 1895–8) and the Boer War of 1899–1902 between the English and the white settlers of South Africa, during which civilian Afrikaners were put into what were called concentration camps.

In all these wars, at both the technical and cultural level, old-fashioned and new features existed side by side. The former were little different from what might have been seen in classic warfare. The latter corresponded to the new characteristics of modern war, involving powerful and deadly means of destruction which affected masses of people, both military and civilian. Without studying all of them, we shall draw on aspects relating to the way death was dealt with and managed.

As far as means of killing are concerned, the significant use of bladed weapons was a legacy of earlier times.

The lance still formed part of the equipment of European armies, even the most 'modern' such as French and German units. The way it was used by the Prussian cavalry in the war of 1870–1 made an impression upon French strategists. Although it was abandoned by the French in 1872 because of its lack of effectiveness, it was reintroduced for dragoons in 1890 and then for chasseurs and hussars in 1913, because the tradition and prestige it enjoyed were so strong. This weapon of a bygone age only disappeared from the armoury of cavalrymen in 1920. Great Britain, Belgium and Russia also had their regiments of lancers. Swords, sabres, and bayonets fixed to the barrel of rifles were used by every army throughout the world until the Second World War. When Poland was invaded on 1 September 1939, the Polish army confronted six armoured divisions lined up by the Wehrmacht with twelve cavalry brigades, only one of which was mechanised.

Used often on the fringes, in particular battles in which enemies confronted each other face to face, bladed weapons meant that forms of close combat continued. This helped to perpetuate an image of an opponent who engaged in single combat with heroic individualism, maintaining throughout the twentieth century the mythology of the warrior, from the disturbingly shadowy figure of the individual clearing trenches to the massive Hollywood figure of the green beret, and including such models of virility as the legionnaire, the SAS commando, the Resistance fighter and the guerrilla.

During the Crimean War, while at the battle of Balaclava the cream of elite British troops was slaughtered with great heroism and futility in the famous charge of the Light Brigade, technical innovations increased the destructive power of the armies involved. Bladed weapons were now rivalled by new means of killing people on a mass scale and from a distance. That changed the relationship between enemy forces, lessening the importance of frontal attacks and bringing whole groups of both combatant and noncombatant people into the firing line. These changes, we repeat, did not take place all at once. To cite one example, the use of the cannon – a radical way of killing at a distance – began in the fourteenth century. But during the period we are concerned with, the marked change occurred in the precision of new weapons; with their range which bore no comparison with that of previous ones, and above all with their power which increased one hundred fold. For example, the cannons with rifled barrels, used by the Prussians in the 1870–1 War, had a range of 7,500 metres for a barrel of 150 millimetres diameter. As Doctor Jean-Charles Chenu made clear in his report on the 1870 war: 'Progress in the art of killing men, that is to say in the manufacture of artillery pieces and huge shells, a new tactic scrupulously adopted by the Germans, considerably reduced injuries from hand-held weapons and increased those caused by long-range shells... We have also witnessed a very small number of injuries from bladed weapons and far fewer bullet wounds than in previous wars.'[2]

The increased fire power of the artillery and the wider use of bombardments are a common feature of these wars. Subsequently, during the two World Wars, 70–80 per cent of injuries sustained by operational troops and recorded by the medical services came from artillery fire, whereas wounds from bladed weapons accounted for less than 1 per cent of the total.[3] In addition, there were new means of killing people, such as sulphur dioxide used in the Crimean War and the American Civil War, which could affect an enemy at a distance who had believed himself to be safe. Similarly, the Crimean War marked a new stage in the development of navies with the building of battleships, for the most part British, the first of which were used in 1854 against the Russian stronghold of Kinburn on the Black Sea. Of the many consequences of these innovations – strategic, financial, tactical, medical – one is aware that they increased the numbers of dead and injured and extended the battle zone beyond the traditional front line. In a parallel development, technological, scientific and organisational progress – notably international conventions – considerably reduced the number of deaths caused by battle fatigue (injuries, illnesses, deficiencies, ill treatment, bodily wear and tear caused by having to move around, etc.). Until 1870, less than 20 per cent of military deaths occurred on the battlefield. In 1914, the proportion was the exact opposite.[4] From that point on, modern conflicts tended more and more to limit death in war to that caused deliberately by the belligerents. From this perspective, the development of aerial bombardment assumes a particular importance. Far from having a strictly military purpose, it represented a strategy to destabilise the civilian population under fire. The role it played in the conduct of warfare in the twentieth century, and the history of bombing itself, is a controversial subject in which strategic and military considerations become entangled with moral and political ones. Be that as it may, destroying an enemy from a distance by dropping bombs from planes demanded special techniques and particular equipment which were above all the concern of the military. But innovations in this field, tried out during the Great War, then in 1935–6 in Abyssinia (with phosgene and mustard gas bombs), and above all in Spain – from the raid on Guernica in April 1937 to that on Barcelona in March 1939 – meant that civilian populations were increasingly caught up in these operations. Whether as a result of experience or visionary prognostication, each camp had its theoreticians of 'strategic bombing', this new way of bringing about mass death, such as William Mitchell in the United States, Giulio Douhet in Italy and Clément Ader in France.[5]

Helping the wounded; collecting up bodies

With new methods of killing came new kinds of help. European military medical services, which were almost non-existent until the Napoleonic Wars, were gradually set up and equipped. In spite of a strong tradition of innovation in this sphere and the creation of field hospitals and permanent ones in the civilian zone, the wounded had little chance of survival because of the lack of medical and surgical remedies and the inadequacy of the measures adopted to rescue them. Most were left abandoned in farms close to the battlefield and depended on the goodwill of the local population which was already hard pressed. During the 1870–1 War, although there had been sufficient progress in surgery to treat wounds with a certain degree of success, the treatment of infection remained so uncertain that, even if an operation was technically successful, it usually resulted in the death of the patient rather than his cure. In other words, to the number of those who died on the battlefield must be added an almost equal number of wounded who died shortly after.

The scale of losses in battle, greater than had been the case hitherto, was one of the new features of conflict in the period beginning in 1854. It made medical services more important, which, as we have said, were previously less well equipped. A characteristic of the change in attitudes was the transformation brought about during the Crimean War, involving the English, the French, the Turks and the Russians, and the Franco-Italian war against Austria, which resulted from the actions of Florence Nightingale and the Swiss, Henry Dunant, who was greatly moved by the slaughter at the Battle of Solferino in 1859.[6] The former made the battlefield an issue of public health, having been distressed by the spectacle of thousands of dead, dying or wounded soldiers lying on the shores of the Bosphorus. The latter provided the impetus for an international conference which took place in Geneva in 1864 and resulted in the creation of the International Red Cross. The first aim of this organisation was to help wounded and sick soldiers during international conflicts by insisting upon the neutrality of health workers and on the duty of care for all the wounded, whichever side they belonged to.[7] In order to achieve this, the idea was to set up a body of volunteer nurses, under the authority of all the military forces engaged.

These principles were initially enacted during the Franco-Prussian War of 1870–1 and the Spanish-American War of 1898. But it was above all during the 1914–18 War that groups of aid workers attached to the Red Cross managed to operate effectively. In contact with the International Committee of the Red Cross in Geneva, which co-ordinated information from all the national organisations of the warring parties, the French section of the Red Cross set up an information office to collect documents relating to the wounded, the sick, prisoners and those who had died, who began to be viewed in a different light.[8]

Until then, the gathering up of victims, as indeed of the wounded, had not been done in an organised and systematic way. Only officers and those of high rank were buried with due and proper ceremony, which was followed by the building of a tomb or the erection of a memorial which were not sited close to the battlefield. Ordinary troops who died, if they were not abandoned or left to local inhabitants to deal with, were hastily buried at the scene of the battle. They were placed in trenches rather than individual graves and sometimes, if there was a lull in the fighting and depending on the goodwill of those who had survived, rudimentary markers were used to designate their final resting place. Until the First World War, in Europe combatants only rarely had individual graves and they were not systematically tended.

New ways of waging war changed attitudes towards the dead and the way they were dealt with. Like Florence Nightingale and Henry Dunant, the belligerents in different conflicts were horrified by the scale of losses. The increase in the number of dead was accompanied by greater consideration being shown to each one of them. It was as if at the dawn of mass killing, the individual became more precious. The greater the number of combatants who perished the more the survivors were concerned to give each one a marked grave, in an identifiable place accessible to the bereaved.

In fact, during this period, changes took place in the numbers and types of troops involved, with regular armies, as a general rule, declining in favour of other forms of recruitment which altered their composition. The Enrollment Act of 3 March 1863, during the American Civil War, was the first time conscription was introduced in the United States, although those with enough money were able to escape it by paying for someone to replace them. The frequency of conflicts in Europe accelerated the change. Thus, in France, various laws passed in 1872, 1889 and 1905 changed the system of army recruitment, gradually bringing in compulsory military service. From then on, six out of ten Frenchmen were conscripted for a period of from one to three years.[9] National Service was in operation at the time of the First World War, France having an army of conscripts at its disposal.

This was not a uniform pattern for all national armies. In Great Britain and New Zealand, for example, the armies were still made up of volunteers until 1916, with conscription then being gradually introduced. In Australia, the voluntary system was not called into question until the end of the conflict. In Latin America, on the other hand, military service had become obligatory from the beginning of the century, a consequence of the political desire to modernise the armed forces and reflecting an aspiration to build nation states on the basis of universal, European models. It happened in 1900 in Chile, in 1901 in Argentina and Peru, in 1902 in Ecuador, in 1907 in Bolivia and in 1916 in Brazil.[10]

Everywhere, to a greater or lesser extent, armies were therefore made up of civilians under arms through regular conscription and those who signed up as volunteers. In July 1862, President Lincoln launched a solemn appeal for 300,000 volunteers to be recruited to defend the Union. A few years later in Paraguay, Marshal López declared a state of general mobilisation. In February 1866, he had the lists of those considered unfit for military service revised and, in 1867, decided that boys from ten to sixteen years old should be mobilised. Refusing to allow Paraguayan women volunteers to bear arms, he let them accompany the campaigning army as nurses, washerwomen or to provide food.[11] Similarly, during the Franco-Prussian War, as well as mobile guards, an 'un-quantifiable number' of irregular troops and *francs-tireurs* were organised. They were volunteers who, under a legal statute of the Imperial Law of 1868, were authorised to serve, but who had to arm and equip themselves at their own expense.[12]

The conflicts which took place during the second half of the nineteenth century within a fairly defined geographical location, which were of relatively short duration, involved intense diplomatic activity and respected – albeit crudely – 'codes of honour' in relation to one's adversary, resembled wars of earlier eras as a consequence. The mobilisation of a large part of the male population, the involvement of civilian populations (women and non-combatants) and the important role which the latter were beginning to play in the whole strategy of war, heralded a new era, of which the 1914–18 War was the turning point.

The historiography of this conflict, which clearly marked the beginning of industrialised and total warfare, emphasises the fundamental break it represented in military history, to the extent that the weapons used during the Crimean War, at Verdun and at Hiroshima seem to belong to different worlds.[13] The changes relating to the numbers of troops involved, the care of the wounded and the way the dead were treated, became more marked with the First World War and represented a decisive turning point. The extension of the battlefield to society as a whole greatly increased the ways in which people were killed by weapons of war. Whereas, until then, the majority of those killed were military personnel and fighting soldiers, war from then on affected the whole social fabric of the countries involved in the conflict, making the distinction between civilian and military more and more difficult. Nations at war had, thereafter, to learn to honour different categories of war dead.

From hero to victim

Without harking back to the glorious death of Greek heroes, the gallant and suicidal charge of the British Light Brigade, celebrated by Tennyson, highlights the powerfully representative image of a glorious death in war in the middle of the nineteenth century. Within the perspective of the long history of anthropological figures, that of the warrior sacrificing his life in a brave and manly way is a constant feature in the depiction of all wars. One can, however, perceive a twin evolutionary process in the course of the period under consideration. Behind the myth of courage are concealed more ambiguous facets of reality, involving horror, fear and cowardice, suffering and pain, which lead one towards a de-mythologising of death in war as something heroic. More-over, the ever-widening status of those considered as vic-tims has raised them almost wholly to the level of active participants.

Over a long period George L. Mosse has studied the birth of the idea of the volunteer, which has its roots in the events of the French Revolution, as a hero whose ultimate sacri-ficial death in combat during the nineteenth century rep-resented an initiation test of his virility.[14] According to the author, the myth survived in the West, despite the ordeals of the 1914–18 War, until the end of the Second World War. After 1945, the myth of the volunteer with his enthusi-asm for combat was more difficult to sustain, because the civilian zone (if that is still a meaningful concept) was too immediately aware of the reality of war for those illusions to be sustained. That doubtless explains the change in the war memorials of the two conflicts. Those commemorat-ing the First World War were above all dedicated to sol-diers, though statues did also represent the rest of society caught up in the war in the figures of weeping widows, inconsolable mothers and frightened orphans. On Second World War memorials, the civilian population has a much greater presence, if only because the names of those who died elsewhere than at the front, in Resistance operations, acts of reprisal and bombing raids, are recorded as well.

Once people were no longer recognised or commemo-rated as war heroes but as victims, our perspective im-perceptibly changed from one of hero-worship to an ac-knowledgement of their status as victims, and this included even those who were victorious. So far as official speeches about the dead were concerned, changes came more slowly, with death in battle still receiving the utmost mark of respect.[15] Throughout the period, vanquishers and van-quished heaped unreserved praise on heroes cut down in battle. American Southerners provide an excellent example of the mythologising of the heroic soldier. After the failure of secession, they sang the praises of the vanquished, lauding their unsuccessful fight and remembering their feats of arms rather than what happened to them. The same thing happened in France following the war of 1870–1, with the public commemoration of the defeat being built in large measure upon celebration of the 'glorious vanquished'.

The same state of mind informed the letters sent by officers and the military administration to families asking to be told about the final moments of their loved ones. If one believes the studies to which they have given rise, these letters, even though detailed and very truthful, minimised the suffering endured, stressing that death was 'instantaneous', and emphasising the courage, bravery and patriotism of the deceased.[16] Marc Bloch did just this on 17 August 1918, when writing to the sister of one of his soldiers who had recently been killed: 'You ask for the truth, and it is my duty to tell you, however painful it might be. Your brother, Corporal Bernard, died for France, on 24 July just past, during a victorious offensive which drove the Boches back to the river Aisne. He was killed by a shell, and I give you my word of honour that he died immediately, without suffering.'[17] Honour here being more in his desire to soften the blow than in his respect for the truth.

From an official and symbolic point of view, the real transformation in the ways things were expressed was reflected in the continuous inclusion by the whole national community of new categories of non-military war dead. In France, the scale of losses during the first year of the war gave rise to the law of 2 July 1915. From that point on, death certificates bore the following statement 'Died for France' (in the masculine), obviously, for soldiers, but also for noncombatants with military status such as 'doctors, ministers of religion, medical orderlies, and female nurses in military hospitals' and especially 'anyone who died from an illness contracted whilst caring for the sick and wounded in the army; any civilian killed by the enemy, either as a hostage, or in public office, whether elected, administrative or judicial, or acting in their place'. A week later, a circular drew attention to the role of civilian officials, who were in no way to be hampered in applying the law by possible delays of the military authorities in providing necessary proof. Article 3 of the law of 28 February 1922 broadened the categories by making clear that the provisions of the law applied to 'any hostage, military or civilian prisoner of war, whether he died on enemy or neutral soil, as a result of wounds, ill treatment, illnesses contracted or which worsened in captivity, an accident at work or as a result of being executed by the enemy.' The legislators omitted neither 'those born in Algeria, the colonies or protectorates', nor 'foreign troops who were killed or who died in the same circumstances.'

Without doubt, the mention that someone had died for their country was a real comfort to those individuals who mourned. Nevertheless, two recent studies of more intimate and personal expressions of grief highlight sharp divisions in the honouring of heroes killed in battle.[18] Focusing upon the Great War, they show, with the help of literary texts and personal papers, the gap between the heroic vision of war, expressed in national speeches of commemoration, and the difficulty of coming to terms with missing individuals whose wretched remains, stripped of their military status, had been first and foremost husbands or children. The mourners who express themselves in these texts – a literary figure in the case of the poet Jane Catulle Mendès, an activist in that of the pacifist Blanche Maupas – do not seem at first to depart from the image of the hero. Jane's son, a young volunteer killed in an attack, and Blanche's husband, shot for having not left his trench, are both mourned as heroes. But what emerges whilst reading these expressions of pain is the depth of private grief, even though it is mediated through writing and militancy. And, if one reads the literature of the First World War closely, one is aware that it rejects the unifying voice heard in the commemorative and sanctifying speeches made on behalf of the dead and returns to the 'dread of the corpse'. In emphasising bodily suffering and the solitude of the dying, these texts move away from the great deeds of heroes. Those who survived could not rid themselves of the vision of human remains that had been part of their daily life at the front and which haunted them at night once peace was re-established.

This evolutionary process began with the horrors of the 1914–18 War. It was intensified by the acute awareness of those who lived through it all that what was to have been 'the war to end all wars' was only the prelude to further conflicts in which the level of violence and cruelty merely increased. Marked by fierce confrontations such as the Spanish Civil War of 1936–9, in which old forms of law seemed inadequate in the face of unheard of suffering on the part of the civilian population, this process became irreversible in the second half of the twentieth century with the defining issue of the extermination of European Jews. Because of the theory which underpinned it, the principle of putting people to death, the desire of the murderers to destroy all traces of their crime as well as of their victims, and because of the number of victims, the massacre which took place gave rise to reflection about mass killing and the possible, subsequent commemoration of it. In asking oneself what kind of reparation would restore to people that which they had permanently lost and what the living might accomplish in lamenting the death of those who had been doubly destroyed, one is led to reflect upon ceremonies for the dead.[19]

Images of battles

The last stage in our attempt to explain what we mean by the phrase 'war dead' leads us to the issue of visual representation. For a long time, images of war have laid emphasis upon death as killing rather than something suffered. Not that heaps of dead and wounded have not been depicted in war pictures since the classical age, but they have served as a framing device for the hero, who was the central figure of the image.[20] His was the face of a victor with positive connotations, and death as pain and loss was almost entirely absent from any representation of battle, except for the silhouettes of civilian victims huddled together as they fled at the bottom of the picture. The first signs of change

came about with the Crimean War and the American Civil
War. Pictures from these wars, whether paintings or photographs, were much less heroic and exalting, and were now
filled with bodies, with prisoners and with the wounded,
expressing the enormous human cost of war. Yet neither
the public nor the civilian and military authorities were
ready to be engaged by such images or to let them be seen.
Despite dispatches – in the modern sense of the term – being widely distributed and realistic enough, images of war
dead at the end of the nineteenth century owed more to
Rimbaud's gentle *Sleeper in the Valley* than to the paint-
ing of 'uncontrolled arms and legs' by Paul de Leusse after Sebastopol. The reluctance to show victims rather than
heroes resulted from the combination of public opinion and
reasons of State; their collective sensibility censured deni-
grating as much as demoralising images.

Once again, the 1914–18 War marked a turning point
in three different ways. Throughout the conflict, photogra-
phers and film-makers on both sides were prolific in their
depiction of various aspects of the fighting. Images of death
in its stark, and therefore unbearable, reality came to the
fore, displacing images of heroism. Realism of this kind, un-
dermining the will to enlist, gave rise to censorship which
has grown in strength ever since. The fact that distressing
images of victims have not been allowed to circulate, have
been confiscated, hidden away in archives or destroyed,
does not alter the fact that their meaning has remained unchanged until the present day. 'The representation of war
has, in the course of two centuries, gone from a heroic depiction of conflict to a heroic depiction of loss, then to the loss of
heroism and to the loss of any sense of meaning.'[21] Though
they have not entirely disappeared, of course, heroes have
got off their horses, in a state of total shock, alongside mass
graves and pitiful rows of children with bloated stomachs,
as well as in televised pictures of Rwandan corpses.

Thus, death as killing has tended to be rejected and replaced by death suffered, as seen in exposed corpses. From
the end of the 1920s, such images have served to denounce
war. For example, the terrible photos taken during the

bombing of Paris, which were censored during the conflict, began to appear at this time. They showed the dis-
membered and disfigured bodies of soldiers, bits of human
remains, a woman's intestines covering her trunk, her un-
damaged vulva the only means of determining her sex, the
obscene remains of a charred, new-born baby, its skull and
chest smashed as a result of the bombing of the Parisian
maternity hospital of Port-Royal. Gruesome or excessively
realistic images of war featured prominently in the 1930s
and during the Second World War.

The aptitude which veterans of the 1914–18 War showed
in conveying to society at large their experiences under
fire probably explains this fracture in the culture. From
then on, in democracies, violence suffered was presented in
an accusatory way against the enemy or to denounce war,
whereas violence as a weapon was not shown, and victims
took the place of heroes. Outside the framework of the traditional glorification of battlefields and warriors which has
been slow to change, the focus upon the victim and mass
killing has been at the forefront in the depiction of conflict
in the mid-twentieth century.

Thus, in 1940, the information department of the Polish government in exile put out booklets showing on the
front page the corpses of massacred Polish civilians, with
the aim of winning the support of Western public opinion.[22]
Similarly, at the Liberation, most of the patriotic material
produced by Resistance workers or on the initiative of the
liberated cultural elite focused upon the victims of Nazism.
The film of the liberation of Paris, shot in 1944 by the Liberation Committee of the French cinema, as well as *Au
Coeur de l'Orage* about the resistance in Vercors, directed
by Jean-Paul Le Chanois, are very restrained concerning
German deaths and the execution of collaborators. These
films do, on the other hand, dwell on close-ups of the bodies
of Resistance fighters covered in flies and of French patriots who had been shot or hanged, their hands tied together. The same thing is true of booklets published after
the war telling of the patriotism of the French in the most
direct images of their martyrdom. They are full of close-ups

of decomposed corpses, of the exhumation of bodies from graves, of human limbs, of charred bodies and remains.[23]

However, from the end of the nineteenth century, people's attitudes changed and they turned away from the presence of death in the world of the living, which they had been used to until then.[24] This change was sufficiently marked by 1907 for the Prefect of Paris, Lépine, to close the morgue. During the Belle Époque, it had become a favourite visiting place of Parisians who willingly came to look at the bodies of unknown individuals which were displayed behind glass awaiting their burial.[25] The decision to close it was taken following a debate which went beyond the small professional group concerned and engaged a wider public. Putting bodies on display had become indecent in an era of changed sensibilities.[26] This dynamic process of change within the civilisation was undoubtedly modified by the two World Wars. The co-existence of the living and the dead in the trenches during the 1914–18 War, and then in society as a whole during the 1939–45 War, introduced a complete break in the representation of death, leading to a rapprochement at the cultural level between those who were still alive and the bodies of those who had died. As at traditional funeral ceremonies, where the living gather around the body of the deceased, at the end of the Second World War, decomposed and martyred bodies not only filled the images of that conflict, they were also a physical presence at the ceremonies which marked its end.

The first of these at the Liberation were characterised by the opening of graves, the displaying of bodies where the enemy were sometimes called upon to show their respect, followed by funerals. At the liberation of Moëlan-sur-Mer, six young girls and an older woman, who had had their heads shaved, were lead by partisans to the graveside of Resistance fighters killed by the Germans. The partisans of the French home army (FFI) took them in pairs and made them look at the bodies and experience the stench of death. 'They told me to get the real smell of bodies', one of them said. They were made to spend the night at the graveside, before being released in the morning.[27]

Are we witnessing here a cultural break, albeit a passing one, created by events as at the time of the Terror?[28] A thirty-year period of warfare as well as the representation of death and of war itself seem to have been telescoped here; the glorification of war has been undermined by the horror of death, which is all the more unacceptable because people no longer see it as the inevitable and expected end of a person's life. In the second half of the twentieth century, conflicts in which Westerners have been directly involved in Indo-China, Korea, Algeria and Vietnam have lost all sense of meaning. Journalists and military information services, propounding the myth of war's civilising and humanitarian function, no longer created war heroes. Nor did they show Western victims, but simply populations of exotic people regularly brutalised by an enemy with blurred faces.[29] The shock was even greater when, at the end of the Vietnam conflict, the media published photos of violent acts committed by the United States army. The picture taken by Nick Ut of little Phan Thi Kim Phuc of Huynh Cong Ut, burned by napalm on 8 June 1972 and published in *Life* magazine, made a deep impression on Western public opinion. It was not until 1980–90 that the veterans of these conflicts, viewed from then on as a group and thought of as victims, could legitimately reintegrate themselves into the national community. Those who had been killed on enemy soil had, for the most part, been discreetly brought home in the course of the conflict.

Were the authorities ashamed of these war dead, given that they no longer sought to create heroes and therefore reduced to a minimum any show of patriotism on their behalf? Or was it society's tendency to consider death indecent which affected equally those killed in war?

Notes

1. Pierre Vayssière, *Les Révolutions d'Amérique latine* (Paris: Seuil, 1991), p. 84.
2. Jean-Charles Chenu, *Rapport du Conseil de la Société française de secours aux blessés. Aperçu historique, statistique*

et clinique sur le service des ambulances et des hôpitaux de la société de secours aux blessés des armées de terre et mer pendant la guerre de 1870–1871 (Paris: Dumaine, 1874), 2 volumes, p. 269, quoted in Corinne Krouck, *Les Combattants français de la guerre de 1870–1871 et l'écriture de soi: contribution à une histoire des sensibilités*, thesis, University of Paris 1, 2001, p. 111.

3. Stéphane Audoin-Rouzeau, 'Au coeur de la guerre: la violence du champ de bataille pendant les deux conflits mondiaux', in Stéphane Audoin-Rouzeau, Annette Becker, Christian Ingrao and Henry Rousso (eds), *La Violence de guerre, 1914–1945. Approches comparées des deux conflits mondiaux* (Brussels & Paris: Complexe/I HTP-CNRS, 2002), pp. 73–97.

4. Michael Howard, *War in European History* (Oxford: Oxford University Press, 1976). *La Guerre dans l'histoire de l'Occident*, (Paris: Fayard, 1986), p. 127.

5. Claude Carlier, 'Clément Ader: premier stratège de l'aéronautique militaire', *Guerres mondiales et conflits contemporains*, 167, juillet 1992, pp. 117–32; Patrick Facon, *Le Bombardement stratégique* (Monaco: Éditions du Rocher, 1996).

6. For a recent account of the work on Florence Nightingale, see Helen Epstein, 'The mysterious Miss Nightingale', *The New York Review of Books*, 8 March 2001, pp. 16–19; Henry Dunant, *Un souvenir de Solferino*, (Lausanne: L'Âge d'Homme, 1986 [1st edn 1862]).

7. Véronique Harouel, *Histoire de la Croix Rouge* (Paris: PUF, 1999).

8. Annette Becker, *Oubliés de la Grande Guerre. Humanitaire et culture de guerre, 1914–1918. Populations occupées, déportés, civils, prisonniers de guerre* (Paris: Noêsis, 1998).

9. Odile Roynette, *'Bons pour le service'. L'Expérience de la caserne à la fin du XIXᵉ siècle* (Paris: Belin, 2000).

10. Alain Rouquié, *L'État militaire en Amérique latine* (Paris, Seuil, 1982), p. 121.

11. Bárbara Potthast-Jutkeit, *'Paraíso de Mahoma' o 'país de las mujeres'? El rol de la familia en la sociecad paraguaya del siglo XIX* (Asunción: Instituto Cultural Paraguayo-Alemán, 1996).

12. François Roth, *La Guerre de 70* (Paris: Fayard, 1990), p. 224.

13. On the pivotal significance of the 1914–18 War, see in particular Jay Winter, *Sites of Memory, Sites of Mourning. The Great*

War in European Cultural History (Cambridge: Cambridge University Press, 1995).

14. George L. Mosse, *L'Image de l'homme. L'invention de la virilité moderne* (Paris: Abbeville, 1997); *De la Grande Guerre au totalitarisme. La brutalisation des sociétés européennes* (Paris: Hachette, 1999).

15. One should refer to the memoirs of officers or to those of other people sympathetic to military values. For example, choosing both a male and female author: Colonel R. Malcor, *L'Honneur de mourir* (Paris: La Colombe, 1962), this book is dedicated to 'officers and soldiers who served in Algeria'; Germaine L'Herbier Montagnon in *Jusqu'au sacrifice* (Paris, Éditions ÉCLAIR, 1960) dedicates her book, which is about pilot nurses of the Air Service, to those 'who lived and died with dignity'.

16. Mark Meigs, 'La mort et ses enjeux: l'utilisation des corps des soldats américains lors de la Première Guerre mondiale', *Guerres mondiales et conflits contemporains*, 175, 1994, pp. 135–46.

17. Marc Bloch, *Écrits de guerre, 1914–1918*, texts collected and presented by Étienne Bloch, with an introduction by Stéphane Audoin-Rouzeau (Paris: Armand Colin, 1997), p. 110.

18. Stéphane Audoin-Rouzeau, *Cinq deuils de guerre, 1914–1918* (Paris: Noêsis, 2001); Carine Trevisan, *Les Fables du deuil. La Grande Guerre: mort et écriture* (Paris: PUF, 2001).

19. Françoise Sironi, *Bourreaux et victimes. Psychologie de la torture* (Paris: Odile Jacob, 1999), p. 124; Boris Cyrulnik, *Un merveilleux malheur* (Paris: Odile Jacob, 1999).

20. Hélène Puiseux, *Les Figures de la guerre. Représentations et sensibilités, 1839–1996* (Paris: Gallimard, 1997).

21. Ibid. p. 243.

22. Polish Government Archives, *L'Invasion allemande en Pologne* (Paris: Flammarion, 1940).

23. Examples include, Albert Béguin, *Le Livre noir du Vercors* (Neuchâtel: Ides et Calendes, 1944); Dr. Pierre Masfrand and Guy Pauchou, *Oradour-sur-Glane vision d'épouvante. Ouvrage officiel du Comité du Souvenir et de l'Association des Familles des Martyrs d'Oradour-sur-Glane* (Limoges et Paris: Charles-Lavauzelle, 1970).

24. See Geoffrey Gorer, *Ni pleurs ni couronnes* (Paris: EPEL, 1995); Philippe Ariès, *L'Homme devant la mort* (Paris: Seuil,

1977); Michel Vovelle, *La Mort et l'Occident de 1300 à nos jours* (Paris: Gallimard, 1983).
25. Vanessa R. Schwartz, *Spectacular Realities. Early Mass Culture in Fin-de-Siècle Paris* (Berkeley: University of California Press, 1998), p. 63.
26. Bruno Bertherat, 'La Morgue de Paris', *Sociétés et Représentations*, juin 1998, pp. 273–93.
27. Gendarmerie statement of 3 October 1944, Pont-Aven brigade, Archives départementales du Finistère, 31 W 631.
28. Antoine de Baecque, *La Gloire et l'Effroi. Sept morts sous la Terreur* (Paris: Grasset, 1997).
29. Fabrice d'Almeida, 'Photographie et censure', in Laurent Gervereau, Jean-Pierre Rioux and Benjamin Stora (eds), *La France en guerre d'Algérie* (Paris: Musée d'histoire contemporaine-BDIC, 1992), pp. 216–27; Jacques Portes 'Voir la guerre. Indochine, Corée et Viêt-nam', in Thérèse Blondet-Bisch, Robert Frank, Laurent Gervereau and André Gunthert (eds), *Voir, ne pas voir la guerre. Histoire des représentations photographiques de la guerre* (Paris: Somogy, 2001), pp. 142–59.

2 Identifying the dead to mourn them properly?

Once the belligerents began to give some thought to providing graves for their dead soldiers they were confronted with the problem of identifying them. It is one thing to gather up anonymous remains in an ossuary, quite another to put up a designated headstone for each clearly named individual, and yet another to erect a cenotaph bearing the names of all those who had been killed – those still missing or who remained unidentified. But weapons of war had become more and more lethal and destructive. The image of men being cut down by such powerful artillery shells that their bodies were obliterated, leaving their survivors with no physical remains to grieve over, does not date from 1914.[1] Such images already fill accounts by veterans of the American Civil War and those of the war of 1870–1. 'The dead were hideous: blackened, swollen, covered in dried blood, riddled with bullets, torn apart by shells', reported one eyewitness of the American Civil War.[2]

Identity discs

As it led the way in other aspects of warfare, the American Civil War first brought in means of identification for individual soldiers who had been killed. To prevent them from remaining anonymous, soldiers were given a small parchment tag, on one side of which was written their name preceded by 'I am', as well as details of their company, regiment, division and corps.[3] A number of them obtained metal identification discs sometimes giving their home town. But the practice was not systematic, and almost half of the graves of the American Civil War bear the legend 'unknown'. A little later, in the course of the 1870–1 War, the Prussian army distributed identification tags, requiring troops to carry an identity card marked *Grabstein* (grave).[4] These first attempts, which proved useful during the bloody battles of Knoxville and Gettysburg, were followed by the more general use of identity discs before the First World War.

In France, the decision was taken in 1881 to provide soldiers with identity discs made of nickel silver (a non-oxidising alloy of nickel, copper and zinc) in order to establish their civil status in case of death and thereby guarantee their estate. In 1883, the nature of the disc was standardised. It was agreed in the 1890s to also give them to colonial troops.[5] On the eve of the First World War, it was a regulation that every serving soldier be provided with a disc.[6] When it first appeared, it was readily worn like a medallion around the soldier's neck, which was easy to accept and to enforce at the end of the nineteenth and the beginning of the twentieth century, given the importance of religious practices and the frequent wearing of images of the Virgin Mary or of a saint, even by men. However, either for superstitious reasons or by neglect, many soldiers did not wear them or indeed removed them.[7] Furthermore, even if directives from 1884 on made clear that the discs of dead soldiers should accompany their military records, in reality various practices were adopted by people on the battlefield up until the Second World War. In some cases they removed the disc and then handed it over to the civilian authorities, in others they left it on the body so that it could subsequently be identified. There was a conflict between these two attitudes: on the one hand, the military wanted the civil status of the individual to be guaranteed, on the other, his comrades in arms wanted the body to retain its identity.

During the 1914–18 War, most European countries had their own type of disc, either engraved on metal or written in ink on cellulose or boiled leather. Thus the British used up to nine different types of identity disc. From 1916

onwards, the Germans decided to use a divisible version
which meant that both the civil status and the identity of
the body could be preserved.[8] In France in 1915, to make
identification easier, Doctor Leclerc, a professor in the Fac-
ulty of Medicine in Lille, proposed a double disc system, one
to be worn around the neck, the other around the wrist. A
new model appeared in 1917, a two-part disc to be worn on
the wrist, one part remaining fixed to a chain which guaranteed that the body would be identifiable if exhumed, the
other, which was detachable, would establish that the person had died.[9] To the extent that a whole policy to codify
the laws of warfare was being established, the absence of a
standard practice was detrimental to the identification of
bodies, especially in conflicts where a great deal of movement occurred and the front line was constantly changing
and in fierce battles over territory which was constantly
lost and retaken.

The value of the identity disc was so obvious that the
military authorities tried to improve its usage, especially
by standardising the information it carried and the way it
was to be worn. At the beginning of the Great War, France,
Italy, Belgium, Sweden and Great Britain, amongst others,
experimented with the use of a bracelet. But, as well as
the frequency of wounds to the upper limbs, 'hands cut off',
and the fear of the evil eye, the reluctance of soldiers to
wear something considered feminine restricted its general
use.

In spite of all these efforts, a large number of dead remained unidentified at the end of the First World War.
In France, out of 1,400,000 soldiers 'killed on enemy soil',
252,900 were declared lost or unidentified. In the United
States, the public authorities wanted to reassure people,
and reported that out of 116,000 killed in this war only
2,896 remained unidentified. But the identification of the
bodies was done with a certain amount of guesswork, and
clear-headed contemporaries worried about the accuracy of
identities. The veterans were not optimistic. According to
one soldier who accompanied a cargo of bodies from the
trenches being repatriated, one coffin in ten might have

contained genuinely identified remains. The others were no more than 'guesses on the basis of skeletons'.[10] In such circumstances, the authorities could not just go on making soothing speeches. They had to improve their methods of identification.

At its twelfth conference in 1925, the International Committee of the Red Cross took the initiative and regularised the use of discs as a necessary, if inadequate, way of identifying those wounded and killed. A commission 'to standardise health equipment' set to work in co-operation with staff officers of the states which had signed the Geneva and Hague conventions, under the leadership of Colonel Rouppert, the head of medical services in the Polish army. A resolution, drafted by the autumn of 1927, was adopted under Article 4 of the new Geneva Convention signed in July 1929. Although each state retained the freedom to implement it as it saw fit, henceforth, soldiers wore a metal disc around their necks, a detachable part of which could be easily passed to the authorities on their own or the enemy side. Besides testing out the strength and form of the identity tag, the standardisation commission was also concerned that an individual's religion should be inscribed. This proposal, intended to make the organisation of funerals easier though ultimately not adopted by most armies, did at least show a feeling of obligation towards the dead.

From the inter-war period on, all soldiers in principle wore identification. In France, for example, the tag, permanently made of nickel silver, bore different information for officers and ordinary soldiers. Officers' had on the front their surname, usual forename together with the word 'officer' and on the reverse their date and place of birth. The name, first forename and rank were shown on the front of soldiers' tags, and on the reverse their regional subdivision and recruitment number. From then on, it was worn around the neck and had to be removed from the body before burial and sent back, if possible, to the accounts and information office with the individual's papers, usually kept in the inside pocket of his tunic. During the course of the Second World War, the United States made an additional effort to organise the tracking of their own dead. In addition to the identity bracelet, which soldiers referred to as the 'dog tag', the military authorities gave the instruction that a hermetically sealed bottle with details of the burial (ROB – Report of Burial) should be placed alongside the body, approximately thirty centimetres beneath the cross. But urgency and the need to improvise often dictated the first burial site. Diggers frequently buried the whole crew of a tank or plane in a common grave. After the war, when they uncovered these graves, those doing the exhumation made an effort to identify the bones, gathering each individual's together, with experts making a guess as to the age and height of the unknown person. The information from Washington made the identification of crews buried in the war zone easier because there were only a limited number of possibilities. Above all, the special cards produced by the American Graves Registration Command which were given to the exhumation parties contained, amongst other information, the dental record of each soldier at the time he was called up. The identification of one body therefore enabled them to name the other soldiers buried in the grave. As a member of one of the French exhumation parties wrote: 'if an identified body costs the American taxpayer a great deal, the body of an unknown soldier is beyond value.'[11]

Recognising civilians as well

So, a huge effort was made to identify soldiers killed in combat and in war zones. Both literature and the cinema have brought to public attention the painful quest of families seeking those who were missing.[12] Organising the identification of individuals, which at first proceeded by trial and error, gradually became more systematic and effective during the Second World War. At this time, the procedures slowly put in place by the military authorities were extended to the civilian population and the teething troubles gradually resolved; and this was done in a similar fashion by all the warring parties. In Paris, for example, in 1942, administrative circulars relating to the procedures to be adopted after civilians were bombed quite properly separated administrative issues from the technical aspects of clearing of rubble and the setting up of temporary shelters. Under administrative tasks, 'duties to the dead' – finding and identifying them, placing them in coffins and giving them a funeral[13] – took precedence over urgent help such as housing, public order, salvage and the organisation of work.

Everything was done so that victims would not remain anonymous. In his report on the Allied bombing raid of 3 March 1942 which killed 316 people, the Prefect of Police could congratulate himself. Having explained how the bodies were removed from the ruins, searched so as to safeguard their personal possessions, placed in coffins and shown to the families who were looking for their missing relatives, he concluded: 'Thanks to the diligence of those involved, most of the bodies have been identified within three days and only twenty-eight remain unidentified. These have been photographed by the Criminal Records Office, their finger prints taken and a description made so that their identity can be established as quickly as possible.'[14] The families of those missing could therefore identify the dead from the photographs held at the town hall.

The identification of non-military personnel involved administrative, medico-legal and psychological issues. In 1941, following the bombing of Rennes, Émile Dupont, who came from Bezons in the Paris region, found himself involved in an administrative tangle: because the body of his daughter had not been identified, her civil status could not be changed. He explained his tragic circumstances to the Prefect of Ille-et-Vilaine six months after the events: 'Having been demobilised on the 27th October last [1940] and returning from the south of Tunisia, I received the very painful news of my daughter, Colette's, death at the age of seventeen during the bombing of the station in Rennes on 17 June 1940. Though a great deal of effort has been made, I have no hope ... of knowing that my young daughter has been identified. My daughter was killed by a bullet through her temple and then torn apart by the explosions. She died in my wife's arms and her death was witnessed by a young friend who was with them. On 2 September in the same year, my wife was knocked down by a lorry not far from Rennes and buried at the cemetery in the eastern part of the town. I would like to know, sir, if the town hall in Bezons which has asked for the death certificates of my wife and daughter can have them.' After his account of these events, the poor fellow asked for a subsidised rail ticket to go to Rennes to reflect on what had happened, adding that his wife had fled during the exodus. The reply from the municipality of Rennes was final. It indicated that a copy of his wife's certificate would be made for the authorities in Bezons, but that so far as his daughter was concerned: 'Given that Mlle Dupont has not been identified, no notification of death has been made in her case.'[15]

In March 1943, after another bombing raid, a young woman had to go to the morgue to identify her mother whose death had been announced. The body was that of someone else! The urgent search undertaken on behalf of the mayor did not find the body, and the police superintendent concluded his report by saying: 'we have grounds for thinking that Mme B's body was either interred as that of an "unknown person" or – more seriously – under another name.'[16]

There are no overall statistics for the number of civilians and soldiers who remain unidentified. Research is still going on today. The armed services in France estimate that between 10 and 15 per cent of the soldiers killed between 1939 and 1945 were either missing or unidentified. However, considerable progress was made from one war to the next. Of those killed in the first four months of the 1914 War 85–90 per cent remain 'unknown' to this day to the Pensions Office of the State Secretariat for Ex-Servicemen. Up until the end of the twentieth century, means of identification have remained uncertain, empirical, relying on the cross-checking of information: the record of the daily movements of units in action and of a soldier's papers, the site of the grave, objects close to the body. But the frequency with which bodies were jumbled together in pits and mass graves has made the subsequent confirmation of identity an illusion. Ninety per cent of unknown soldiers of the First World War are those who fell in 1914 and were buried in mass graves. Only the will to implement identification and the more widespread use of individual graves, which was far from feasible on all occasions, guaranteed the possibility of truly recognising those who had been killed.

Since the 1990s, the use of DNA or, more recently still, sophisticated techniques enabling facial recognition using identification parameters have allowed people to establish almost beyond question the identity of bodies which had been discovered but had remained unknown. These have included the 'disappeared', secretly buried by agents of the dictatorship in Argentina, Russian soldiers hastily buried in mass graves in Chechnya, the remains of those buried in the ruins following the attack on the twin towers of the World Trade Center in New York on 11 September 2001. Until now, these laborious and costly procedures have only been used on a limited number of occasions.

Counting the dead

Following on from identification, the dead and missing had to be counted. From the historian's point of view, telling the story and presenting the results of this numerical process is never easy. One has to determine who is being counted and the basis on which it is to be done. One also has to elucidate absolute and relative values and the social and political implications of selecting one outcome as opposed to another. For example, it is difficult to compare the dead of the two World Wars, not only statistically, but also in terms of how public opinion experienced the scale of the losses incurred. France lost a million and a half soldiers during the 1914–18 War and then in the 1939–45 conflict another 600,000, of whom 170,000 were soldiers, 150,000 citizens of metropolitan France and 280,000 people displaced by the Germans. The cost in human lives was therefore significantly lower in the Second World War than in the First, and indeed less than the number usually cited.

One can truly talk of a society in mourning over the First World War. But, on a strictly statistical basis, one cannot legitimately make the same claim for the Second. And yet the dominant feeling at the end of the 1940s and during the following decade was in fact one 'of shared grief and mourning on the part of the nation as a whole without exception'[17] If, in 1945, France did not lament the loss of as many men as in 1918, the memory of the scale of the losses was based upon a contrary impression. The different political situation during the two periods (on the one hand the Sacred Union, on the other the fracture caused by the Vichy regime), as well as the discovery of the world of concentration camps and the changing ideological basis of conflicts, partly explain this alternative perspective.

It was less a question of getting in perspective the exact numbers of dead, though they were used for political and commemorative purposes, than of using this 'error' as a yardstick with which to measure the omnipresent sense of death, which was based upon a mental construct that transformed a quantitative process into a qualitative one. Both in people's minds and in reality, the advent of mass killing reinforced and modified the effect of battlefields becoming bigger; and with the distinction between the front and the rear being less clearly defined, the whole population of a country at war now deserved to be honoured.[18]

Providing, that is, such gestures could be made. Gradually, states and armies designed regulations and practices for honouring the dead, and they went to a great deal of trouble to count and classify them. On this basis, history can be told. Similarly, one can endeavour to enter into the intimate grief of the families of soldiers, and the widening population of those killed in war. There remain those who were either not honoured or not fit to be honoured; those who were not accepted or were rejected by the whole national community or a section of it. These were individuals whose complicated status reminds us that, despite things having changed, the military man, once his work was done – and the historian in his wake – is more comfortable with soldiers on the field of battle, whether sent to their death or mourned. During the two World Wars, it was common for prisoners and the wounded to be killed on the spot, before they could be taken either to a camp or to a hospital.[19] Though these contraventions of the Geneva and Hague Conventions occurred above all on the Russian and Pacific fronts during the Second World War, the practice of killing prisoners and the wounded was already 'widespread and commonplace' between 1914 and 1918.[20] What happened to all these bodies? Who dealt with them? What were the circumstances? We know very little, except what we have learned from mass graves discovered afterwards; those around Metz and Sedan in 1871; the one at Katyn and those in Sétif after 1945, which do not tell us much about what happened immediately after the killings.

Equally unknown is the fate of clandestine personnel who suffered such an 'anonymous, cruel and lonely' death that they were not even included in the figures.[21] Amongst their number was the machinist and fitter Garnier, a Resistance worker brought out of obscurity by Laurent Douzou. Although he was fatally wounded during a failed sabotage operation in December 1942, all trace of him had to be eliminated for security reasons. All his personal effects were removed by his comrades and his body placed in a cloth sack and thrown into the nearby canal. His widow was told nothing of what had happened and all trace of him disappeared. For him, as for so many clandestine individuals, there were no ceremonies, though money was given to the family which knew nothing of his death. Above all, no posthumous mention was made of him other than as someone who had disappeared, until the chance discoveries of an archivist rescued him from oblivion.

His case raises the question of how one defines a war victim. Mention has already been made of prisoners executed on the battlefield, and one can only imagine how they were piled into mass graves by civilians ordered to do so by the military authorities who controlled the sector, by the army itself or by the Engineers. Clearly, one also has to include all the victims of extermination. What gradually happened was that society at large strove to get the public,

military and governmental authorities to grant equal status to civilian and military victims, apart from outcasts and
'clandestine' individuals. A good example is the express
wishes carried out by the family of a young female refugee
from Lille, killed in the bombing of Paris on 5 February
1918. In the letters notifying people of her death, they included after her name the words 'She died for France'.[22]

In Paris again, but this time during the 1939–45 War, the
same similarly expressed attitude led to a hidden struggle between the Germans and the French over the burial
of those who had been executed or who had died on the
premises of the occupying police forces. The Germans tried
to transport bodies anonymously and by night; the French,
without any written orders, arranged to have personal details placed on the cemetery records. They served a useful
purpose when bodies were exhumed for identification and
for proper burial at the end of 1945 and during the spring
of 1946.[23] In the case of the young refugee and of those who
fought in the shadows, we see how the community to which
they belonged – the family in the case of the girl from Lille
and the nation in the case of those who were victims of the
Nazis – nonetheless took responsibility for their dead, who
were not strictly 'worthy of honours' in the eyes of the military and political establishment at the time of the fighting.
Thus, they were shown respect in death by being reinte-
grated into the community of those at war either at the
time or some years after they had died.

Circumstances did not allow certain other categories of
'unworthy people', of 'irredeemable dead', to be recognised.
For example, the denial of proper burial to Nazis condemned by the Nuremberg War Crimes Tribunal was a kind
of inverted liturgy. After they were executed and cremated,
their ashes were not scattered with any form of ritual respect, but as a mark of disapproval and disdain.[24]

A bloody death, whether instantaneous or delayed, only
accounted for a proportion of the losses sustained by the
warring armies and societies. To understand how societies
experienced the presence of death, this macabre analysis
has to include details of those who died as a consequence

of very varied illnesses resulting from the exceptional circumstances of war. We are familiar with the ravages of epidemics – typhus during the 1870–1 War, Spanish flu at the end of the 1914–18 War – but we are only just beginning to take into account in our evaluation of the deaths which occurred such things as TNT (trinitrotoluene) poisoning which killed several tens of thousands of women working in munitions factories in England during the First World War.[25] To these must be added specific groups such as old people. Becoming more frail during the war, for psychological, economic and health reasons, men and women over sixty in large European cities died in greater numbers during the First World War.[26]

So far as the huge area of mental illness is concerned (referred to in French and English medical literature under the generic heading of shell-shock), which was usually incurable, recent studies have shown how attitudes have changed from a denial of any illness at the beginning of the century and the shameful death of soldiers overcome by the terror of war, to the recognition and even the prevention of these illnesses.[27] Similarly, suicide, which for a long time remained ignominious according to army codes of behaviour, and which could not be cited as the cause of death in military documents making it difficult to ascertain, is today viewed by historians as a way of escaping from war.[28] These personal dramas were very commonplace, and one has to break family secrets and invade people's privacy to have any sense of the degree of trauma which existed during a particular period.

A study of young French men who chose military collaboration with the Germans during the Second World War has revealed that they belonged to a generation who were fatherless, their male forebears having been killed in the Great War.[29] This is true of Christian, an eighteen-year-old only son, who enlisted in a division of the SS at the time of the invasion. His paternal grandfather had fallen at the battle of Dixmude during the First World War, and his maternal grandfather, suffering depression after that war, had committed suicide in 1931. His only experience of his father, who joined up as a volunteer in 1918, was of a very sick man who was paralysed as a result of a brain seizure.[30] The father of another young man, born in 1919 and a member of the same SS division as Christian, had received the Military Cross, had been in a state of depression since the war ended, and had committed suicide in 1922. The boy's maternal uncle had also committed suicide around the same time. The psychiatrist who examined the young man, who died during the purges at the Liberation, reported what he said: 'He told us that the experience of having lived for a number of years in an exclusively female environment had not prepared him for the struggle for life.'[31]

Can one imagine what this society was like in which hundreds of thousands were missing or had disappeared and whose memory was inviolate because 'everything was owed to them', and where millions of insomniac veterans were haunted at night by the thunder of the guns and the rattle of rifle fire?

If, so far as those who grieved were concerned, individuals expressed similar sorrow, by and large, in the way they honoured a soldier who had fallen in battle, a hostage who had been executed or a child who died of dysentery, from the collective point of view of groups or nations an evolution had taken place since the middle of the nineteenth century in their perceptions of a noble death and of the victims of war. How did the authorities, states and armies change over this period in their treatment of military death?

Notes

1. Blaise Cendrars, *L'Homme foudroyé* (Paris, 1945).
2. Général de Trobriand, *Quatre ans de campagne à l'armée du Potomac*, 2nd edn (Paris: Librairie Intern. A. Lacroix, 1874), quoted in Renée Lemaître, *La Guerre de Sécession en photos avec un choix de textes de témoins français* (Brussels: Elsevier Sequoia, 1975), p. 110.
3. Lt-Colonel Francisco Trigueros Penalver, 'La placa militar de identidad', *Ejercito*, October 1959, pp. 29–34 (Service historique de l'armée de terre, Centre interarmées de documentation militaire, trad. no. 7166).

4. H. Wayne Elliot, 'Identification', in Roy Gutman and David Rieff (eds), *Crimes de guerre. Ce que nous devons savoir* (Paris: Autrement, 2002), pp. 235–6.

5. Official military paper from 1881–1909.

6. Lieutenant A. Froment, *La Mobilisation et la préparation à la guerre* (Paris: La Librairie illustrée, no date [end of the 19th, beginning of the 20th century]).

7. Franc-Nohain and Paul Delay, *Histoire anecdotique de la guerre de 1914–1915* (Paris: P. Lethielleux, 1915), p. 143.

8. Thierry Hardier and Jean-François Jagielski, *Combattre et mourir pendant la Grande Guerre (1914–1925)* (Paris: Imago, 2001), p. 187.

9. Jean-Yves Le Naour, *Le Soldat inconnu vivant* (Paris: Hachette, 2002), p. 47.

10. Mervyn Burke, *Journal inédit*, Carlisle Barracks, quoted by Mark Meigs, 'La mort et ses enjeux: l'utilisation des corps des soldats américains lors de la Première Guerre mondiale', *Guerres mondiales et conflits contemporains*, 175, 1994, p. 144.

11. Claude Sudry, 'L'exode des cadavres', *La Nouvelle Équipe Française*, 59, 1949, p. 43.

12. Claude Simon, *L'Acacia* (Paris: Minuit, 1989); Bertrand Tavernier, *La Vie et rien d'autre* (1989).

13. Circular from the Prefect of the Seine to the mayors of *arrondissements* and *communes* of the Seine, 30 March 1942, Archives de la Préfecture de police de Paris, BA 1756. Similar circulars exist for other towns. (Departmental archives of Calvados, Loiret, l'Indre, files on 'bombing raids').

14. Raid of 3 March 1942, Archives de la Préfecture de police de Paris, BA 1756.

15. Letter from Émile Dupont of Bezons to the Prefect of Ille-et-Vilaine, sent to the Mayor of Rennes on 6 December 1940, Archives municipales de Rennes, 6H23.

16. Statement of the police chief of Rennes, 26 March 1943, Archives municipales de Rennes, 6H23.

17. Pieter Lagrou, 'Les guerres, les morts et le deuil', in Stéphane Audoin-Rouzeau, Annette Becker, Christian Ingrao and Henry Rousso (eds), *La Violence de guerre, 1914–1945, Approches comparées des deux conflits mondiaux* (Brussels & Paris: Complexe/IHTP-CNRS, 2002), pp. 313–27.

18. Susan R. Grayzel, *Women's Identities at War. Gender, Motherhood, and Politics in Britain and France during the First*

World War (Chapel Hill & London: The University of North California Press, 1999).

19. Stéphane Audoin-Rouzeau, 'Au coeur de la guerre: la violence du champ de bataille pendant les deux conflits mondiaux', in Stéphane Audoin-Rouzeau, Annette Becker, Christian Ingrao and Henry Rousso (eds), *La Violence de guerre*, pp. 73–97.

20. Ibid.

21. Laurent Douzou, 'Les morts de la Résistance', in Olivier Dumoulin and Françoise Thelamon (eds), *Autour des morts. Mémoire et Identité* (Rouen: Publications de l'Université de Rouen, 2001), pp. 409–17.

22. Police records, 'Physionomie de Paris', 2nd quarter 1918, Archives de la Préfecture de police de Paris, BA 1587.

23. Record of exhumations, December 1945–March 1946, Archives de la Préfecture de police de Paris, BA 1821.

24. Louis-Vincent Thomas, *Rites de mort* (Paris: Fayard, 1985), p. 117.

25. On female war victims, see Carine Trevisan, *Les Fables du deuil. La Grande Guerre: mort et écriture* (Paris: PUF, 2001), p. 114; Claude Nières, *Faire la guerre. La guerre dans le monde de la préhistoire à nos jours* (Toulouse: Privat, 2001), p. 184.

26. Jean-Louis Robert and Jay Winter, 'Un aspect ignoré de la démographie urbaine de la Grande Guerre: le drame des vieux à Berlin, Londres et Paris', *Annales de Démographie Historique*, 1993, pp. 303–29.

27. Louis Crocq, *Les Traumatismes psychiques de guerre* (Paris: Odile Jacob, 1999).

28. Christian Ingrao, 'Le suicide comme sortie de guerre', paper given at Stéphane Audoin-Rouzeau's seminar on mourning and escaping from war, May 2001.

29. Luc Capdevila, 'The quest for masculinity in a defeated France (1940–1945)', *Contemporary European History*, 10: 3, 2001, pp. 423–45.

30. Report on the protection of children and adolescents of May 1945 and the psychiatrist's analysis of April 1945, Archives départementales d'Ille-et-Vilaine, 213 W, Cour de Justice CG 1945.

31. Psychiatrist's report, June 1945, Archives départementales d'Ille-et-Vilaine, 213 W, Cour de Justice JM 1945.

3 Armies and states faced with their dead

Wars in the industrial age have been conducted by armies and states faced with ever more complex logistical problems. Amongst other issues, the military and politicians have been confronted with too many bodies for them to be able to ignore them. As well as the material question of public order, they have had to negotiate with society at large how best to deal with them. Having given them their children in the prime of their lives, people in general gradually came to consider it their right to have some say in the way the bodies of their dead were treated. The process of negotiation, which led to the establishment of a regulated system of dealing with bodies, took place over a period during which there were four specific times when new practices were introduced.

In conflicts at the end of the nineteenth century, armies had to deal immediately with the dead even during battle, given the significant increase in losses. What were they to do? How did they identify them? Where did they put them? How did they notify families?

In a second phase, the civilian and military authorities began to gather them together in provisional and then permanent cemeteries. This passage from the temporal to the eternal meant that a record of the dead had to be drawn up, that the sites of graves had to be recorded on maps, that bodies had to be exhumed, transported, transferred and even repatriated.

This brought about a third phase in the discussion and choice of location for cemeteries and the form funeral ceremonies should take.

The fourth phase had to do with remembering and commemoration, the physical upkeep of cemeteries and the
preservation of the spiritual dimension of memory. This
evolutionary process, which was chronological since with
each new war the belligerents moved forward from the position which they had already reached, was also diachronic
because it was shaped by the specific national, political and
mental contexts in which it took place.

The actions of the authorities

Before 1914, the authorities had not been totally indifferent
to the war dead. Nevertheless, the way bodies were dealt
with, in particular those of ordinary soldiers, had scarcely
changed since the 'Ancien Régime' when the pits dug on the
battlefield marked the end of fighting.[1] The hurried burials, carried out by the local population mobilised for 'the
task', demonstrated an instinct for survival in the face of
the obvious need to guard against disease, at the same time
making the soldier's death a matter of concealment, something unobtrusive, like the death reserved for paupers, who
were also buried in communal graves at the time. From
the seventeenth to the nineteenth centuries, battlefields
became mass graves; the thousands who fell at the battle
of Rocroi in 1643 would have been buried within a few days
in potholes in the area;[2] likewise the battlefield of Waterloo, strewn with corpses on 18 June 1815 and turned over
by ploughs, yielded up bones many years later.[3]
When the fighting was over, the victorious army took
charge of burial operations. However, up until 1914, as
warfare for the most part involved moving around, armies
which were extremely mobile did not always have the time
to deal with their dead. It therefore fell to the civilian authorities, generally mayors, to bury the bodies in local cemeteries. If there were really too many, they had to be placed in
a grave dug on the battlefield and covered with lime for reasons of hygiene.[4] A soldier's death therefore had lower status than that of a civilian, to the extent that a decree of the
23 Prairial of the year XII (12 June 1804), which regulated

cemeteries, stipulated individual graves and an obligatory coffin. From that date, even if the poor were buried in mass graves, they were placed side by side rather than in heaps, and a coffin was compulsory even for them.[5]

Within this perspective, the treatment of war dead had hardly changed when compared with practices of the seventeenth century. In 1726, Lieutenant-Colonel Hans Friedrich von Leming gave orders to his higher command – with the threat of corporal punishment or even execution – that they should prevent 'the dead from being plundered because wounded officers are sometimes killed so that they may be stripped of their possessions'.[6] They had also, he went on 'to inform the enemy that the dead are to be buried so that they may come and look for high-ranking individuals who have been declared missing. The dead are then buried and a sermon is preached on the battlefield ... A general who is aware of this and acts accordingly earns fame and glory within his own army, from the enemy and from worthy society.'

In fact, from the time of Louis XIV, funeral honours for the military were strictly regulated. The ceremonial, which was first seen as far back as the sixteenth century (the presenting of arms and firing of salvos), was even extended to ordinary soldiers in the first half of the eighteenth century. In a very hierarchical society, it varied, of course, according to rank.[7] Five rifle salvos were fired for a lieutenant-general, three for other ranks, but cannon rounds were fired for field marshals. The detachment which accompanied the body had to be made up of fifty men for a captain and ten for an ordinary soldier. Only those of the same rank lifted the body and carried it to the tomb. Under the Restoration, the prescribed rituals for mourning remained equally precise. Officers wore military mourning for a month, attaching a black band to their sword, whereas 'family' mourners wore a band on the left arm.

Yet, at this time, little concern was shown for bodies left where they fell. In the *Dictionnaire militaire*, published in 1745 by La Chesnaye des Bois, the only reference to the dead appears under the heading 'enemy remains', which

then refers one to 'booty', and makes clear that taking spoils
or causing damage after the fighting had ended was rep-
rehensible, unless the troops had been duly authorised to
do so.[8] From the time of the Napoleonic wars, the State
assumed responsibility for the funeral of anyone killed in
battle or who died of his wounds within three months of receiving them.[9] Signalling a change in attitudes, the decree
of the 23 Prairial of the year XII, the first text to establish de facto the existence of military cemeteries, required
communities to provide a burial place for soldiers. In practice, and according to customary law, towns and villages
used the same communal grave or ossuary for soldiers as
it did for the poor in order to economise. But one of the
first signs of change which came about during the revolutionary wars was the creation of the first graves for officers
and the erection of the first monuments honouring troops
on the field of battle. One was put up at Valmy bearing the
names of all the soldiers killed in the battle. At Waterloo,
families had tombs built for, mainly British, officers who
fell on 18 June 1815. At least two graves of cavalrymen are
equally accounted for in and around the farm referred to
as Mont Saint-Jean.[10]

Furthermore, it was the responsibility of the civilian and
military authorities to record details of those killed. At the
beginning of the nineteenth century, the officer responsible for records kept the regimental details of the unit. After each battle, he counted those who were missing and
recorded their names, with the help of three witnesses who
were required by law. The cause of death was noted if it
had been caused by war: death in battle, as a result of
wounds received, 'from disease caused by stresses of war',
or from 'ordinary' diseases. On no account were deaths in
ignominious circumstances, such as suicide and duelling,
to be mentioned. The officer then informed the authorities
of the place where the person came from, if known. When
the first identity tags appeared at the end of the nineteenth
century, the procedure remained unchanged, except for the
fact that they were collected up so that the dead could be
identified and their names registered.

Thus, from the middle of the nineteenth century, the broad outlines of the way bodies should be dealt with and the numbers of those killed in battle recorded were enshrined in military law governing armies engaged in warfare. Beyond what was prescribed, there were customs and practices. In 1870–1, soldiers wore no individual identity tag and bodies were piled up and buried with their effects in pits, officers and men together with no account taken of their nationality. The priority was to clear the battlefield where machine gun and heavy artillery fire had produced heaps of corpses within a small area. As happened during the Crimean War, during the battles of August 1870, the new fire power of the artillery caught the staff officers unawares and led to massacres during cavalry charges and ordinary attacks. The infantrymen of the Prussian Guard were wiped out in a few minutes at Saint-Privat, with 8,000 Germans and 5,000 Frenchmen losing their lives. At Morsbronn, the French cavalry was slaughtered in a single charge; and on 6 August at Froeschwiller, those killed or wounded exceeded 20,000 on the two sides.[11]

Thousands of bodies had to be quickly buried, for fear that the piles of human remains might cause the spread of opportunist epidemics, which occur at times of disruption and when troops are on the move. But the dead stretched out on the ground had to await burial until the survivors were able to organise themselves or until the firing ceased momentarily, which was not peculiar to this particular 'terrible year' but was true of warfare in general. Doctor Henri de Beaunis, who visited the site of the battle a week after it happened, recalled his impressions: 'It was indeed ghastly, but from another point of view the scene had a certain grandeur. The dead were still lying on the ground, their weapon beside them where they had dropped it; the earth, trampled by men and horses and strewn with wreckage of battle, retained the chaotic atmosphere of what had taken place. One could feel the heat of battle and the poetry of combat.'[12]

The main concern of the authorities, other than dealing with the bodies, was the taking of spoils. Both the military

and civilian authorities tried to stop 'those who would have
stripped the dead and injured' from getting near them and
kept an eye on the activities of second-hand dealers close to
battlefields. They supervised the collection and recording of
dead people's possessions. Once they had been parcelled up
and sealed, they were handed over in exchange for a receipt
from the Deposit and Consignment Office of the main town
in the area.[13]

The conflict of 1870–1 marked a break in the history of
death in war, so far as France was concerned. The Treaty
of Frankfurt, signed on 10 May 1871, stipulated in Article 16: 'the French and German governments undertake
to maintain the graves of soldiers buried in their respec-
tive countries.' This was in fact done. In Germany, the law
of 2 February 1872 regulated the setting-up of graves for
both armies, in Alsace and the old department of Moselle.
It was therefore possible to prepare French burial grounds
as a result of these measures: in Metz (7,636 bodies were
placed in an ossuary and 178 in individual graves), and in
Forbach, Gravelotte, Haguenau and Woerth. In France, after the law of 4 April 1873 had been passed, the State took
charge of Franco-German burial sites, buying up plots in local cemeteries or taking over unenclosed land where there
were other graves. These purchases took place over a period from 1873 to 1878. The graves were put in order, each
with a standard cast iron surround and stamped 'military
graves, by law 4 April 1873'. Twenty-five large ossuaries
with a monument on top were built at Lunéville, Chartres,
Le Mans and Champigny as well as at the Père Lachaise
cemetery and at Montmartre in Paris. In total, the State
took charge of 87,396 burials, with most of the brave souls
lying anonymously and scattered in ossuaries.

In fact, the first large French military cemetery had been
built abroad to bring together the remains of those members of the Eastern army killed at the siege of Sebastopol. It
was completed in the 1880s and was made up of a number
of funeral chapels erected over seventeen vaults containing the bones of officers and soldiers who had perished in
the Crimea between 1854 and 1856. Surrounded by high

walls, with a commemorative monument in the centre and shaded by trees, it served as a model for the commemorative ossuaries of the 1870–1 War. Elsewhere, the graves of those killed during the campaign of 1859 were looked after by colonies of the French in Italy.[14]

Though there were differences between them and the old continent, a similar pattern of events unfolded in the United States. From the time of the War of Independence, and after that of 1812, the first communal graves appeared with a hastily erected marker. These were followed by individual graves, each having a commemorative memorial, often in the form of an obelisk, symbolising eternity and inspired by the Egyptian pharaohs. The first military cemetery was created by the State of Kentucky in 1847. Here they buried the bodies of their dead who had been killed in the Mexican War, having organised and paid for their repatriation. A few years later, the federal State established a permanent military cemetery in Mexico City for the soldiers who fell between 1845 and 1847. The bones of soldiers and officers were gathered up from the surrounding area and placed in permanent graves in a cemetery surrounded by a wall. In the course of the American Civil War, military cemeteries were built for Union soldiers. In 1862, Maryland opened one for the Unionists who fell at the battle of Antietam, as did Pennsylvania in 1863 following the battle of Gettysburg. Indeed, in 1862, Congress adopted measures which allowed the federal authorities to create permanent cemeteries for Union soldiers.[15]

Individual graves therefore became established much earlier in the United States than in Europe, where, until the end of the nineteenth century, it was the custom to bury common soldiers in communal graves; mass sites and ossuaries being used for unidentified human remains. Though few in number, individual burial plots were not necessarily reserved just for superior officers, as we have already seen at Waterloo and as was the case for the Voulminot and Linck National Guards buried in the cemetery at Colmar. They were, however, a minority.[16] Military ossuaries remained the favoured form of burial site for those

killed in the war of 1870–1, as well as for those who fell in
colonial wars or who simply died in their barracks, at the
end of the nineteenth and at the beginning of the twentieth
century.

Much more archaic practices for dealing with those killed
in war were the custom in the Southern Cone of Latin
America. Following the war of the Triple Alliance, the disruption of Paraguayan society was such that many victims
had no grave at all, which observers took to be an obvious
sign of the chaotic state of affairs,[17] an opinion expressed
by the review *La Tour du Monde*. It published a report by
L. Forgues who, during a two-month stay in Paraguay just
after the fighting had ceased, gave a startling eyewitness
account of victims 'left to rot'.[18]

In this geographical region, the principle of the military
cemetery had not yet been adopted, although the funerals of officers had proved to be important occasions during
the conflict.[19] At the beginning of the twentieth century,
their graves became places of commemoration, as in the
case of the mausoleum of General Díaz in the cemetery of
Recoleta in Asunción.[20] Certainly, the officers, often with
a European background, established rules relating to the
dead. Brazilian officers, though offended, sanctioned mutilation, which was carried out on enemy corpses by their na-
tive recruits.[21] When the fighting was over, the bodies were
buried in graves surmounted by a cross on which the number of dead and their country of origin were recorded. But
often, enemy corpses were abandoned if they were too numerous, or when the army was on the move. Clearly, there
was widespread killing of the wounded to make pillaging
easier and bodies were stripped by other soldiers, by auxiliaries and by poor people who followed the armies around.
Similarly, bodies were dug up from their graves so that any
salvageable possessions could be taken. Paraguayan officers sometimes tied themselves to their horses in the hope
that, if they were wounded, their uninjured mount would
bear their body back home so that it might lie in Guarani
soil, which was doubly dear to them because its natural red
colour had been revitalised with the blood of the brave.

When the Brazilian army occupied Asunción in 1869, it created a cemetery at Mangrullo for its own dead. Brazilians continued to be buried there until they left in 1876. At that point and quite spontaneously, the Paraguayan population took the place over. In 1915, it was closed and turned into a public park by municipal decree.[22] This was equally true of most Paraguayan war graves which received no special upkeep. They were still in a neglected state until the early years of the twentieth century when nationalist intellectuals, trying to stir up heroic memories of the *Guerra Grande,* became interested in these special places and rediscovered some of them.[23] The chronology of these events, without being totally different, followed a different time scale in North America, the Southern Cone and in France.

In France, despite a supposedly State-organised system, nothing was put in place to enable families to fulfil their obligations as mourners before 1914–18. It seems that no particular precautionary measures were adopted for the breaking of bad news. Above all, because of the physical circumstances of burial, it was difficult for relatives to come and meditate at the graveside of those they had lost, either because the burial site was unknown or because the grave was a long way from home. That is why the first war memorials of 1870–1 for those killed 'on enemy soil' were erected in the region from which they came and stood in place of graves. We are reminded of this in the patriotic poem published in 1885 honouring the memory of those who died far from home:

> Rest peacefully there beneath the earth
> Which you defended with such courage!
> Sleep . . . France keeps in her maternal heart
> The memory of your devotion.
> The land to which you bring such glory,
> Dearest Poitou which was your cradle
> Has, in bronze, honoured the memory
> Of those, its children, who have no grave.[24]

Nonetheless, in France, the United States, and to a lesser extent in the Southern Cone, national wars marked a turning point in the treatment of those killed in battle. There was both a declared willingness to preserve their remains and a resolve to honour those individuals who had sacrificed themselves on behalf of the national community. Whilst acknowledging the differences between what was said and what was done, and bearing in mind that circumstances and situations varied in civil and international wars, attitudes towards bodies lying on the ground after battle began to change at the end of the nineteenth century. The care with which the living took charge of the dead, the physical remains of war, revealed the change in the way death in war was seen and in the accompanying mourning rituals of those who survived.

Responding to the expectations of families

During the First World War, especially in France, the authorities made the individual treatment of each body the key factor in the handling of the war dead. Although there was gradual and consistent progress, the political will in the response to the needs of families concerning funeral rites was not in evidence at the beginning of the conflict. It was the fruit of bitter negotiations between the society at large and the civil and military authorities, which dragged on from the summer of 1914 until the 1920s.

Despite intense legislative activity to organise society to meet the challenges of war, no measure was adopted for dealing with the dead until the autumn of 1914.[25] Directives put out by the military hierarchy still envisaged the use of a communal grave for ordinary soldiers.[26] The rules governing the medical service in the field made soldiers camped on the spot responsible for burying the dead, supervised by medical officers once the armies had advanced. The German offensive made these orders obsolete, and French troops were buried by the enemy as and when they could in communal graves, individually over a wide area and in cemeteries, often without the necessary measures being taken for their identity to be ultimately established. In the autumn of 1914, once the front was established, it became customary to bury the dead where they fell, at the edge of a wood, in a shell hole, near a house. From then on, all those engaged in combat adopted these practices.[27]

At the beginning of the conflict, the authorities were confronted by civilian codes of behaviour. The great majority of combatants – who were after all only civilians in uniform – were not prepared to adopt military practices. Their behaviour in particular posed organisational problems for the hierarchy. Whenever they could do so, soldiers buried their comrades in individual graves and informed their relatives by letter or when they went on leave as to the place and circumstances of a son's death or the disappearance of a husband. Many families wished to have a body repatriated, and some did so without delay. The funerals of combatants brought back from the front were the first large, patriotic ceremonies to take place away from the front in the summer of 1914.

Legislation was urgent and, in a circular of 19 November 1914, the army High Command forbade the exhumation and transportation of any soldier killed in battle and buried in the war zone. The ban did not affect soldiers who died in military hospitals away from the fighting. The directive was repeated in 1915, so that the intentions of the administration concerning exhumation and transportation, now a clandestine activity, would be clearly understood. Prefects made their subordinates aware that there were to be no exceptions to this rule and that all transportation of bodies by the army was to be refused. As they had to reassure relatives, however, the note reminded them that instructions had been given that 'the location of graves should be identified and respected as much as possible, and that all information should be gathered which would make the subsequent identification of a dead soldier possible.'[28]

There was cause for concern. Firstly, the practice of using communal graves, which still seemed normal to the military hierarchy at the beginning of 1915, made the return of authenticated remains quite uncertain. Then, the authorities, worried about the number of bodies and the risk of infection, considered the large-scale incineration of enemy

as well as of unidentified French and Allied corpses during
the first half of 1915. A bill was even voted upon in the
National Assembly on 18 June 1915, to which we shall return in a later chapter.[29] Emotions ran high, because there
was a conflict between, on one side, the political and military establishment, which was anxious to organise on a
rational basis the decontamination of battlefields and the
protection of the armies from the danger of epidemics, and
on the other, elected members and the Catholic hierarchy
and press. The latter, as the bearers of the families' anguish and inspired by their own religious feelings, refused
to countenance the idea that parents, one day, would not be
able to meditate upon a genuine grave.

After a parliamentary battle, the bill was thrown out by
the Senate on 27 January 1916.[30] At the last sitting, Senator Martin's counter-measure which proposed the simple
and rapid embalming of bodies, something that could 'even
be done by women', so as to meet the demands of combatants and their families, was rejected. There was however a
precedent in the United States when, during the Civil War,
a similar plan had been devised to repatriate the bodies of
those killed in combat. Embalmers were, at the time, one
of the professions active on and around battlefields.[31] In
France, the statement made by Senator Cazeneuve – that
'the bodies of soldiers should be buried whenever it can be
safely done, which will allow families to come and meditate
and place flowers upon their graves' – was the decisive argument which ended the debate and caused the bill to fall.

This trend had already manifested itself in 1915 in several directives and pieces of legislation which, in defining
what was meant by 'those who died for France', made their
status clear.[32] On 19 July 1915, General Headquarters set
up a state registration service, referred to as the 'battlefield'
unit. Their orders required them 'to abandon the use of communal graves, to gather bodies together thereby avoiding
scattered burials, to place them either in individual tombs
or in rows of ten (laid side by side rather than on top of each
other.' By 1915, therefore, those killed in action were to be

treated exactly as had been decreed for civilians more than a century earlier in the decree of the 23 Prairial, year XII. Furthermore, the use of a 'battlefield notebook' to record the exact location of graves became compulsory, and it was recommended that a lead disc should be attached to the bodies bearing a number which would be recorded in the notebook so that they could be identified if they were subsequently exhumed.[33] Though it is clear that these instructions were rarely carried out, the fact that they existed was a sign of new thinking.[34]

Under a law of 18 February 1916, the Ministry of War created a general pensions department to centralise and deal with the vast amount of data relating to the dead. It also had the job of collecting their belongings and their wills – whether they were French, from the colonies, allies or enemy combatants – in order to protect their estates.[35] This administrative body gathered information relating to isolated graves. It had to identify unknown persons, to establish cemeteries in military zones and away from them, and to keep families informed.[36] Those dealing with civil matters and with graves did a great deal of work so far as information and research were concerned, co-operating with municipalities and the police in order to identify and locate the closest relatives of the victim who had to be notified. In telegrams, which generally informed people simultaneously of a death and burial, the bearer was often reminded to show proper consideration in breaking the news. 'I respectfully request you, with due regard in the circumstances, to inform Mr Robillard ... of the death of the soldier Jean Texier who enlisted in 1905 in Rennes and who was killed in action on 10 October 1914 at Mercatel (Pas-de-Calais). I shall be very grateful if you would offer the condolences of the Minister for War and inform me when you have carried out this task.'[37]

The authorities made a distinction, however, according to the way people died. On the list drawn up by military administrators to inform families, regulations required them to differentiate the unremarkable deaths of those persons

or their sons who had died for their country from those who
were to be recorded as 'unworthy', 'having died in dishonourable circumstances'.[38]

Though it was not systematically used, the phrase 'show
due regard when notifying families', which one might have
expected, did appear regularly in letters. Usually, the
mayor or his deputy visited the family with the sad news.
In Paris, special employees of the municipality, dressed in
black, or widows chosen for their tactfulness, were employed to express patriotic condolences. They were asked
to make enquiries from concierges and neighbours before
visiting the families concerned.[39] Throughout the conflict,
the attention paid to families remained a political concern,
heralding the psychological support for families in subsequent conflicts. During the Second World War, the principal
role of female assistants in the Air Force was to meet and
comfort the parents of pilots and other crew members who
had disappeared on a mission.[40]

To return to the beginning of this process, a special civil
unit was also set up in 1916 initially to look for isolated
graves and to bury bodies which were not adequately protected. This work was already under way when the German
offensive of 1918 occurred, but the fierce fighting which took
place almost totally destroyed what had been achieved.
Once the armistice was signed, this body had to recom-
mence its methodical work. The territory comprising the
former war zones was divided into fifty-five sectors, plus
seven in Alsace and Lorraine, and these sectors were sub-
divided into clearly delineated squares. This would allow
metre-by-metre exploration so that exhumations and reburials could take place, necessitated by the regrouping of
graves. The average rate was three thousand reburials a
day according to the authorities.

In order to track down graves for which there was often no
visible marker, information obtained from earlier searches
was used, as well as records provided by the Engineers and
details obtained from families and associations set up to
look for those missing. The excavations were supervised
by officers and the remains examined, according to the

administration, so that 'no possible identification mark was overlooked'. Each body was then placed in a coffin and buried in an individual grave within a 'concentrated' cemetery, a precise plan of which was drawn up. Copies were sent to families who would thereby discover the exact location of their loved one's resting place.

Because the work had to be done quickly, relatives could not be invited to witness the exhumations and reburials, as this would have caused hiccoughs in the operations, but the War Office allowed representatives to be there. To this end, the federation of associations set up to look for the missing sent two delegates to each sector to help supervise the collecting of bodies.

After the armistice, it was difficult to maintain the ban on families bringing their dead back to their local cemetery from the war zone. But such a ban was crucial whilst they were being informed as to the exact location of a grave, prior to transporting the body back home, because mistakes were inevitable. During the first exhumations, it was discovered that wrong information had been put on crosses placed over graves, that there were several bodies in those bearing only one name, and that crosses had not always been put back on exactly the right spot when they had been displaced by shell fire. A whole process of re-identification therefore had to take place, which was difficult and uncertain and raised issues of conscience for the Engineers who usually did the work.

Furthermore, aid for the repatriation of those killed in action seemed, to the authorities, to be a matter of general or public concern and they thought it should therefore be administered democratically. Was it acceptable to allow only wealthy families to bring home a child who had died for his country? Prolonging the spirit of 'sacred union' which had informed the prosecution of the war, an organisation was set up for the exhumation and free transport of bodies, which depended on the restoration of the railway system, and this process determined the granting of permits. Long delays were inevitable and the authorities assured those who were grieving and impatient 'that the graves of their dead would be respectfully tended by officers in the sector responsible for them.'[41]

The reason for these measures did not deter people from bringing bodies home. A number of families, who were prepared to pay a great deal for this, contacted clandestine transport companies who defied the ban because it was a lucrative business.[42] Mayors were given orders to pursue them, by preventing any coffin from entering their area if the driver had not been granted permission to exhume and transport bodies under the regulations in force. Convoys were halted until the police arrived, though these measures were unpopular and unacceptable in the eyes of public opinion.

Thus, in the course of the war, the authorities were brought to the point where they made certain that funeral rites took place which were acceptable to civil society. These included the identification of the body, the placing of it in a coffin – which had gradually become common practice during the nineteenth century –, the funeral itself, the surveillance and upkeep of the grave, the gathering together of bodies, and, lastly, when the law of 28 September 1920 was passed, the handing over of the body to families which requested it. Without setting down all the regulations which governed these military practices, we can acknowledge their actual implementation throughout the conflict. Indeed, the provision of individually marked, military graves for most of those who died for their country was accepted de facto before it was enshrined in law after the armistice. Though soldiers were honoured in death in the middle of the nineteenth century, even if they often remained anonymous, their death became both public and individual during the First World War. The face, name, history and remains of each were known.

Every dead man has a face

Documents provided a point of reference. In practice, the identification of bodies posed enormous problems. Soldiers killed by artillery fire were not always identifiable and they did not necessarily wear their identification tag. During exhumation, skeletons were often jumbled together, a sign they had been buried hurriedly, itself a consequence of the reality of war. After the battle of the Marne, it took eight days to collect up the bodies and bury them, as time and resources were so limited. At Rozelieures (Meurthe-et-Moselle), a grave might have contained 1,500 bodies in 1915, whereas at Saint-Pierremont and Magneux in the Marne only a hundred would be found at that time. But the authorities were beginning to respond to society's expectations. For example, the High Command had numbers of softwood coffins constructed as a precautionary measure. Anticipating losses, they had graves dug before launching an attack. And if bodies were left where they were whilst the battle raged, stretchers which had only just been made were drying in the open close to the front line, waiting for a lull so that the dead and wounded could be evacuated.

One can understand the anguish or the anger of troops going forward when they came upon the things that had been prepared. Canon Le Douarec reported: 'At Mourmelon, the day before an attack, a regiment was marched past the cemetery where territorials were busy digging. The enraged soldiers almost killed the unfortunate gravediggers. They accepted the fact they were being sent to be slaughtered, but not that they should see their own graves being dug.'[43]

The search for those missing went on after the war, and continues to this day. Between 1926 and 1935, 122,000 bodies of French and German soldiers without graves were found on the battlefield. The unidentified bones of those who fell in battle were placed in massive ossuaries. The reason for their construction, like the burial of the unknown soldier on 11 November 1920 which we shall return to, was to create something like a tomb with a body so that families could mourn those they had lost. Calling to mind the pilgrims who came to meditate at the ossuary at Douaumont, Henry de Montherlant, Secretary General of the body responsible for this monument wrote: 'Thousands of people have gone away from this incomprehensible charnel house some grieving others without grief. They only knew of some obscure name on a map. Everything which was found out there is in this tomb, they were told... There they kneel confronting the possible. An astonishing source of comfort.'[44]

The restitution and repatriation of bodies already occurred during the Crimean War and the Italian campaign when coffins sealed with lead began to be escorted home. Similarly, senior officers who died in the colonies were repatriated. During the 1870–1 War, families had dead bodies brought back. 'The 15th militia from Calvados paid their final respects the next day to their brave and loyal leader, to whom it owed its spirit of strength. After a solemn service, with heartfelt emotion, everyone accompanied his mutilated body to the station so that his honoured remains could be taken home to his family. The whole town of Dreux shared the grief of the militia, because townspeople and soldiers alike realised that the country had lost one of its most loyal and valiant servants.'[45]

Real revolutionary change occurred after 1918, with the systematic repatriation of bodies, paid for by the State, to those families who requested it, as provided for in Article 106 of the Finance Bill of 31 July 1920.[46] The budget of the Special Service for the Repatriation of Bodies set up by André Maginot, the Minister for Pensions, was considerable. The overriding desire to 'satisfy the families' encouraged them to spend large sums from the public purse. In 1922, the press denounced 'Dealers in Death'. These businesses had exploited the State by providing standard coffins at exorbitant prices.[47] Between 1921 and 1923, 240,000 bodies were exhumed and taken to parents all over France, which represented 30 per cent of those who had been identified. This democratic principle of respecting the grief and suffering of families remained in force in subsequent conflicts.

One can only talk about families if one does not isolate their reactions from the attitude of the authorities. The debate about the principle of handing bodies back which divided the political class also divided the society at large.

The National Commission for War Graves, presided over by General Castelnau, was asked to examine the bill to be presented to parliament in the first half of 1919. Many were impatient at having to wait for the maximum number of bodies to be identified and of missing to be found so that all families would be satisfied. One of them, Louis Barthou, the deputy for the Pyrénées-Atlantiques, was inconsolable since the death of his son. Others, like Paul Doumer who had lost four sons in the fighting, did not want to see bodies scattered all over the battlefield. The senator from Corsica maintained that a son, whether an officer or a simple soldier, should 'lie alongside those with whom he fought; he led his men into battle and I want him to remain with his comrades, so that for him the battle goes on and that he is at the front and inspires future generations with the desire to defend their country, if there were to be another attack.'[48]

Thus, their desire to demobilise the dead, which was as crucial to them as the demobilisation of the living, led some veterans and relatives to demand their repatriation. And this is what Demachy, one of the soldiers in Roland Dorgelès novel *Les Croix de bois*, did in his own way. 'After Nourry died, writes Dorgelès, two letters arrived addressed to him. We could have sent them back, with the blunt statement written on one corner "recipient could not be contacted", indicating that he had died. Demachy thought it better that he kept them. He took them out of his cartridge pouch, tore them up without opening them, and scattered them like petals over the regulation military grave, as square as a barrack room bedstead, so that the soldier might at least rest beneath words sent from home.'[49] This man had truly enacted a demobilisation of his dead comrade.

Parliamentarians therefore decided to allow families a free choice. For those who wished to have a body brought home, the State assumed total responsibility for everything, including exhumation, transportation and reburial in a cemetery chosen by the family.[50] That gave rise to a great wave of funerals after the war, which was the inspiration for Marcel Pagnol's first comedy *Marchands de gloire*.[51] Military graves still in a national necropolis or in special

sections of local cemeteries were looked after by the State
and families were granted the right of an annual pilgrimage paid for out of public funds. So that the graves might
be more personal and informal, they were set up 'in such a
way as to allow families to place any object to honour the
memory of their dead'.[52]

In fact, the initiative for the return of bodies to their families had come from the United States. During the Mexican
and also the Civil War, repatriation had been scrupulously
carried out. At the beginning of the twentieth century, the
federal government decided that soldiers who died on foreign soil should be automatically returned, both during the
Spanish-American war in Cuba and the insurrection in the
Philippines. They were then interred in the Arlington National Cemetery.[53] The engagement of the United States in
1917 against the central powers forced the Wilson administration to undertake a massive public relations exercise,
one aspect of which related to the burial of American soldiers who fell in Europe. The American Red Cross set up
a funerary service with the intention of sending a host of
embalmers to France to ensure that bodies were properly
treated.

The State Department rejected this proposal and immediately created the Graves Registration Service of the
Army, the role of which was to manage, register and regroup
graves, even though troops had not yet crossed the Atlantic.
Immediately after the armistice, an intense public debate,
just like the one taking place in France at the same time,
divided North American society. Some, under the banner of
the American Field of Honour and ex-President Roosevelt –
whose son Quentin had died in Europe – wanted the bodies
to remain for ever in cemeteries on the other side of the
Atlantic, so that thereafter they would be in consecrated
American soil, as a reminder of American involvement in
the war and as a symbol of their bond with France and
England. Others, following the lead of the League for the
Repatriation of Bodies, asked the federal government to
honour its commitment by consecrating a tomb in America
for those American soldiers who had died abroad.

A few months before the French, the Americans opted for the repatriation of bodies if families so wished and decided that those brave men who had died in battle and who were not reclaimed should remain in Europe. This applied to those on Allied soil. The bodies of American soldiers who died on enemy soil, whether in Germany, in the former Austro-Hungarian Empire or in Russia, were automatically repatriated. Around 70 per cent of families asked for the return of those who fell in Europe, and more than 45,000 coffins crossed the Atlantic once France had authorised the movement of bodies on its territory in March 1920.

Families who had accepted the retention of burial in Europe formed associations such as the Gold Star Mothers. They engaged in intensive lobbying of the federal authorities, requesting that their pilgrimages to graves on the other side of the ocean be paid for. Congress allocated a budget of five million dollars to enable mothers and widows to go to Europe 'as guests of the nation'.[54] The question of fathers had been raised but, in the end, Congress only authorised payment to women, the aftermath of war being a time of great celebration of motherhood in the United States. So, between 1931 and 1933, mothers and widows crossed the Atlantic at public expense, whites travelling on luxury liners whilst the Hoover and Roosevelt administrations felt that blacks could make do with ordinary commercial shipping lines, despite protests from Afro-American associations.[55]

Thus the United States and France made the return of bodies to families a great principle in the treatment of their war dead. In this they were the exception. The Germans and the British, for example, left bodies in military cemeteries near where the soldiers fell. But the major principles underpinning these new patriotic funeral rites were respected by the other Western nations. In Great Britain, the Crown sent out on average four thousand gravestones a week to France between 1920 and 1923.[56] On 11 November 1920, Britain buried an unknown soldier in Westminster Abbey. He would remain there for all eternity alongside kings. In France, on the other hand, despite hesitation between the

Panthéon and the Arc de Triomphe, the 'sky-blue' National
Assembly finally opted for the latter. In comparison with
a church becoming the resting place of certain great men
honoured by the nation, the arch had more military connotations, commemorating all the victories achieved by the
army. Lastly, in the eyes of the conservative right, its patriotic status was beyond dispute, as the pure body of an unknown soldier could not be laid to rest alongside the ashes
of Zola, a defender of Dreyfus!

Other symbolic tombs were erected in memorials in
Washington, Lisbon, Brussels and Rome in 1921, in Prague
and Belgrade in 1922, then in Budapest, Warsaw and
Bucharest.[57] In the Southern Cone, during the war between
Paraguay and Bolivia from 1932 to 1935, military cemeteries were built along the same lines in the northern Chaco region. Wooden crosses marked individual graves which were
lined up for all time in orderly fashion. Immediately after
the Chaco War, on 12 October 1936, the tomb of the unknown soldier was inaugurated in the Pantheon, the place
of heroes, in the centre of Asunción,[58] and books of martyrs
and of commemoration attempted to list all the 'defenders
of Chaco' who fell during the three years of war.[59]

'Vast cemeteries beneath the moon'[60]

Although there were national variations, a Western pattern for dealing with war dead became established around
1914–18. From this time on, the authorities took responsibility for bodies on the battlefield and extended to all who
died in war the same military funeral rites which were imbued with the spirit of bourgeois funerals. In the United
States, the principle of a permanent individual grave for
all Union soldiers, irrespective of race and class, had been
adopted by Congress in 1866.[61] In France, this was enacted
under the law of December 1915, and in England the Imperial War Graves Commission was set up in 1917. On the
German side, during the First World War, officers were appointed to set up and look after cemeteries. However, when
the fighting was over, things were so disorganised that the

authorities abandoned the upkeep of military graves and handed it over to private associations.

Directives given during the inter-war period simply confirmed and perfected the system which had been put in place during previous conflicts. In 1939, official orders governing burials and the decontamination of battlefields stipulated that bodies should be buried as quickly as possible. But it was to be done without undue haste, so that military doctors could clinically confirm death and administrators attached to the medical services could complete details of civil status, helped in their identification process by the systematic wearing of identity tags.[62] When a body could not be identified, a detailed description was made of the place where it lay, of all the objects found on and around the individual, of the kind of clothes he was wearing, and of any weapons nearby. The names of bodies which had been identified in the vicinity as well as the number of the regiment to which the men belonged were to be noted. Finally, the death had to be reported to the accounts and records services.

Orders were clear: 'Bodies must always be buried, whatever the number of dead . . . ' The instructions contained all the technical information about digging graves for up to eighty corpses. To avoid polluting the soil and contaminating water courses, bodies were stripped of all equipment. In addition, the use of lime, which was essential to mask the smell, was restricted so that insects and flesh-eating larvae did their job.

When circumstances dictated the burial of soldiers in communal graves, everything had to be done to make sure that each body was treated as an individual.[63] 'Before being placed in a grave, the body is stripped of equipment and part of the clothing, and limbs are straightened if they have been distorted by rigor mortis. It is put in a shroud, together with its identity and number tags, which is then secured with bindings. A strong, rust-proof metal wire can then be attached, the other end of which is fixed to the cross or tombstone placed above the grave.'[64] The grave, with its mound, had to be marked and guarded.

Orders stipulated – 'if at all possible, when the number of corpses is not too great' – that the body be placed in a coffin and in an individual grave. This was recommended because it was 'the custom', but also in case of subsequent exhumation. Throughout the war, and when it was over, armies exhumed bodies to identify them, place them in coffins, group them together, move them, hand them back, repatriate and re-inter them in permanent graves. Respect for the identity of each soldier meant that military administrators could specify the appropriate religious rites for those who came from various continents, as was done in national cemeteries.

'Each grave must have a cross or a funeral tombstone which will vary according to the religion of the dead soldier.' Instructions indicated what form the tombstone should take depending on the religion. The graves of Moslems were to be aligned on a south-west/north-east axis, with the body placed in a shroud rather than a coffin, lying on its right side, facing Mecca. From the beginning of the First World War, with the arrival of African contingents, the Minister of War gave orders to company commanders and the heads of medical services that the funeral rites and customs of Moslems were to be respected, to reassure those foreign troops who had come to fight in Europe. In Paris, coffins were still used, but, in order to cause the least offence to Moslem sensibilities and to respect in some way the rite of burial straight into the ground, it was decided to line the bottom with sand and to wrap the corpse in a shroud.[65] The funeral tombstone for Jews took the form indicated in the Tablets of the Law. The Indo-Chinese, whose nails were cut and whose arms were placed at their sides rather than folded across their chest, were dressed in clothes having no metal attachments, fasteners or buttons and wrapped in a white shroud. Anyone whose mother or father was still alive wore a white turban around his hair. Finally, it was reiterated that no body was to be burnt, except by order, and unless there was a real danger of infection or if the remains were so mutilated that they could not be identified.

On the eve of the 1939–45 War, experience gained from previous conflicts led the authorities to set up a system for the mass handling of bodies in an individualised manner and to envisage a succession of exhumations and reburials taking place after the war. During the 'phoney war', the decree of 22 February 1940, bringing up to date the legislation relating to military burials, made the same arrangements for both Allied and enemy graves.[66]

The Second World War did not alter the rules and practices relating to death. In France, given the exceptional circumstances of the Occupation, the German authorities, in discussions with the Armistice Commission during the summer of 1940, demanded that their own First World War Department for War Graves should be responsible for all military cemeteries, whether German, Allied or even French.[67] In fact the occupation forces handed over the upkeep and financing of them to the French civil authorities, concerning themselves only with the burial and registering of Germans and with the upkeep of German graves.[68] Moreover, three German officers were allocated to look after war graves to the south of the demarcation line 'in unoccupied France'.[69]

The major difference compared with the First World War was the proportion of civilian deaths amongst the victims. Whereas in the 1914–18 War there were approximately 40,000 civilian victims in France, around 250,000 were recorded in 1945. Moreover, the law of 28 February 1922, which readopted many of the provisions of the previous one passed on 2 July 1915, stated that all civilians should have the same rights as military victims and that 'any civilian killed as a result of enemy action'[70] should be honoured as having 'died for France'. Those killed in bombing raids as well as those deported as forced labour were included under this new heading. The 1922 law was also retroactive. From that date, civilian victims of the Great War could be found alongside soldiers in military cemeteries: ten or so at Cerny-en-Laonnais, and some Belgians and a few French forced labour deportees in the one at Effry in the department of Aisne, and so on.

On the other hand, most civilian victims of the Second World War were not granted a permanent grave maintained by a government department. The law of 27 August 1948 only permitted civilians belonging to the Resistance to be buried in a national cemetery, which reflected a contradiction between the right to be named as having 'died for France' and to be granted a permanent resting place.[71] In fact, Article L.115 of the law relating to pensions for soldiers and war victims stipulated that a burial place was restricted to those civilians whose death 'was the direct result of a deliberate act undertaken in the struggle against the enemy, their death certificate bearing the inscription that they "died for France".' Thus, unlike civilians in the Great War, the families of hostages, of Compulsory Labour Service conscripts who died in Germany and of the victims of bombing could not request that they be buried in military cemeteries, despite having died as recognised patriots 'for France'. Civilian graves of the 1939–45 War, which today are protected within the military section of local cemeteries, are looked after by municipalities or by families.

Second World War cemeteries furnish evidence of these differentiated identities which, from the Liberation on, have led us to discriminate in the way we remember. In the eastern cemetery in Rennes, there are quite different sections for the graves of those who 'died for France' during the First World War and for the various categories of those who died during the Second World War: the graves of the victims of bombing, the graves of the Allies, all with rows of crosses or white stones, and then the Resistance fighters who had been shot and placed in civilian graves bearing patriotic symbols which mark the dividing line between the military section of the graveyard and the part where everyone else is buried. Though almost two thirds of the combatants of 1940 are in military graves in national cemeteries (that is to say the same proportion as of veterans of the 1914–18 War), the urge to discriminate between victims, and for families to categorise them, has meant that barely 1,500 Resistance fighters who 'died for France' have been buried in a State-maintained grave out of the 30,000 whose official records indicate that they too belong to this category.[72]

In practice, society extended to all victims of war the same patriotic funeral which had been introduced during the Great War. The ceremonies for those killed in bombing raids gave rise to large-scale patriotic demonstrations both in 1914–18 and in 1939–45. Their remains were placed in graves similar to military ones paid for by the municipality. In 1944, anticipating an increase in the number of deaths with the intensification of bombing prior to the D-Day landings, certain municipalities undertook to extend their cemeteries, ordered hundreds of coffins in advance and planned for funerals to be speeded up so that each person and each family could have a basic ceremony. With the Liberation came the digging up of sites where the Germans had buried the bodies of hostages and Resistance fighters.[73] In the early weeks, municipal authorities exhumed bodies for identification purposes, handed them over to families and organised 'dignified' funerals, that is to say religious ceremonies, at which they were also often given military honours.[74]

Similarly, the principle of handing over bodies to families was reintroduced in 1946.[75] This time, the law adopted was that of 1920: all victims of war, both military and civilian, were to receive the same treatment. Families who wished could have the body of their loved one repatriated. If the person had died as a consequence of war, he or she was automatically said to have 'died for France', whether they were a Resistance fighter, had been conscripted or killed by enemy or Allied bombing. Thus ended the process whereby distinctions were drawn between civilian and military victims of war.

The conflicts in North Africa, moreover, did not bring any appreciable change to the way the State and the military organised funerals. Whether those who died during operations were regular or conscripted soldiers, they were said to have 'died for France', even though the country was not officially at war.[76] They received military honours and their families were by statute to be shown public sympathy, though certain survivors had to wait until 1998 before being recognised as veterans. With the war in Algeria, funeral practices, the formalities of which had long been established, were modified because of the particular political circumstances. Those members of the expeditionary force in Indo-China who died were buried on the spot in colonial military cemeteries. It is true that conscripts were not mobilised for this conflict. In Algeria, once the 'events' had begun, soldiers who 'died for France' were buried in provisional plots before being handed over to those families who wanted them back. Then, they were systematically repatriated to metropolitan France.

Everything was carried out to the letter. Each individual was said to have 'died for France', was given military honours both by the hierarchy and his comrades, his coffin was draped in the tricolour, there was a minute's silence, decorations were pinned to a red cushion. Finally, his bodied was repatriated to France for permanent burial in a national cemetery or in one near his home. But the funeral occurred in two stages. In Algeria itself, the medical services dealt with things in a matter-of-fact way, leaving trestles erected on which the coffins were placed and always using the same flag. Military funerals were often organised discreetly at dawn, and in a hurry, revealing the authorities' desire to conceal the vulnerable situation of the expeditionary force. Before bodies were repatriated in groups, their brothers-in-arms who mourned gathered together one last time in a chapel of rest.[77] There was, therefore, a mixture of punctilious respect for what was proper and the cold insensitivity of warfare.

The repatriation of corpses was handled by the Central Office of the service responsible for the movement and transfer of bodies. It was attached to the interdepartmental agency which looked after the interests of war veterans and the victims of war and which achieved its final form in December 1958. The family was initially informed by a telegram which expressed the 'sincere condolences of his superiors and comrades'. A few days later, the mayor and father of the deceased received a letter stating that he had 'died for France'. The body followed some weeks later in a lead-lined coffin. In metropolitan France, all the pomp of a patriotic ceremony was displayed at the funeral. This was a reminder of what had taken place when bodies were brought back at the end of the two World Wars, with various people present including school children, the authorities, associations of three generations of veterans, families and local people. Patriotic symbols were displayed: the tricolour covering the coffin, decorations pinned to a cushion held by a soldier, and above all a guard of honour led by an officer. The latter had been recommended by the army's psychology department both as a mark of respect and in case of any hostile reaction or pacifist demonstration.[78]

Thus, 'the war which never was' resulted in patriotic deaths; deaths which were kept hidden in North Africa and deaths which were an embarrassment in metropolitan France, since they reminded people who were not terribly involved and who no longer wished to sacrifice their children, of the realities of war. In choosing to hold ceremonial funerals, the authorities tried to mobilise the population, as they had done in previous conflicts.[79] It was a question also of treating the dead somewhat differently from the living. In a war which had not been officially declared and which produced no veterans, men nonetheless fell in battle, and if they died for France was it not the case that the repatriation of their bodies, albeit a nationally enshrined practice, suggested that at some time in the future territory would be given up which was already not entirely French?

Despite having different traditions, the United States behaved similarly in Vietnam. The decision was taken at the end of the Second World War to repatriate as a matter of course all Americans whose bodies were buried in places which were difficult to get to or not secure. From that point on, only territory belonging to the United States or its European allies was considered sufficiently secure as a last resting place for their brave compatriots. The bodies of Americans who died in Africa and Asia were taken back home, which was not the case so far as the British, Australian and Dutch authorities were concerned. Because of their imperial past, these countries retained military cemeteries overseas, for example in Thailand and Burma where the bodies of prisoners who died during the construction of the railway line across the river Kwai still remain to this day.[80] The same practice was adopted during the Korean War. The federal authorities buried soldiers together on a temporary basis in cemeteries in Asia before taking them back home.

In South Vietnam, provisional burial was rare and the military authorities systematically flew the bodies of its soldiers to America.[81] The federal government did what it could to locate those 'missing in action', initially on its own and then, when diplomatic relations were re-established with the North Vietnamese, in collaboration with them, which meant that the remains of around two hundred men 'missing in action' were repatriated between 1981 and 1989.[82] During the same period, the Vietnamese authorities were asked by the French government to return the bodies of those who died during the war in Indo-China. It then organised their repatriation and reburial in metropolitan France, most of them being interred in the memorial cemetery in Fréjus.

Armies and states have spent vast sums of money and expended a great deal of energy in assuming responsibility for bodies, even when one takes into account their expenditure on weapons of destruction. But it was not automatic. The municipal council of Trélazé, near Angers, took the decision on 18 December 1920 not to erect a war memorial in the community, for anti-militarist and financial reasons. In a written statement, which was however withdrawn by the Prefect of Maine-et-Loire, the council said that 'the dead need nothing. They wanted to live and they were sent to their death. What has happened to them cannot be undone. A memorial will alter nothing... The materials, money and labour used to create memorials would be better spent on projects for the living, especially houses.

With what would be spent on this object in our community, a number of houses could be rebuilt in areas which have been liberated.'[83] It was not until 1947 that a memorial 'to the children of Trélazé who died for France, and to all victims of war' was erected there in the cemetery.[84] Between the debate stirred up by this municipal council during the 1920s and the clear consensus underpinning the compassion felt for those who had suffered in the war three decades later, attitudes towards the war dead had changed.

Taking France as a single example, the numbers of war cemeteries bear witness to the widespread conflicts in which her soldiers have been involved.[85] At the end of the twentieth century, there were 720,000 bodies in 252 national cemeteries and 115,000 others lay in local ones. Almost 200,000 were in cemeteries in other countries. All these people who had 'died for France' included soldiers and civilians who had fallen in combat since the second half of the nineteenth century, the largest number being those who died in the Great War. To them must be added those soldiers and civilians who also died for their country and, having been handed back to their families, had become ordinary citizens. The remains of 240,000 in this category were brought home at public expense at the end of the Great War. Another 144,274 were also returned at the end of the Second World War, and in most cases conscripts killed in Algeria were repatriated and handed over to their loved ones. In addition, one could include those hundreds of thousands of other combatants: British, Americans, Italians, Belgians, Poles, Portuguese, Serbs, Russians, and so on.

As well as these, there were the 1,024,027 Germans, mostly soldiers, whose bodies have been brought together in forty or so designated cemeteries and in sectors of approximately fifty local ones in the aftermath of three wars and three invasions of French territory. This almost equals the number of Frenchmen in national cemeteries. What ventures and what negotiations led to these foreign combatants being buried in an alien land? How were the enemy seen and what was done with their bodies?

Notes

1. André Corvisier, 'La mort du soldat depuis la fin du Moyen Âge', *Revue historique*, juillet 1975, pp. 3–30.
2. Jean-Philippe Ollier, 'Une nouvelle lecture de la bataille de Rocroi', *Histoire et Défense. Les Cahiers de Montpellier*, 28, 1993, pp. 109–34.
3. André Corvisier, *Les Hommes, la Guerre, la Mort* (Paris: Économica, 1985), p. 388.
4. Un officier supérieur en retraite, *Les Devoirs des maires en cas de mobilisation générale* (Paris: Paul Dupont, 1889), pp. 64–6.
5. Philippe Ariès, *L'Homme devant la mort* (Paris: Seuil, 1977), p. 510.
6. In Chapter 32 'Après avoir gagné la bataille' in his huge work *Le Parfait soldat allemand*; quoted in Hans Soltau, *Volksbund Deutsche Kriegsgräberfürsorge. Service pour l'entretien des Sépultures Militaires Allemandes – ses origines et son action* (Kassel, 1987), p. 10.
7. André Corvisier, *Les Hommes, la Guerre, la Mort*, p. 384.
8. *Dictionnaire militaire ou recueil alphabétique de tous les termes propres à l'art de la guerre*, by De la Chesnaye des Bois (Paris, 1745), 2 volumes.
9. *Instruction provisoire pour le service des troupes en campagne*, printed on the orders of the Minister of War (Paris: F. G. Levrault, 1823).
10. Jean-Charles Jauffret, 'La question du transfert des corps: 1915–1934', in Rémy Cazals (ed.), *Traces de 1914–1918*, colloque de Carcassonne (Carcassonne: Les Audois, 1997), pp. 133–46.
11. François Roth, *La Guerre de 70* (Paris: Fayard, 1990); Stéphane Audoin-Rouzeau, *1870, la France dans la guerre* (Paris: Armand Colin, 1989).
12. Docteur Henri de Beaunis, *Impressions de campagne (1870–1871)* (Paris: Félix Alcan, 1887), pp. 134–5, quoted in Corinne Krouck, *Les Combattants français de la guerre de 1870–1871 et l'écriture de soi: contribution à une histoire des sensibilités*, thesis, Université Paris I, 2001, p. 119.
13. Un officier supérieur en retraite, *Les Devoirs des maires en cas de mobilisation générale* (Paris: Paul Dupont, 1889), pp. 65–6.

14. Le Souvenir Français, 'Allocution du général Cosseron de Villenoisy', *Rapports de l'assemblée générale du 24 mai 1896*, Paris, 1896, p. 2.
15. G. Kurt Piehler, *Remembering War. The American Way* (Washington, DC & London: Smithsonian Institution Press, 1995), pp. 40–9.
16. Antoinette Le Normand-Romain, 'La guerre vue à travers la sculpture funéraire', in Philippe Levillain, Rainer Riemenschneider (eds), *La Guerre de 1870 et ses conséquences* (Bonn: Bouvier, 1990), pp. 494–505.
17. Alfredo Viola, 'Asunción bajo la dominación extranjera', *Historia Paraguaya*, Asunción, XXV, 1988, pp. 91–140.
18. L. Forgues, 'Le Paraguay. Fragments de journal et de correspondances, 1872–1873', *Le Tour du Monde*, 701, juin 1874, p. 398.
19. National Library of Asunción, Emiliano Solano López collection, *Honores funebres. Discursos pronunciados sobre la tumba del general ciudadano José Diáz* (Humaïta: Imprenta del Ejercito, 1867).
20. *Apoteosis del general Diáz* (Asunción: Talleres nacional Krauss, 1907). Summary and speech at the unveiling ceremony of the bronze bust of General Diáz at the cemetery of la Recoleta (Asunción), 23 September 1907.
21. Alfredo de Taunay, *La Retraite de Laguna. Récit de la guerre du Paraguay, 1864–1870* (Paris: Phébus, 1995 [1st edn 1867]), p. 109.
22. Alfredo Viola, 'Cementerios del Paraguay', *Historia Paraguaya*, vol. XXVII (Asunción: 1990), pp. 167–200.
23. 'Cimetière de Pasó Pucú, la sépulture de Natalicio de María Talavera', in Arsenio López Decoud (ed.), *La República del Paraguay un siglo de vida nacional 1811–1911* (Buenos Aires: Talleres Gráficos de la Companía General de Fósforos, 1911), p. 169.
24. An extract from J. Philippe, 'Gloria Victis! Aux mobiles des Deux-Sèvres', in *Union des Femmes de France, Almanach pour 1885* (Niort: Typographie A. Boureau, 1885), p. 30.
25. *Guerre de 1914. Documents officiels, textes législatifs et réglementaires, 31 juillet–15 octobre 1914* (Paris: Librairie Dalloz, 1914).
26. Jean-Charles Jauffret, 'La question du transfert des corps: 1915–1934', in Rémy Cazals (ed.), *Traces de 1914–1918* (Carcassonne: Les Audois, 1997), pp. 133–46.

27. Yves Pourcher, 'La fouille des champs d'honneur. La sépulture des soldats de 14–18', *Terrain*, 20, 1993, p. 45.

28. Note of 17 July 1915 from the Prefect of Ille-et-Vilaine to the sub-prefects, sub-prefecture of Vitré, Archives départementales d'Ille-et-Vilaine, 6 Z149.

29. *Journal officiel de la République française* (parliamentary debates) of 19 June 1915, Chamber of Deputies, sitting of 18 June 1915.

30. *Journal officiel de la République française* (parliamentary debates), Senate, sitting of 27 January 1916.

31. Michel Vovelle, *La Mort et l'Occident de 1300 à nos jours* (Paris: Gallimard, 1983), p. 622.

32. *Journal officiel de la République française*, 9 July 1915, law of 2 July 1915 relating to the citation 'died for France' in death certificates.

33. Summary of the way burial arrangements were organised between 2 August 1914 and 10 January 1919, Paris, le 10 mai 1919, Archives nationales, BB18-2607-1484 A 18, ministère de la Guerre, sous-secrétariat d'État de l'Administration, service général des Pensions.

34. Yves Pourchet, 'La fouille des champs d'honneur. La sépulture des soldats de 14–18', pp. 45–6.

35. Bulletin officiel militaire, partie permanente, 1916, classement à l'édition méthodique no. 28, 'Instructions pratiques concernant la constatation aux armées des évacuations, disparitions, décès et inhumations' [Practical instructions concerning army registration of deaths, burials, bodies evacuated and the missing], 2 juin 1916, pp. 439–73.

36. *Journal officiel de la République française*, 20 February 1916, p. 1422, law relating to the creation in the Ministry of War of a service for pensions, aid and information for families, dealing also with personal details and details of soldiers' wills.

37. Correspondence from Captain Quéro, head of the accounts office of the 71st infantry regiment to the mayor of Rennes, 11 April 1916, Archives municipales de Rennes, H 54 – notification of death.

38. Bulletin officiel des armées, édition méthodique, 1916, circulaire no 62 du 22 juin 1916, 'Diplôme d'honneur à remettre aux familles des officers, des sous-officiers et soldats morts pour la patrie' [Honourable mention to be conveyed to the families of officers, non-commissioned officers and ordinary soldiers who died for their country].

39. Françoise Thébaud, 'La guerre et le deuil chez les femmes françaises', in Jean-Jacques Becker (ed.), *Guerre et cultures, 1914–1918* (Paris: Armand Colin, 1994), p. 109.

40. Note of 31 January 1945 to the head and those in the social service section of the Air Force, Service historique de l'armée de l'air, 4D54 – SPAA.

41. Fortnightly circular number 4 of 15 September 1919, from the Prefect of Ille-et-Vilaine to the sub-prefects and mayors in the Department, Archives municipales de Rennes, 119 W 9.

42. Letter from the Minister of the Interior to prefects, 16 September 1919.

43. Chanoine Le Douarec, *Un Bleuet, de la peur à l'héroïsme*, Éditions Alsatia, 1938, p. 244, quoted in Thierry Hardier and Jean-François Jagielski, *Combattre et mourir pendant la Grande Guerre (1914–1925)* (Paris: Imago, 2001), p. 206.

44. Henri de Montherlant, *Chant funèbre pour les morts de Verdun*, 1st edn 1924, *Essais* (Paris: Gallimard, 'Pléiade' edn, 1988), p. 198.

45. *Notice historique sur le mobile du Calvados 1870–1871*, 'This booklet is sold in aid of the fund to erect a memorial to those born in Calvados who died for their country during the 1870–1871 war', Caen, Imp. H. Delesques, no date (last quarter of the nineteenth century), p. 9.

46. *Journal officiel de la République française*, 2 October 1920, 28 September for the decree of its implementation.

47. Béatrix Pau-Heyries, 'Le marché des cercueils (1918–1924)', *Revue Historique des Armées*, 3, 2001, pp. 65–80.

48. National Commission for war graves on the proposed law forbidding the exhumation and transportation of the bodies of French, Allied and enemy soldiers on French soil for an unspecified period, 1919, Archives nationales BB18-2607-1484A18. Quoted in Yves Pourcher, 'La fouille des champs d'honneur. La sépulture des soldats de 14–18', p. 47.

49. Roland Dorgelès, *Les Croix de bois* (Paris: Albin Michel, 1919), p. 150.

50. *Journal officiel de la République française*, 3 October 1920, decree of 28 September 1920 concerning the return of bodies to families.

51. Marcel Pagnol, *Marchands de gloire* (Paris: Éditions de Provence, 1964), first performed in Paris in April 1925.

52. *Journal officiel de la République française*, 30 September 1920, decree of 25 September concerning cemeteries and war graves.

53. G. Kurt Piehler, *Remembering War. The American Way*, pp. 90–1.

54. D. M. Kennedy, *Over Here. The First World War and American Society* (New York & Oxford: Oxford University Press, 1980), p. 367.

55. G. Kurt Piehler, *Remembering War, The American Way*, p. 104.

56. M. Eksteins, *Le Sacre du printemps* (Paris: Plon, 1991), p. 296.

57. C. Vilain, *Le Soldat inconnu. Histoire et culte* (Paris: M. d'Artoy, 1933); Annette Becker, 'Du 14 juillet 1919 au 11 novembre 1920. Mort, où est ta victoire?' *Vingtième siècle. Revue d'histoire*, 49, 1996, pp. 31–44.

58. El Mariscal Francisco Solano López Presidente de la República del Paraguay y General en Jefe de sus Ejercitos. APOTEOSIS, Asunción, Paraguay, 1936.

59. Alfredo M. Seiferheld, *Cincuentenario de la Guerra del Chaco (1932–1935)* (Asunción: El Lector, 1985). Memories of the war of the Triple Alliance and the Chaco War and on contemporary political culture in Paraguay, cf. Claude Castro, 'Le panthéon des héros à Asunción del Paraguay: l'histoire en question', in *Lieux du pouvoir et pouvoirs du lieu dans les Amériques*, GRAL, Toulouse, 27–29 septembre 1995, volume III, pp. 45–55; 'La guerre du Paraguay: un espace pour diverses interprétations de l'histoire', in Jacqueline Covo (ed.), *Historia, Espacio e imaginario* (Lille: Septentrion, 1997), pp. 229–36; Guido Rodriguez Alcalá, *Temas del autoritarismo* (Asunción, 1994).

60. This refers to *Les Grands Cimetières sous la lune* (1937), in which the writer Georges Bernanos denounced fascist atrocities during the Spanish Civil War. [Translator's note]

61. G. Kurt Piehler, *Remembering War. The American Way*, p. 51.

62. Hygiene service in the field, *Notices. Volume à jour au 24 juillet 1939* (Paris: Charles-Lavauzelle, 1939, directive no. 9, 'Inhumations – assainissement des champs de bataille', pp. 123–8.

63. Ibid. chapter 1. Guerre de mouvement (document abrogé: notice no. 9 du 12 avril 1913), p. 21.

64. It would appear that this practice began during the First World War, cf. Thierry Hardier, Jean-François Jagielski, *Combattre et mourir pendant la Grande Guerre (1914–1918)*, p. 209.

65. Franc-Nohain and Paul Belay, *Histoire anecdotique de la Guerre de 1914–1915*, volume 5 (Paris: P. Lethielleux, 1915), pp. 96–9.

66. *Journal officiel de la République française*, 25 February 1940, decree of 22 February 1940 on war graves.

67. Correspondence of the Field Commander, the officer in charge of graves to the Prefect of Ille-et-Vilaine and to mayors of the Department, 10 August 1940, Archives départementales d'Ille-et-Vilaine, 31 W 3.

68. German requisitions, invoices: burial expenses (1940–1944–1945), German requisitions, invoices: upkeep of German war graves (1940–1944), Archives départementales d'Ille-et-Vilaine, 170 W 851 and 170 W 785.

69. French delegation to the German armistice commission, *Recueil de documents publié par le gouvernment français, tome 1, 29 juin 1940-29 septembre 1940* (Paris: Alfred Costes, 1947), p. 315.

70. *Journal officiel de la République française*, 1 March 1922, law of 28 February relating to death certificates of military personnel and civilians who 'died for France'.

71. *Journal officiel de la République française*, 28 August 1948, law of 27 August 1948 relating to permanent graves for civilian war victims. The decree of 20 February 1952 concerning the public administration of the law of 1948 gives details of civilians to be granted permanent graves: 1) those deported and those Resistance fighters who were interned and who 'died for France' and who were given a card posthumously indicating they were deportees or internees; 2) Resistance fighters who 'died for France' and received posthumously a card stating they were volunteer fighters in the Resistance; 3) Resistance fighters who 'died for France' and were granted a military pension as a result of their death or of being invalided.

72. Serge Barcellini, 'La gestion du deuil par l'État français au lendemain de la Seconde Guerre mondiale', in Francine-Dominique Liechtenhan (ed.), *Europe 1946 entre le deuil et l'espoir* (Brussels: Complexe, 1996), p. 135.

73. Prefect's office, investigations of victims of the German occupation and of the Milice. Heroic acts of resistance, damage

caused, Archives départementales d'Ille-et-Vilaine, 134 W 42. The documentation relating to 'German atrocities' which contains much information on funeral practices, comprises reports of the French Red Cross, material from the archives of the gendarmerie, the regional services of the CID (SRPJ) as well as from the archives of the prefecture.

74. René Coustellier, *Le Groupe Soleil dans la Résistance* (Périgueux: Fanlac, 1998).

75. *Journal officiel de la République française*, 17 October 1946, law of 16 October 1946 relating to the free transportation and to the restitution to families of the bodies of war veterans and other war victims.

76. Jean-Charles Jauffret, *Soldats en Algérie, 1954–1962. Expériences contrastées des hommes du contingent* (Paris: Autrement, 2001), pp. 312–17.

77. Jean-Yves Jaffrès, *La Vie des soldats bretons dans la guerre d'Algérie, 1954–1962* (Bannalec: Éditions Nos Photos Témoignent, 2000), p. 261.

78. Claire Mauss-Copeaux, *Appelés en Algérie. La parole confisquée* (Paris: Hachette, 1998), p. 29.

79. Charles-Robert Ageron, 'L'opinion française à travers les sondages', in Jean-Pierre Rioux (ed.), *La Guerre d'Algérie et les Français* (Paris: Fayard, 1990), pp. 25–44.

80. Hugh V. Clarke, *A Life For Every Sleeper. A Pictorial Record of the Burma-Thailand Railway* (Sydney: Allen & Unwin, 1986).

81. G. Kurt Piehler, *Remembering War. The American Way*, p. 168.

82. Danielle Fernandez, 'L'opinion publique américaine et la question des "missing in action"', in Jean-Michel Lacroix and Jean Cazemajou, *La Guerre du Vietnam et l'opinion publique américaine (1961–1973)* (Paris: Presses de la Sorbonne Nouvelle, 1991), p. 136.

83. Minutes of the municipal council meeting of 18 December 1920, Archives municipales de Trélazé (Maine-et-Loire).

84. Équipe de recherche historique d'ECA3, *Les monuments aux morts du Maine-et-Loire. Mosaïque et miroir de l'histoire communale* (Angers: Georges Bodet, 1999), p. 33.

85. The following information was obtained from the office of the Secretary of State responsible for war veterans and other victims of war – the section dedicated permanently to Commemorations and Historical Information, cf. the atlas *Les*

Nécropoles nationales en France, cf. also Catherine Grive-Santini, *Guide des cimetières militaires en France* (Paris: Éditions du Cherche-Midi, 1999); for German cemeteries see *Deutsche Kriegsgräber. Am rande der Strassen. Frankreich, Belgien, Luxemburg und Niederlande* (Kassel: Éditions du VDK, 1997). These are approximate figures, as the number of war graves is in the process of being firmly established. Indeed, the remains of several tens of French and foreign combatants are still being found by chance each year.

4 What should be done with enemy corpses?

Since the middle of the nineteenth century different forms of warfare have produced three sorts of reaction to enemy bodies – respect, fury and the urge to annihilate. These attitudes did not coincide precisely either with specific chronological periods or with particular geographical areas. They co-existed, manifesting themselves simultaneously or being mutually exclusive in turn.

Of these forms of behaviour, the easiest to grasp and to define historically is respect. Though not the most widespread, it was nonetheless robustly theorised over and affirmed. It belonged to a form of warfare which was codified in terms of internationally recognised rules of engagement accepted by most states. In such confrontations, the enemy was a fellow human being with whom, in some way or another, one would ultimately negotiate. But the violence of war could not be contained within the narrow bounds of fair and chivalrous combat, and killing on a grand scale also changed the way the enemy was seen. The breaking of established social norms, which international law tried to restrain, led to excesses in the way enemy bodies were treated since no boundaries had been set. The third stage in the way the enemy was perceived resulted in him no longer being viewed as a foe or an opponent but as someone radically different from oneself, a wholly antipathetic being who should be obliterated even when dead. Of course, these three reactions were never wholly separable. The treatment of enemy bodies was, therefore, a function of the way war was seen, of the way one saw oneself as well as one's opponent, and the kinds of relationships one enjoyed with the living both

Plate 1 Battlefields during the American Civil War. Photograph
taken by A. Gardner in Renée Lemaître, *La Guerre de Sécession en
photos* (Paris/Brussels: Elsevier Séquoia, 1975).

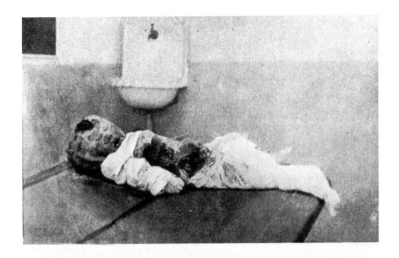

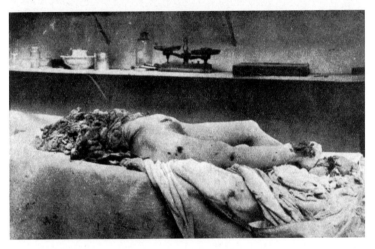

Plate 2 After the bombing of a Parisian maternity hospital, March 1918. These photos, censured at the time, were published in 1933 in the first number of a pacifist review, *Témoignages*, devoted to *Images secrètes de la guerre. 200 photographies et documents censurés en France, recueillis et commentés par Paul Allard en collaboration avec F. Drach* (Paris: SA Les Illustrés français). Rights reserved.

Plate 3 Scene of the German invasion of Poland, September 1939. This photograph was used on the cover of a pamphlet published by the Polish government in exile in 1940: *L'Invasion allemande en Pologne. Documents, témoignages authentifiés et photographies, recueillis par le Centre d'information et de documentation du gouvernement polonais* (Paris: Flammarion, 1940). Rights reserved.

Plate 4 Mass grave at Bron (near Lyon). The opening of graves at
the Liberation, September 1944. This photograph was reproduced
in *Le Livre noir du Vercors* (Neuchâtel: Ides et Calendes, 1944)
with the following caption: 'In July 1944, hundreds of prisoners of
the Gestapo, Jews, political detainees and soldiers of the Forces
Françaises de l'Intérieur (FFI) were taken to bomb craters where
they were shot in the back of the head. Having been thrown one on
top of the other into the hole, earth was piled onto them by
another group of prisoners who then suffered the same fate. Young
French volunteers of fifteen to eighteen years of age disentangle
the putrefied corpses jumbled, intertwined and stuck together in
death.'

Plate 5 Mass grave at Bron. This photograph was reproduced in *Le livre noir du Vercors*, op. cit., with the following caption: 'A chapel of rest was set up in the only part of the massive hangar which remained standing at the aerodrome of Bron near Lyon. Helped by young lay volunteers, a Franciscan brother is about to lay out the bodies and place them in deal coffins.' Rights reserved.

Plate 6 Bodies dug up to be placed in coffins, 1941. American agency photograph reproduced in *Voir, ne pas voir la guerre. Histoire des représentations photographiques de la guerre* (Paris: Somorgy, 2001). MHC-BDIC collection. Rights reserved.

Plate 7 *Top* Representation on a bank note of the Panthéon which contains the body of the unknown soldier of the Chaco War. *Bottom* Paraguayan military cemetery of the Chaco War. This photograph is taken from Alfredo M. Seiferheld (ed.), *Cincuentenario de la Guerra del Chaco (1932–1935)* (Asunción: El Lector, 1985).

Plate 8 Reims, 1918. Identifying the dead: sorting out bodies. French on the right, Germans on the left. Photograph taken from *Témoignages* No. 1 (see Plate 2 caption). Rights reserved.

Plate 9 Kanchanaburi (Thailand). Cemetery for prisoners of war who died building the railway which crossed the River Kwai.

Plate 10 Near Qui Nhon, Vietnam, 1967. Taken from a helicopter:
the scattered bodies of North Vietnamese soldiers who have been
dragged by ropes to the centre of this piece of ground so that they
can be buried together. Photographed by Henri Huet (AP), taken
from *Requiem par les photographes morts au Viêt-nam et en
Indochine* (Paris: Marval, 1998). Rights reserved.

Plate 11 One of those hanged at La Mûre-en-Vercors. This photograph was reproduced in *Le Livre noir du Vercors* (Neuchâtel: Ides et Calendes, 1944), with the following caption: 'Peasants in the hamlet of La Mûre were discovered hanged in conditions of truly the most refined form of satanic cruelty. Their hands tied behind their backs with telephone wire, a rope around their necks, they were left to die slowly over several hours or indeed several days, as their torturers had left them standing on one leg, the other stretched out horizontally and tied to a fence. With his leg giving way as he grew tired, strangulation began until, in a desperate act of exertion, the individual managed to push himself up until he collapsed again.'

Plate 12 Silhouette of a pregnant woman in Buenos Aires, around 1980. Protest by poster at the disappearance of pregnant women opposed to the regime together with their child, during the dictatorship. This photograph was taken from Rita Arditi, *Searching for Life. The Grandmothers of the Plaza de Mayo and the Disappeared Children of Argentina* (Berkeley: University of California Press, 1999). Rights reserved, Association of Grandmothers of the Plaza de Mayo.

Plate 13 Desecration of tombs in Barcelona. These images, from the film about the Spanish revolution by Mateo Santos and made at the instigation of Republican groups (*Reportaje del Movimiento revolucionario*, CNT-FAI, July 1936), were used for a different purpose when they were reproduced the following year in an indictment of the Spanish Republic (*La Persécution religieuse en Espagne* [Paris: Plon, 1937], with a poem-preface by Paul Claudel). Rights reserved.

Plate 14 Saint Alexander Square, Warsaw. Temporary graves of civilians killed in bombing raids, September 1939. This photograph was taken from *L'Invasion allemande en Pologne* (see Plate 3 caption).

Plate 15 Monument to the Bir-Hakeim maquis.

Plate 16 Hiroshima. A man atomised 250 metres from the epicentre. All that remains of him is a shadow left on the stone. This photograph was taken from Shuntaro Hida, *Little boy. Récit des jours d'Hiroshima* (Paris: Quintette, 1984). Rights reserved.

Plate 17 The first war memorial put up in the local school at Laurens in 1919.

Plate 18 *Top* War memorial and tomb of the soldiers killed during the war in the municipal cemetery of Laurens, 1923.
Bottom Memorial plaque attached to the railings surrounding the monument in Laurens.

Plate 19 Reproduction of the cover of the pamphlet published by France libre, *Tania la partisane*. Rights reserved.

in the present and the future affected equally the manner in which enemy remains were treated.

The way international law evolved

There were three stages in the evolution of international law regarding enemy dead, marked by the widening geographical and growing demographic implications of warfare. The earliest codifications dealt particularly with the identification of the dead so that records could be kept up to date, the numbers killed established, and control maintained over the gathering together of personal belongings left on the battlefield. Then there were regulations concerning the actual bodies. Finally, account was taken of the dead as individuals to whom one had obligations.

Until the First World War, the material care of bodies was part and parcel of army practices and not specifically codified. The first laws during that period dealt with the living, namely prisoners, the wounded and the sick. Thus, the law drafted by Lieber at the request of Lincoln in 1863, which was a source of inspiration to lawyers when they drew up documents concerning the practices and conduct of war published at the end of the nineteenth century, made no mention in the instructions given to fighting armies of what was to be done with the bodies of the enemy killed in battle.

Nonetheless, before any new principles were enshrined in law, some thought had already been given to their treatment by the belligerents. Henry Dunant, in his book *Un souvenir de Solferino*, made readers aware of the dead being abandoned. In 1867, in a report to international conferences of agencies engaged in aid to soldiers and sailors, he addressed this very point in an article about prisoners who died in captivity. He demanded that they be given 'individualised graves' so that their families could 'at all times' locate their loved one and ultimately have his body repatriated.[1] At a conference held in Berlin in 1869, delegates of the International Committee of the Red Cross proposed that victorious armies should, if at all possible, seek

to identify bodies on the battlefield and that exchanges of
information should take place between the opposing parties. Subsequently, in his manual of the laws of warfare
adopted by the Institute of International Law in Oxford on
9 September 1880, Gustave Moynier – one of the founding
fathers of the Red Cross – considered this issue in more
general terms. Article 19 prohibited the plundering and
mutilation of the dead left on the field of battle, and Article
20 stipulated that measures be adopted to identify the dead
before any were buried and all information concerning the
enemy be passed on to their army or government.

These texts represent first thoughts concerning the treatment of enemy dead. They were used as reference documents when the proceedings of the conferences at the
Hague in 1899 and 1907 and at Geneva in 1906 were drawn
up, and recommended that belligerents should inform each
other of the death of prisoners and of the identity of enemy
dead in the area under their control. As much as an exchange of information enabling civil records to be updated
for the sake of good administration, it was a question of
handing back to their rightful owner effects found on the
battlefield. Recognising the enemy as a fellow human being to whom one had obligations was a matter of principle.
Ideas such as these began to be put into practice in 1871 in
the peace treaty of Frankfurt. Article 16 charged the two
governments who signed it to care for war graves on territory under their control, embodying a spirit of reciprocity
towards the enemy. What had been achieved was not challenged and, in 1919, Articles 225 and 226 of the Treaty of
Versailles established the same principles.

The second stage, which came about after the First World
War, was marked by the Geneva Convention of 1929 making each belligerent responsible for those killed and left
behind on the battlefield. From then on, bodies were to be
sought out, identified, and protected from pillaging and ill
treatment. It involved opposing states in looking after each
other's dead, rather than simply exchanging information.
Each also had to hand over part of the identity tag taken
from the body before burying it 'in a dignified manner'. This

meant that the State had to keep a record of graves so that they could always be precisely located and make sure that a doctor was available to certify death before authorising burial. Article 4 stipulated that 'to this end and from the beginning of hostilities, [the belligerents] were to set up an official war grave service to make possible ultimate exhumation and to guarantee the identification of bodies wherever they might subsequently be moved to.'[2] Under the second convention, the same obligations were applied to prisoners who died in captivity and who were even guaranteed the right to make a will and to have it sent to those concerned.

About fifty states had ratified these two conventions on the eve of the Second World War, the future principal belligerents of which (Australia, the United States, France, Great Britain, Greece, Poland, the USSR, Yugoslavia as well as Germany, Italy and Japan) respected them to a greater or lesser extent.

Up until then, international humanitarian law was concerned with soldiers involved in military action and prisoners of war. Following discussions which took place during the 1930s and as a consequence of the Second World War, the law specifically included civilians in 1949 and, in 1977, was extended to cover all victims caught up in 'non-international conflicts'. As well as including all victims of war, the 1949 conventions reinforced those of 1929 relating to the treatment of bodies. From that date, the identity of those killed had to be respected. As a consequence, the incineration of corpses could only be considered 'for urgent health reasons or where the religion of the deceased person demanded it.' Belligerents had to bury bodies ensuring 'if possible . . . that the funeral was conducted according to the religion of the individual concerned' and that the graves should be grouped 'according to the nationality of those killed'.

The authors of these reference documents sought to prescribe how people should behave in situations of extreme violence. As the fatalistic Henry Dunant had written, they merely hoped to 'alleviate the horrors of war'.[3] But this shows how, from the end of the nineteenth century, those

killed in war, whose identity was increasingly better established, were treated more and more as individuals. First of
all, this is seen in the way states exchanged information
about the dead and then, as set out in the convention of
1977, in the way bodies, whether of friend or foe, received
'a decent burial'.

Practices ranging from respect to transgression

Of course, these rules were not always obeyed. In each situation codes and practices were sometimes respected, sometimes ignored. The case of prisoners of war, who were the-
oretically a protected group, allows us to measure the gap
between the conventions and what was actually done. As
soldiers, they were shown respect by their adversaries, who
were also in uniform and who saw them as enemy combatants essentially like themselves. Viewing the enemy in this
way explains the particular treatment received by captured
French officers during the 1870–1 War. Some were allowed
to keep their arms. Others avoided captivity by giving their
word that they would no longer fight in the war. They were
also referred to as prisoners on parole.[4]

Similar consideration was shown in the way soldiers were
interred and was particularly marked in those cemeteries
situated in former territory of the German Empire where
French prisoners of the 1870–1 War were buried. Most of
them have a grave. At Bydgoszcz in Silesia, as in Gdansk,
Szcsecin and even Poznan where 573 bodies were laid to
rest, lines of crosses were carefully set up to mark the burial
place of dead French prisoners a long way from home. Similarly, German prisoners who died in captivity during the
First World War and who were buried in plots in French
cemeteries remained for the most part in what were both
civilian and enemy surroundings. German military cemeteries in France in which the dead of both the 1914–18 War
and the Second World War were buried were also carefully
tended.

Looking at the way the dead were treated, the burial
grounds of Allied prisoners of the 1939–45 War – principally

Australians – situated in Thailand and Burma are particularly instructive. During the conflict, in order to construct the railway line linking Ban Pong and Thanbyuzayat, the Japanese army employed 60,000 prisoners and recruited 200,000 'Asian workers'. The mortality rate was very high, due both to bad sanitary conditions and poor food and to the terrible working conditions. The painful memory of heroic suffering on the part of prisoners who endured the brutality of their captors was what remained uppermost in the collective memory of Australians when they recalled this episode. The death toll of Allied prisoners was, however, half that of the Asian workers. The difference is explicable essentially in terms of the healthcare available to the former. By preserving their hierarchy and keeping their medical officers they were better able to guard against infectious diseases, notably cholera, in comparison with conscripted workers who lacked organisation. Above all, most of the Allied troops who died as a consequence had a marked grave which was looked after, as opposed to the 80,000 Asians who died in similar circumstances. They were buried in pits, their deaths unrecorded by the Japanese authorities.

Furthermore, those officially classified as prisoners gave their dead proper funerals, with the agreement of the Japanese, burying them for the most part in individual graves, sometimes scattered throughout the jungle. There were cremations, probably for health reasons, but possibly also on account of the person's religion, as there were Indians and Burmese amongst the prisoners. The fact that records were kept of burials meant that bodies could subsequently be regrouped in three military cemeteries, where today only 1.2 per cent remain unidentified.[5]

Throughout various conflicts, the way people behaved was at variance with the rules of conduct, either sporadically or on a massive scale depending on the circumstances. Such lapses were systematic on the eastern front during the Second World War, where Soviet prisoners were killed in huge numbers by the Germans and dumped on top of each other in vast graves, at the place where they had been executed.[6] Any reference to funeral rites at the time of these burials would have been meaningless. Likewise, the 1929 Geneva Convention, which had been ratified by the Soviet Union on 25 August 1931 and by Germany on 21 February 1934, seemed a mockery. Indeed, respect for the enemy was only shown towards prisoners viewed as such by their captors. Things were wholly different for captives who were not covered by the rules of war either for reasons connected with the culture of the belligerents, the circumstances of their capture, or their supposed identity. Referred to as irregulars, rebels, subversives or terrorists, the way they were viewed reflected an imaginary concept of the enemy as someone other than a fellow human being.

The kind of relationship you imagine you might have in the future with the enemy as an adversary would affect fundamentally the manner in which you treated his dead body. Thus, in the history of warfare, concern shown for the enemy dead might limit the amount of brutality used. Assuming responsibility for the burial of one's opponent or allowing him to bury his own dead represented equally a break in the cycle of violence. However, to look beyond the enemy at the person with whom a peace treaty would be concluded, to show marks of respect, has multiple meanings: fidelity to one's own image of oneself, a concept of military honour, political engagement. It also acts as a signal – whether as a promise or a warning – to public opinion on one's own side, to one's allies, one's enemies and to neutral parties.

Because warfare was not conducive to periods of reflection, formal funeral ceremonies for those on one's own or the enemy side punctuated lulls in the fighting. On every occasion that the violence abated ceremonies took place, the importance and the nature of which were a measure of the degree of tranquillity restored and of relations established between adversaries: cease-fires in the midst of battle permitting the evacuation of the wounded and the gathering up of the dead,[7] quick burials and furtive ceremonies once the battle was over, the regrouping of graves whilst fighting was in progress and the normalisation of funeral practices when tensions had eased. Agreements about the administration of cemeteries and about the handling of family mourners, which had been tried out during periods of calm, were extended in peace treaties and then in the normalising of diplomatic relations after the war.

There were countless periods of reduced tension during which enemy funerals temporarily interrupted the warring cycle of violence. In the winter of 1941–2, soldiers who fell during the campaign for France the previous spring were exhumed from the temporary graves which had been dug for them during the debacle of May–June 1940 in what had become a forbidden zone, and were re-interred in local cemetery plots in northern France by prisoners of war and civilians, with the permission of the occupying forces.

The repeated confrontations between France and Germany meant that these two warring nations had acquired considerable experience in the management of enemy war cemeteries.[8] In the middle of the 'phoney war', with the revised decree of 22 February 1940 relating to permanent war graves, the French government reaffirmed what had been agreed in this respect in the peace treaties of Frankfurt and Versailles, namely that the measures adopted concerning Allied graves should be extended to those of the enemy. In so doing, France merely reinforced the spirit of the Geneva Convention which she had ratified on 21 August 1935.

A generation after the end of the 1939–45 War, the issue had to be re-examined. Arising out of the speech given by General de Gaulle on the fiftieth anniversary of the battle of Verdun, in which he said he was ready to engage in 'direct and preferential co-operation' with Germany, an agreement was signed on 19 July 1966 between France and the Federal Republic relating to German war graves on French soil. In wishing 'to give definitive legal status to German graves of the 1914–1918 and 1939–1945 wars situated on French soil',[9] France sought, in its compassionate treatment of the war dead, to give formal expression to Franco-German rapprochement and to reinforce a European axis at a time of 'new departures'[10] in this sphere. In implementing Article 3 of the agreement, France freely granted the Federal German Republic free rights for all time to the land on which war cemeteries were built. In addition, the French government offered a 50 per cent reduction on train travel to one thousand eligible Germans so that they could make a pilgrimage to the grave of a loved one. For individuals and for the two states, it was a significant rapprochement between French and Germans so far as rights concerning permanent war graves were concerned.

A century earlier, in the United States, war graves were also included within a similar policy of reconciliation. In 1865, at the end of the Civil War, the federal government decided to transfer the bodies of Union soldiers from isolated graves to cemeteries in which they were grouped together. There within stone walls they could be protected against vandalism by Southerners. Late in the day, during the 1890s, the federal executive made several gestures of reconciliation. President William McKinley granted the Confederates a military plot in the cemetery at Arlington. Theodore Roosevelt brought under federal administration the upkeep of Confederate graves in the north, while President William Taft (1909–13) authorised the erection of a Confederate monument within the Arlington cemetery. Finally, in 1929, just before he left office, Calvin Coolidge saw to it that official memorial stones for private Confederate graves were provided by the Secretary of State for War. This was an identical measure to the one adopted in 1879 for the graves of Union soldiers.[11] More than three generations had passed before the federal government enshrined in law the same treatment for Confederate dead as for Unionists and before peaceful relations were restored between former enemies.

'After a civil war, genuine peace always begins in the cemeteries. It is there that one must always start to make peace.' These were the words of Georges Bernanos, writing about Spain in 1938.[12]

Using enemy bodies as a weapon

Using bodies as a weapon was contrary to the conduct of warfare as codified by international law since the end of the nineteenth century. But it was the way soldiers behaved; something they did in combat.

The idea that enemy bodies might be used as weapons developed in peacetime, as dangers increased. One has only to call to mind the myths of war spread by the authorities in times of conflict, without detailing what was thought up and put into practice by political and cultural elites to mobilise public opinion. But there was a gap between these myths and the way people behaved because of the general mood of aggression and the fact that they had grown accustomed to death. A study of newspapers produced in wartime enables one to see how both civil and military authorities described enemy bodies in such a way as to reflect public opinion and their own propaganda.

Until the end of the 1914–18 War, it was legitimate to show whatever violence had been inflicted.[13] Papers devoted column inches to realistic photographs of human remains – friend and foe alike – which had been torn apart by weapons of war: burns, bones, limbs, shattered bits of flesh, limbless torsos, bodies caught in their death throes. In 1914–18, one could still mobilise people not engaged in the fighting by illustrating the dire consequences of an attack: showing them the charred corpse of a German pilot, or the broken body of an enemy officer on the cover with the caption: 'It is the mission of the best German marksmen to aim their fire at our officers. This one, killed by a shell, remains perched where he was, a wretched scarecrow who no longer frightens crows.'[14]

Nevertheless, even then, images of death inflicted and suffered were not common in the official press. At the beginning of the twentieth century, there was a tendency not to use such visual images to mobilise people in times of war. The practice became more established in subsequent conflicts, with images of death inflicted upon others disappearing and being replaced by those of death suffered during the macabre events which characterised the Second World War. Even death itself became less visible in media depictions of warfare somewhere between the years 1980 and 1990. During the Gulf War of 1991, information systems controlled by the Western allies fed the press corps images from which all evidence of enemy soldiers killed had been eliminated. Marcel Trillat, a correspondent for Antenne 2, reported that before allowing accredited journalists to enter Khafji, where violent fighting had taken place, United States soldiers systematically cleared the streets, removing bodies and even cartridge cases.[15]

Variations in the way war has been depicted during conflicts have revealed the evolution of contemporary sensibility and its denial of death, which was particularly marked after the Second World War, and its ambivalent relationship with – desire for/rejection of – war itself. Individuals whose direct experience of combat has given them prolonged contact with dead bodies and a daily experience of death have developed a different outlook.

Combatants followed their own practices on the battlefield. Acts of violence inflicted on bodies varied in different cultures and at different times. Symbolic ritual mutilation of a body reflected the victor's desire to have some tangible sign of his bravery, to take away his opponent's strength, to prolong his suffering in the afterlife.[16] In antiquity, the remains of the enemy, his body and his shield, were a trophy. The photograph has become its modern equivalent. Once soldiers were able to obtain small cameras (from at least the time of the 1914–18 War), considerable numbers took pictures of enemy bodies. They kept these images of those who had been killed and showed them to whoever wished to hear about their exploits in war. The photograph was not so much evidence of the horrors of war but an affirmation of victory achieved and a proof of virility.[17] It fixed that timeless moment of male intoxication experienced by Drieu la Rochelle at Charleroi on 24 August 1914.[18]

Whether as simple acts of disfigurement or having a deeper meaning, these practices were concentrated on sensitive and symbolic areas of the body, protruding parts and orifices. The pillaging of corpses resulting in mutilation (the removal of gold teeth or of rings) and cutting off a part of the body as a trophy were still current practices in the twentieth century. Even the removal of ears from enemy corpses, which Senegalese infantrymen were often wrongly accused of, occurred as well. Léon Bloy referred to it in the description of his experiences as a volunteer in 1870–1.[19] American soldiers in Vietnam and Soviet troops in Afghanistan spoke of it as something which happened regularly.[20] The chopping off of heads and the removal of limbs in order to parade them as spoils of war, the gouging of eyes which disfigured the face and filled the sockets with blood, the simple act of kicking a body on the ground or of urinating into the mouth to humiliate the dead victim and intimidate those still alive were frequent occurrences which lie beyond the scope of this book.

Sexual mutilation (castration and impalement) was part of the ritual of victory for a warrior, which took away the victim's human virility. It was at once a humiliating attack upon a body which still had something in common with the living, a negation of the person as a human being, and a way of possessing his strength. Cases of castration were reported during the sacking of Nanking in 1937. Quoting Iris Chang, Joshua S. Goldstein reported that the Japanese ate the penises of Chinese men to increase their virility.[21] Similarly, during the Spanish Civil War, those on each side castrated the bodies of the other. Franco's Moroccan troops often resorted to this ritual practice, but officers in the rebel camp, who were repelled by it, preferred to expose the sexual organs of Reds who had died before throwing their bodies into pits as a way of defiling their manhood.[22] Combatants who found themselves under fire in a very enclosed world characterised by extreme aggression developed archaic means of attack. They re-enacted the ritual behaviour of hunters and warriors who, in refusing to accept their own death, immediately denied the humanity of the adversary lying at their feet.

Of equal interest to the historian are forms of aggression generated by specific social organisations, in differing circumstances and at particular times, as well as the violent acts of individuals which are inevitable in the context of war.

There are moments of paroxysm in war when aggression shown to the living is directed equally towards the dead. This occurs particularly at times of extreme tension between the warring parties, at the precise moment of an attack, during invasions, when troops are falling back, or during periods of repression when enemy bodies are used as weapons to terrorise the enemy and to take away his humanity. Following the Allied landings in Normandy, on 6 June 1944, when the German army was retreating and victory for the Allies looked more and more likely, the bodies of Resistance fighters and of hostages were put on display for several days, suspended from balconies and from the branches of trees in Tulle, Trégastel, La Mûre-en-Vercors, or abandoned without burial in Oradour-sur-Glane.

At Vassieux-en-Vercors, the German airborne commandos who had massacred seventy-six villagers and about a hundred partisans on 21 July 1944 occupied the place for three weeks, surrounded by dozens of corpses which began to rot increasingly quickly because of the hot weather.[23] According to Maurice Rouchy, who went to inspect the site after the German soldiers had left, 'the smell was unbearable, the houses were full of bodies, the spring and wells had been contaminated, the dogs ... were mad. This was the picture of the village the peasants who accompanied us described, and who refused point blank to go any further. You have to understand these poor devils whose eyes revealed the horrors they had witnessed ... A poor old lady of about eighty who had been shot was lying in the middle of the road, her arms outstretched, as if to stop us from entering this dreadful place. Walking ahead of the group, I was stopped in my tracks by seventeen corpses in a state of advanced decomposition lying scattered amidst the rubble ... Bodies lay everywhere, in the ruins, on the road, in cellars, on dung-heaps, exactly where they had met their death, some for almost a month ... Then, we halted suddenly, confronted by the even more terrible spectacle of young people who had been hanged using parachute harnesses, their bodies hanging limply. Their eyes had been torn out, their tongues cut off, their fingers crushed, their feet left touching the ground. They had suffered an unspeakably refined act of cruelty; one of their legs had been attached to a nearby fence. Unable to support their weight for very long, the poor wretches had slowly hanged themselves... '[24]

Dreadful scenes involving the bodies of civilians, who had previously been tortured, were reported as having occurred in Eastern Europe at the front during the two World Wars.[25] In France, the hatred and fear of irregular troops influenced the behaviour of the German army, both in August 1914 at the time of the invasion and at the end of the Occupation some thirty years later. On the eve of the Normandy landings, at a time when the actions of armed Resistance fighters were intensifying, orders were given within the army of occupation to increase repressive measures against the partisans. In February 1944, a circular from the *Militärbefehlshaber in Frankreich* (the Military Commander in France) gave orders for 'terrorists' to be fired upon. German officers confirmed after the war, at the time of the investigations into war crimes, that they received secret orders around June 1944 to make bodies unrecognisable and to conceal the burial places after partisans had been condemned to death by a court martial.[26]

Not all enemies were alike. The French army, for example, modified its behaviour depending upon whom it was fighting and its theatre of operations. In 1925–6, officers who had fought in the trenches and given a dignified burial to those Germans they had killed, when they led the expeditionary force in Syria against the Druze insurgents, gave orders for bodies to be put on display for several days before they were burnt. Bennett J. Doty, who was a member of the Foreign Legion at the time, remembered clearly what he had seen and wanted to testify about it: 'Colonel Andréa ordered that enemy bodies should be lined up right through the village and beyond it as an example. In punishing the treachery of this village which had declared itself *subdued* and pretended to accept French authority and pay taxes, those who shot the people were aided by Druze prisoners, who were given all the worst tasks. The bodies, brought down from terraces and up out of cellars were dragged through the streets to the sinister spot where they were to be displayed... Horses, which had died in their stables or on the streets, were also dragged out of the village as part of this macabre display.'[27] The intention of placing the carcasses of horses alongside human remains was without doubt to increase the suffering of the Druzes, whose love of the animals they rode was traditionally very strong.

Similarly, public executions and the displaying of dead insurgents were common forms of repression during the war in Algeria.

It is true, however, that the treatment of enemy bodies and national practices between friends have evolved in the direction of norms which have become more and more controlled, under the influence of international regulation. On the other hand, so far as perverse forms of behaviour are concerned, different sorts of social organisation as well as ideological and warlike situations have led groups of human beings to seek the destruction of their enemy and to co-ordinate even the obliteration of their dead.

Killing the dead

Perverse practices carried out on enemy dead are in large measure a function of the way in which they are viewed: demonised, dehumanised, bestialised and even feminised in societies where masculinity is claimed as universal. Every person attacking someone else draws on some form of system which allows him to represent and understand his relationship with the world and its otherness and which permits him to eliminate an identified opponent. What he in fact draws on is a complex pattern of ambivalent images through which his perceptions of 'the stranger' are in a permanent state of flux. For, if the dynamics of conflict are based upon changing manifestations of hatred between adversaries, one has to come to terms with the reversal of alliances and with the fact that wars also allow different nations to come together, to discover, get to know and appreciate each other.

In the post 1870 context, patriotic visions led people to imagine scenes of cannibalism, as Léon Bloy did with such pleasure in *Sueur de Sang*. Moreover, there was a very fine line to be drawn between the image of the ancient enemy dating from the period before the 1914–18 War and that of the barbarian capable of every kind of atrocity at the beginning of the conflict. But fellow sufferers in the misery of the trenches were viewed as fellow human beings, and this led to more realistic and less exaggerated perceptions of the Germans during the inter-war period. In a similar fashion, the propaganda machine in the United States, especially through the Hollywood studios of Warner Brothers, portrayed Russian communists in a favourable light during the Second World War, to persuade people they were suitable partners in the Grand Alliance. They then used exactly the same techniques to reverse these stereotypes during the McCarthy period. An identical process occurred in France where clichéd nationalistic images of their German neighbours were prevalent before the European project got underway.

This continuous process of adjustment in the way the other was seen, the constantly alternating stereotypes of people as sub-human or fellow human beings, meant that there was considerable inconsistency in the way enemy bodies were treated in times of war. Attitudes ranged from respect for the dead according to acknowledged codes of behaviour to acts of desecration.

Here, one has to distinguish between the pressure which was put on the living by displaying their dead and the way totalitarian systems have sought to destroy their adversaries. In the first case, human remains were additional instruments of aggression used against the living, the aggressor often showing minimum respect in the way bodies were treated. In the second, the dead were one element in the politics of annihilation. The desire to exterminate the enemy led to the destruction of every generation of a whole population, which included both sexes of the living, their progeny and even the dead, all memory of them and of their aggression.

At the time of the Liberation in France, the punishment of collaborators which took place outside the law in certain communities was tantamount to an act of annihilation. Those who sought vicious revenge could not conceive of a 'renaissance of France' in which 'bad Frenchmen' would in any way take part. At Pamiers in the department of Ariège, those condemned to death by the people's tribunal set up by the Resistance in August 1944 were buried in a communal grave and their families were forbidden to mourn in public.[28] At the beginning of the 1950s, following long negotiations with the civil authorities, their bodies were eventually handed over. Similarly, at Kerfot, near Paimpol, French citizens executed by the Maquis in August 1944 were buried in a grave away from the local cemetery.[29] The civil authorities did not issue death certificates at the time, as if to deny all memory of their execution. One year later, in 1945, the civil court had to rectify this. But here too, families had to wait several years before the bodies were handed back to them. At Kerfot as in Pamiers, where the families of those condemned by the people's tribunal left their homes, memories of the Liberation have remained strong until the present day.

Putting pressure on the living by ill-treating their dead has been a common practice. During the different periods when France has endured occupation, the German authorities have been flexible in their use of this repressive measure. Thus, in departments in the north and the east which were invaded between 1914 and 1918, the German High Command, as a general rule, allowed civilians to bury their dead in almost normal conditions, supervised by the occupying authorities. Funeral cortèges simply had to have a military escort.[30] Gatherings were permitted for the funerals of those who died as a result of British and French bombing, but also of those who were victims of German repression. Bodies were handed over to families and only a shortage of materials, it seems, was to blame for the simple ceremonies where the dead were buried without a coffin. Repressive measures involving the dead had not, however, entirely disappeared. David Hirsch, a shopkeeper in

Roubaix, wrote in his diary of the constraints imposed upon a prisoner when his wife, herself a hostage who had died in prison, was to be buried: 'Thursday, 1 February 1917: poor Mme Dispa was buried this morning. The German authorities had allowed M. Dispa to accompany her to her final resting place – guarded by a German soldier. He had to leave the burial service at one o'clock, as he did not have enough time to accompany his wife to the cemetery before returning to the prison at Loos at the prearranged hour.'[31]

Relying on the accounts of hostages who had been deported, David Hirsch revealed what survivors felt about the death of their own people, and showed how the German authorities graduated the coercive measures they used: 'Monday, 29 April 1918: hostages returning from Miliégani because of illness told of all they had suffered there. A lack of food; those who had no more money were left gathering up crumbs from the table, and it was impossible to receive money because it was forbidden... out of 150, 19 died... Amongst those unfortunate souls who died and remained unburied, though the other poor wretches had complained, one had his head eaten by rats; our compatriots could not obtain the coffin they had paid to have made; in order to prevent the same dreadful thing happening to the other unfortunate people, our compatriots strung them up on wires until they were buried.'[32]

The same inconsistent behaviour on the part of the belligerents was common throughout the Second World War with, on the one hand, people being allowed to do what they wanted and then being repressed by way of their dead. When Poland was invaded in 1939, all funeral gatherings were forbidden by the Germans. The dossier established by the information service of the Polish government in exile reported that, on 11 September 1939, at Karvina in Silesia, following the assassination of Doctor Olszak (the chairman of the village council), the Germans forbade the villagers to ring the bells and to go to his funeral. 'Despite that, the crowd which gathered at the roadside and in the ditches, to pay their last respects to their benefactor, if only with a silent prayer, were dispersed with blows from rifle butts.'[33]

Such repressive behaviour was not, however, standard practice. Less public funerals were authorised at that time. The same dossier reported the case of a Polish civilian whose wife was exhumed in October from a communal grave by a German officer, following a request made by the Pole. He was then allowed to rebury her in her own grave. It is true that in October there was already a lull in the fighting, but this episode shows that the German authorities had at least some record of her identity and of where she was buried. In Warsaw, it was the Germans again who exhumed the victims of the September bombings who were buried at the time in provisional graves scattered throughout the city. They were then brought together to be re-buried in cemeteries on the edge of the city.

The bodies of French Resistance fighters were treated in similar ways by the German occupying forces between 1940 and 1944. This was true at least for those who died on French soil. Those deported to camps were subject to measures other than simple political repression. Depending on the circumstances, the bodies of partisans were handed back to their families or to the French authorities, buried incognito at night in cemeteries, burnt to prevent identification immediately they had been removed from police stations, put on display to terrorise the population, or buried in secret graves.[34] The strength of the Resistance and its confrontations with the forces occupying their country explained in large measure the move towards an increasingly brutal attitude on the part of the Germans to the bodies of Resistance fighters. This was all the more the case as those involved did not share, in their eyes, the same code of behaviour as soldiers in uniform.

The identification of human remains which would enable proper funerals to take place became possible at the Liberation thanks to those who, throughout the whole process of having to deal with the dead, had taken steps to remember who the victims were. Police officers in Paris saw to it that personal details were entered in cemetery records, though they were not ordered to do so.[35] In one way or another, the identity of the victims of torture buried in these graves was preserved, either because the German authorities gave a list of the dead to the French police, or because the local people and the Resistance group knew when and where individuals had disappeared. After the Liberation, families were summoned to the opening of the graves by the local prefecture or by the French Forces of the Interior to identify bodies. The information was usually correct; though sometimes an unknown body was unexpectedly discovered.

The colonial authorities and the French army acted in a similar fashion when dealing with the bodies of Algerian nationalists. The actions of the settlers and the authorities were a product of the colonial situation, as was the behaviour of the army. Following the massacres which took place after the nationalist uprising in the region of north Constantine in May 1945, the bodies of local people in and around Guelma were initially buried rather hastily in communal graves. As temperatures rose in summer, paramilitary militiamen and gendarmes gave orders for the bodies to be exhumed and they then had them burnt in a lime kiln by Italian prisoners of war.[36]

During the war itself, it was the responsibility of officers to put corpses on display and speed up the judicial process in order to regain the initiative in the psychological battle between the French army and the Army of National Liberation.[37] In 1959, as a direct response to attacks by the Algerians and having arrested those presumed responsible for the crime, the army had their bodies displayed on the public highway and their wounds left clearly visible to show passers-by how they had been killed. On 6 May 1959 at Miliana and on the seventeenth of the same month at Affreville, bodies were also paraded through the streets in military vehicles 'their heads hanging down outside the trucks'.[38] Following fighting in the Tsaneur mountain region, on 29 March 1959, the Sixth Parachute Regiment of the Marines had the heads of district chiefs embalmed to prolong the image of their defeat.[39]

Although Lieutenant-Colonel Argoud introduced these tactics at the beginning of 1957 with public executions, so far as the army in Algiers was concerned, he was only imitating what had been done during periods of repression throughout the Empire since the nineteenth century. Captain Jacquot noted in his diary, in July 1892, how the bodies of natives were dealt with, abandoned and then burnt to terrorise the population during the Legion's campaign in Dahomey.[40] Andrée Viollis referred to similar happenings in Tonkin during the repression of 1931.[41]

The act of concealing bodies as a political weapon was widely used during the war in Algeria. From the time of the battle of Algiers in 1957, there was a considerable increase in the number of bodies of tortured insurgents which disappeared.[42] There were thousands of them, including more than 3,000 within his own area according to the prosecutor for Algiers.[43] But, unlike what happened in South America in the 1970s, the army and police practice of concealing the whereabouts of their opponents was more a practical means of repression than a calculated instrument of terror. In the first instance, it was a question of concealing what could not be admitted, namely the bodies of those insurgents who died as a result of torture. This is what the First Parachute Regiment of Cavalry did with the body of Maurice Audin. Such behaviour also developed out of a sense of impunity on the part of the army and the police, who adopted whatever oppressive measures they considered appropriate against the Algerians. This is the main explanation too for the disappearance of dozens of supporters of the National Liberation Front, who were thrown into the Seine on the night of 17 October 1961, or secretly buried in common graves within cemeteries in the Paris region in the days which followed. By denying people a grave, those responsible prolonged the suffering of families with a repressive measure which left them totally unaware of what had happened to their relative.

However, the expeditionary force did not systematically persecute the families of insurgents to the extent that it affected the way they mourned their dead. Suzanne Torres, the wife of General Massu who commanded the northern sector of the Algiers region, set up a service herself to help the families of those who had disappeared. Paul

Aussaresses, in a robust plea on his own behalf, insisted that when communal graves were dug for insurgents they were aligned with Mecca. It is unlikely, however, that French soldiers showed systematic respect for the basic funeral rites of their opponents. Bodies left abandoned were usually buried by villagers. Whether his testimony was credible or not, the fact that he took the trouble to say what he did, revealed his desire, at least after the event, to rectify a possible wrongdoing.

A coded record of the death of those who disappeared was also kept in Algiers.[44] Andrée Viollis confirmed too that hospital records included details of those who died as a result of torture by the security services on the Indo-Chinese peninsula in the 1930s.[45]

Thus, in Algeria as previously in occupied France, the dead were used as an instrument of repression against an enemy who was despised, yet with whom co-existence was envisaged, at least in a selective and limited fashion. Such acts of terror were as much practices borrowed from earlier conflicts as new tactics arising from an actual situation, but these acts of terror which included using the dead were in no way thought out or truly organised. Acts of aggression against both the living and the dead committed by certain military dictatorships in the Southern Cone during the 1970s were somewhere between measures of repression and the complete annihilation of their opponents.

Within the armed forces who were behind the coups d'état in Chile on 11 September 1973 and in Argentina on 24 March 1976, there were those who sought to eliminate what was referred to as the 'communist cancer' in Chile and agents of 'subversion' in Argentina.[46] The most hardline officers of these juntas, who felt they were dealing with the enemy within, thought that national renewal could only take place with the physical elimination of groups held responsible for the decline of their country. This ranged from neutralising them politically to executing them or sending them into exile.

The Chilean Commission for Truth and Reconciliation, set up by President Aylwin in 1989 to investigate the worst cases of human rights abuses by the Pinochet regime, concluded in its final report published in March 1991 that 'it was indeed convinced an underlying plan to exterminate certain categories of people was systematically carried out for political reasons.' As a consequence of these conclusions, in October 1998, the Spanish government instituted proceedings against Augusto Pinochet who was under house arrest in London. Amongst the charges made against him was the crime of genocide.[47] One can measure the extent and the nature of the coercive measures adopted by these states in the years 1970–80 by comparing Chile, where repression was centralised and organised, and Argentina where, within a weak state, it was carried out by a multiplicity of official and unofficial agents, which vastly increased the number of victims.[48]

Destroying the living through the dead

Striking at the living through their dead was characteristic of the terror tactics orchestrated by the agents of repression. There were two stages to the terror campaign used in Chile. At the time of the coup in September 1973, the junta resorted to brutality to show that there would be neither negotiation nor reconciliation with their opponents, but only total victory over them.

This is when large stadiums were transformed into detention camps, when brutal mass arrests were made in public places; a time also when summary executions occurred on the streets, and when bodies were thrown into rivers and allowed to wash up on the banks. Such deliberately theatrical forms of repression led people to think that the savagery was greater than it in fact was. Whereas the opposition reported 50,000 deaths directly after the coup d'état,[49] the different investigations undertaken by the National Commission of Truth and Reconciliation uncovered a little over 4,000 immediate victims of the coup in 1996.[50]

The same thing was true concerning those who disappeared. People talked of large numbers, up to 11,000 for example.[51] Now, the Commission and the families have agreed that the actual number of those who were 'forcibly taken and who disappeared'[52] amounted to 1,198. This first illustrative phase was followed by a second period of repression in which sophisticated methods convinced those opposed to the junta that they were vulnerable.

Between 1974 and 1977, the National Intelligence Agency orchestrated disappearances in a systematic regime of terror aimed at demoralising their opponents.[53] The policy of concealing bodies was directed at specific groups, in particular officials of extreme left-wing political organisations and those of the left-wing Popular Unity coalition, with often phoney reappearances being staged. Mutilated and charred corpses emerged from the shadows; most often of those who had been assassinated. Sometimes the police used the bodies of vagrants and unknown individuals. Such reappearances were a trap, raising false hopes. As for what happened to the bodies, some were buried without a cross or in unidentified graves, with just 'NN' on them, an abbreviation of the Latin *nomen nescio*, name unknown. Others were thrown into the sea, and a few were burnt.[54] To this day, the bodies of 85 per cent of those who disappeared have not been found.

The concealment of bodies was much more widespread in Argentina. There too, they were thrown into the ocean, dropped to the bottom of lakes, buried anonymously in graves marked 'NN' or in pits. Whereas the National Commission on Disappearance (CONADEP) has acknowledged 8,960 cases of 'forced disappearance', the families of victims say there are more than 30,000.[55] Unlike Chile where the National Intelligence Agency used sophisticated techniques, disappearances in Argentina were more part of a badly controlled repressive strategy by the central authority which, whilst seeking to terrorise opponents within, sought to reduce international pressure – coming principally at that time from the Carter administration with its new diplomacy of human rights in the region.

The Argentinian military did, however, resort to more hidden forms of totalitarian oppression in eradicating their opponents. As well as the almost systematic concealment of bodies, children born in prison to 'subversive mothers'[56] also disappeared. By systematically seizing children and denying them any link with their biological parents agents of the dictatorship sought to cut off the source of potential enemy recruits. New-born babies were given to families which were politically reliable. The explicit aim of these abductions was the total annihilation of their opponents, physically, through their progeny, as well as all memory of them. Thus, there was no trace of the parents' bodies or graves, and the children had a completely different identity. The practices adopted by the military, in this instance, were exactly the same as those used in colonial and post-colonial wars of the region. When groups of American Indians were massacred, the settlers would spare the children, seize them to use as servants or even adopt them.

'NN', *nomen nescio, Nacht und Nebel* (night and fog[57]): these initials resonate, recalling as they do disappearances which happened under the Nazis, others which occurred in colonial wars of independence and those which haunted the Southern Cone in the 1970s.[58] From the colonies of exiles who went to live in this region, refugees of the Third Reich, many of whom were in the Andean piedmont, to members of the OAS[59] who joined Argentinian death squads, the most brutal elements of the military in power drew, at least in part, on the experiences of their predecessors in Europe. Augusto Pinochet was an avid reader of the Nazi military journal *Ejercito-Marina-Aviacion* at the end of the 1930s and during the Second World War.[60] As for the Argentinian military, they claimed to have been inspired by the repressive techniques employed by the French army in its fight against subversion in Algeria: the doctrine of the revolutionary war.[61] General Camps declared in the newspaper *La Razón* on 4 January 1981: 'In Argentina, we have been influenced first by France and then by North America... France and the United States have been principally responsible for spreading the doctrine of the fight against subversion.'[62]

In both Chile and Argentina repression in the form of disappearances rebounded on the authorities. At the height of the repressive measures in the two countries, families mobilised against the juntas, initially seeking to be told where the disappeared were. Not knowing what had happened to them and unable to mourn properly, they endlessly confronted the dictatorship in public to discover the truth. Subsequently, having formed associations, they turned into movements of civil resistance. The Association of the Families of the Disappeared in Chile was formed in 1975, whereas mothers and grandmothers began to come together in May Square, Buenos Aires from April 1977. Because it was more difficult for parents to mourn not having seen a corpse and, more importantly, because they had no information about the person who had disappeared, in the long term the concealment of bodies was revealed as an ineffectual instrument of terror. All it did was to mobilise and energise the living instead of weakening their will to fight. As a result, the concealment of bodies did not eradicate the memory of individuals with their physical remains. On the contrary, the latter became a more potent force, because survivors refused to accept a death which they had not verified. General Harguindéguy, the Minister of the Interior of the Argentinian junta throughout its rule, disclosed in 2003: 'certainly disappearances were a mistake because, compared with those which occurred in Algeria, the situation there was very different. Those who disappeared belonged to a different nation, and the French went back home to get on with other things! Here, on the other hand, each person who disappeared had a father, a brother, an uncle, a grandfather who continue to feel resentment towards us, which is natural...'[63]

One can make a comparison with the regimes which tried out ways of totally destroying their opponents during the 1930s and 1940s.

During the Spanish Civil War, Franco's supporters developed a real culture of death. The extermination of the 'Reds' was seen as necessary for the regeneration of the nation, their massacre part of Spain's expiation. In fact, they carried over to Spain techniques they had used in Morocco. The 'Africans', as they called themselves, modelled on other colonial troops, subjugated the Moroccans by massacring them and displaying their bodies, and especially the heads of their victims.[64] But during the Civil War in Spain, what had been a battle tactic became a political strategy. Franco's Press Attaché, Gonzalo de Aguilera, said: 'We must kill, kill and kill... Our programme is to exterminate a third of the Spanish male population. In this way, the country will be cleansed and we shall rid ourselves of the proletariat.'[65]

Franco himself said he wished to eliminate half of Spain, and General Gonzalo Queipo de Llano defined the *movimiento* as a 'war of extermination' directed at the 'Marxists'. The repression of the Republicans by Franco's forces also involved massacres, especially during the initial assault in the summer and autumn of 1936. There were mass executions in the streets and in the cemeteries, and for a while bodies were abandoned all along the public highway.[66] In Seville, at the height of the repression, dozens, indeed thousands, of bodies were left in the streets where they fell, simply pushed aside and heaped against the walls so that military vehicles could pass.[67] They were then buried in communal graves, which became a feature of the Spanish landscape as the Nationalists advanced.

In the areas which remained under Republican control, members of the militia organised mass assassinations and macabre rituals: the desecration of graves, the displaying of bodies, and human remains being subjected to morbid acts of a bestial nature and to mockery. But these things were not part of an organised and clearly defined political project. They were condemned and curbed by both the civilian and military authorities on the Republican side, by the hierarchy and officials of the Spanish Communist Party as well as by the leaders of the Iberian Anarchist Federation and the National Confederation of Work (CNT).[68] The massacres committed by the militia in Republican areas and the macabre scenes which they set up occurred mainly during the counter-attack following the military coup d'état of 17 July 1936.

The desire of Franco's supporters to eliminate all the living who opposed them was extended to the dead, whose bodies disappeared. At the beginning of the Civil War, orders were given to the authorities in Galicia and in Asturias that they should not register those killed in the repression. Families did not receive a death certificate. It was only from February 1937 that deaths were officially recorded in Andalusia when the repression began to acquire legal status with the setting up of martial courts. But the persecution of the living through their dead went on longer. In 1939 in Cordoba, the sister of a communist, who had been tortured and committed suicide, was arrested for wearing black as a sign of mourning. Her head was shaved and she was forced to drink castor oil. Many suffered similar punishments.[69] Franco's insurgents used the dead as a concerted part of their terror campaign.

The rape of Republican women was also seen by the military hierarchy as a way of forcing the Reds to give birth to little fascists.[70] The Falangists displayed the same mentality when they forced mothers to drink castor oil and shaved their heads simply because they had brought 'Red vermin' into the world.[71] Thus, together with their aim of killing all male opponents, by raping and purging Republicans, Franco's supporters and the Spanish far right entertained the hope of eliminating those opposed to or who did not fit in with their project of creating a Spain freed from the Popular Front.

Acts of aggression involving the dead were part of the plan to annihilate people. By denying them death certificates, Franco's insurgents demonstrated their refusal to accept even a dead Republican as a member of the national community. By not allowing deaths to be officially registered, the Nationalists persecuted the living, denying them their widowhood and their right to mourn, and symbolically banished the dead from the nation. Thus, the State decided not to keep records for a section of the population. But, as in Armenia, South America and elsewhere, memories were stronger than any ban on mourning. In the mining towns of Asturias, the names of more than 50 per cent of the

victims of Nationalist repression reappeared in the regis-
ters after 1975, following Franco's death.[72] Sixty years after the event, democratic Spain is itself divided over the
problem of the 'disappeared' during the Civil War.[73]

The extermination of European Jews by the Nazis during
the Second World War has remained unequalled on account
of the scale and the radical nature of what took place. As
in Spain, from the start, it aimed to eradicate all memory and to deny the dead any place within the national
community. In Germany in 1935, the Nazis refused to allow the names of Jewish war dead to be inscribed on all
memorials.[74] However, the headstones of Jewish soldiers,
with crosses beside them, were preserved in military cemeteries. Subsequently, as in other places, Nazi aggression
towards the Jews included the usual acts of terror: massacres, the abandonment of bodies on the public highway,
the displaying of corpses.

The unique aspect of the Holocaust, compared with what
had been witnessed previously, was that the industrial-
scale massacre of all the Jews of Europe – babes in arms,
young and old – by the Nazis was not simply a consequence
of the war, but one of its motivations and ultimately its
goal. The deportation of Jews, the organisation of their
round-up across Europe and transportation to extermination camps because of their racial origin, constituted one
of the unprecedented features of the Holocaust. The genocide was the logical consequence of viewing the enemy as a
sub-human element, harmful to the superior species which
those carrying it out claimed to represent. Because there
was no question of a confrontation between armies, any
distinction between civilians and military, combatants and
non-combatants, and above all between men of a fighting
age and women, children and old men had no meaning. In
this mass murder planned and carried out by Nazi ideo-
logues, one cannot separate the methods of execution and
what happened to bodies.[75] This is, however, something we
have to return to.

Firstly, we have to do so because of the huge numbers
of corpses at the places where people were killed. After the

initial executions by firing squad, principally in Poland, the bodies were thrown anonymously into pits.[76] Later on, in Ukraine and Belarus, they were shot lying down in ditches, partly to speed up the rate of execution and to avoid having to transport and deal with the bodies.[77] In August and September 1941, the numbers of executions reached tens of thousands per day. On 29 and 30 September at Babi-Yar (Kiev), 33,371 people were killed and 11,000 were executed on 14 September in the Nikolajew region of Ukraine.[78] Alive, the enemy was not quite human; dead, his body was mere debris. How was it to be dealt with?

The industrialisation of mass slaughter brought with it the incineration of bodies. The extermination camps were equipped with crematorium furnaces from 1942 to reduce corpses to ashes. It was a way of getting rid of them at the same speed as they were being killed. As symbols of the genocide, the crematoriums were not the only inhuman means of dealing with bodies. A system of incineration pits was tried out at Auschwitz. According to Filip Müller, channels had been dug for the fat to feed the combustion chamber. This revealed a mental outlook symbolic of the Nazi's wilful extermination policy where everything was to be used and reprocessed.[79] Ideas of a similar kind were discussed concerning the exploitation of bodies for experimental purposes, with the collection of hair and the manufacture of soap.[80]

Was it premonition or a wretched fantasy? In January 1916, Senator Cazeneuve of the Army Committee, referring to rumours of the enemy's monstrous behaviour, claimed in the Luxembourg Palace that bodies were 'being transported by railway wagon and then burnt in tall furnaces in the northern region',[81] as a way of getting rid of them. Other rumours at the time suggested that their enemies were using bodies as raw materials for industrial purposes.

Throughout the long process which led to the extermination of the enemy, secrecy was an essential component of the ultimate denial of his death.[82] To expunge their memory and eradicate all trace of them as well as of their own actions, the Nazis set out to deny the existence of the Jews by causing the dead to disappear and by removing the evidence of their crime. In a system where bureaucratic obsession affected the whole administration, everything was done to cover up the final solution, by encoding letters, plans and orders, and by not registering those who died immediately they arrived at the camps at the end of their journey of deportation. From November 1944, Himmler ordered the destruction of all installations used for industrialised killing to preserve secrecy.[83] The special commando units formed in the extermination camps were periodically liquidated, so that no traces remained either of the victims incinerated in the crematorium furnaces and on pyres in the open air or of the implements used by the murderers. By reducing to ashes the bodies of those who had been gassed, complete extermination was to be achieved. Even the ashes were then scattered in the surrounding fields, ponds and rivers.

Holocaust deniers today seek to recreate a veil of secrecy, clouding the whole issue of extermination. But within the Jewish community and most of the western hemisphere, the destruction of the dead has created a cult of memory out of the inability of people to mourn, as happened on a different scale in other places. Since the period 1960 to 1970, it has made the Holocaust the central occurrence of the war, influencing almost every interpretation of events and affecting the way the whole twentieth century is understood.

There is a great difference between the body of an enemy mourned as an equal, to whom a last tribute is paid with due ceremony and compassion, and human remains which, on account of their identity, are treated as mere refuse by their adversaries. Yet, in all conflicts, however the enemy has been viewed and his body treated, whatever the nature of the war and the means of killing, the fact of death has remained enigmatic for those still alive, if only provisionally. Do soldiers and societies at war become accustomed to death? We have seen in this chapter how contact with bodies, enemy ones obviously more than those of comrades, has created a sense of repulsion. Having to deal with them seemed to involve such a risk of contamination, whether real or symbolic, that the task was left as far as possible to the vanquished, to inferiors, or to someone else. Mention has been made of interments and exhumations carried out by assorted prisoners, Italians and Russians here, French and Germans there, of the obligatory burial of civilians under occupation, of workers in the camps being made to carry out the final tasks of extermination. Beyond the fear of being sullied or contaminated, one can understand the refusal to touch corpses as a way of not having to perform rites to separate oneself from the dead.

Notes

1. Henry Dunant, *Un souvenir de Solferino* (Lausanne: l'Âge d'Homme, 1986 [1st edn 1862]), p. 134.
2. *Les Conventions de Genève de 1929*, Genève, Siège du CICR, p. 4.
3. Henry Dunant, *Un souvenir de Solferino*, p. 113.
4. François Roth, *La Guerre de 70* (Paris: Fayard, 1990), pp. 422–3.
5. *Hellfire Pass Memorial Thailand-Burma Railway* (Bangkok: Australian-Thai Chamber of Commerce, 2000), p. 15; Hugh V. Clarke, *A Life For Every Sleeper. A Pictorial Record of the Burma-Thailand Railway* (Sydney: Allen & Unwin, 1986).
6. Catalogue of the exhibition on the crimes of the Wehrmacht, *Vernichtungskrieg Verbrechen der Wehrmacht 1941 bis 1944* (Hamburg: Hamburger, 1996), p. 131.
7. These truces, although rare, were often reported during the First World War. Thus, on 12 May 1917, on the Chemin des Dames, a week after the major French offensive near Cerny, a ceasefire was agreed between 1300 and 1700 hours so that hundreds of corpses could be gathered up, because their advanced state of putrefaction as well as the sight and smell of them had become intolerable to the troops. Cf. Thierry Hardier and Jean-François Jagielski, *Combattre et mourir pendant la Grande Guerre (1914–1925)* (Paris: Imago, 2001), p. 185.
8. Ariarig Sauvage, *L'Ennemi enterré chez soi. Sépultures militaires allemandes et culte funéraire sur le sol français, de 1870 à nos jours*, master's degree thesis, Université de Rennes 2-CRHISCO, 2001.

9. *Journal officiel de la République française*, 23 May 1967, decree no. 67–408 of 5 May 1967.

10. Maurice Vaïsse, *La Grandeur. Politique étrangère du général de Gaulle, 1958–1969* (Paris: Fayard, 1999), pp. 582–3.

11. G. Kurt Piehler, *Remembering War. The American Way* (Washington, DC: Smithsonian Institution Press, 1995), pp. 51–66.

12. Georges Bernanos, *Les Grands Cimetières sous la lune* (Paris: Plon, 1938), p. 162.

13. Two fortnightly patriotic magazines, both illustrated, *Le Miroir*, and *Le Pays de France* have been systematically studied. They appeared regularly throughout the First World War. Although images of those killed in action remain marginal (78 photos in the 230 numbers of *Le Miroir* and 53 in the 245 numbers of *Pays de France*, during the period from 1914 to 1918), one is aware that mostly enemy bodies are shown (90% of those in *Pays de France* and 68% in *Le Miroir*). Half the macabre pictures (depicting suffering, mutilated or injured bodies) so far as *Le Miroir* is concerned (images of this kind did not appear in *Le Pays de France*) were of enemy corpses, and a third were those of 'exotic' allies, predominantly Serbs.

14. *Le Miroir*, no. 54, 6 décembre 1914, on the cover.

15. Testimony of Marcel Trillat, quoted in Michel Collon, *Attention Médias! Les médicamensonges du Golfe. Manuel anti-manipulation* (Brussels: EPO, 1992), p. 132.

16. Lawrence H. Keeley, *War Before Civilization. The Myth of the Peaceful Savage* (New York & Oxford: Oxford University Press, 1966).

17. Michael Herr gave the following account of the war in Vietnam. 'The photos were in a small leatherette file, and one could tell from the attitude of the Marine standing near us, who smiled in anticipation as we turned the protective plastic pages, that it was one of his favourite objects... There were hundreds of these albums in Vietnam, thousands even, and you had the feeling they all contained the same images...; the photo of a head which had been cut off, often placed on the dead man's chest or held by a smiling Marine, or a row of heads each with a lighted cigarette in its mouth, the eyes open...' Michael Herr, *Putain de mort* (Paris: Éditions de l'Olivier, 1996 [1st American edn 1968]), pp. 199–200.

18. Pierre Drieu la Rochelle, *La Comédie de Charleroi* (Paris: Gallimard, 1934), p. 57; Maurice Rieuneau, *Guerre et révolution dans le roman français 1919–1939*, thesis, Université de Paris IV, 1972, (Lille-III, service de reproduction des thèses, 1975), p. 542.

19. Léon Bloy, *Sueuer de sang (1870–1871)* (Paris: Georges Crès et Cie, 1914), pp. 25–34.

20. Michael Herr, *Putain de mort*, p. 41; Svetlana Alexievitch, *Les Cerceuils de zinc* (Paris: Christian Bourgois, 1991), p. 162.

21. Joshua S. Goldstein, *War and Gender. How Gender Shapes the War System and Vice Versa* (Cambridge: Cambridge University Press, 2001), p. 367.

22. Marcel Oms, *La Guerre d'Espagne au cinéma. Mythes et réalités* (Paris: Éditions du Cerf, 1986), p. 91.

23. Georges Menkès, *Le Livre noir du Vercors* (Neuchâtel: Ides et Calendes, 1944), pp. 16–17.

24. Quoted in Louis Jacob, *'Crimes Hitlériens', Ascq, Le Vercors* (Paris: Mellottée, 1946), pp. 110–15.

25. Omer Bartov, *L'Armée d'Hitler, La Wehrmacht, les nazis et la guerre* (Paris: Hachette, 1999).

26. The Karl Groenwald case (14 April 1945), report of the CID in Rennes, enemy war crimes investigation of 10 August 1945, Departmental archives d'Ille-et-Vilaine, regional CID service 1045 W 4 No. 19, quoted in Sébastien Louezel, Julien Louyer and Mickaël Perrin, *La Violence de guerre en Bretagne (1940–1944)*, master's degree thesis, CRHISCO-Rennes 2, 2002 (in progress).

27. Bennet J. Doty, *La Légion des damnés* (Paris: Stock, 1930), p. 109.

28. Pierre Laborie, 'Entre histoire et mémoire, un épisode de l'épuration en Ariège: le tribunal du people de Pamiers, 18–31 août 1944', in Michel Brunet, Serge Brunet and Claudine Pailhes (eds), *Pays pyrénéens et Pouvoirs centraux (XVIe–XXe siècle)*, Conseil général Ariège et Amis des Archives de l'Ariège, 1995, pp. 267–83.

29. Pierre Labusset, *Résistance et Occupation, mémoire de la Seconde Guerre mondiale dans les communes littorales de la région de Paimpol*, master's degree thesis, CRHISCO-Rennes 2, 2002 (in progress).

30. Richard Cobb, *Vivre avec l'ennemi. La France sous deux occupations: 1914–1918 et 1940–1944* (Paris: Éditions du Sorbier, 1985), p. 47.

31. 'Diary of David Hirsch', in Annette Becker, *Journaux de combattants et civils de la France du Nord dans la Grande Guerre* (Lille: Presses Universitaires Septentrion), pp. 270–1.

32. Ibid. pp. 294–5.

33. *L'Invasion allemande en Pologne. Documents, témoignages authentifiés et photographies, recueillis par le Centre d'information et de documentation du gouvernment polonais* (Paris: Flammarion, 1940), p. 47.

34. *Rapport concernant des cadavres incinérés au four crématoire du cimetière du Père-Lachaise sur instruction des autorités d'occupation*, Archives de la préfecture de police de Paris, BA 1804.

35. Exhumation dossier, December 1945–March 1946, Archives de la préfecture de police de Paris, BA 1821.

36. Jean-Louis Planche, 'La répression civile du soulèvement nord-constantinois, mai–juin 1945', in Anne-Marie Pathé and Daniel Lefeuvre (eds), *La Guerre d'Algérie au miroir des décolonisations françaises* (Paris: Société Française d'Histoire d'Outre-mer, 2000), pp. 112–14.

37. Raphaëlle Branche, *La Torture et l'armée pendant la guerre d'Algérie, 1954–1962* (Paris: Gallimard, 2001), p. 283.

38. Ibid. p. 285.

39. Jean-Charles Jauffret, *Soldats en Algérie, 1954–1962. Expériences contrastées des hommes du contingent* (Paris: Autrement, 2000), p. 265.

40. Capitaine Jacquot, *Mon journal de marche au Dahomey, 1892–1893*, 20–21 July 1892, manuscript quoted in Douglas Porch, *La Légion étrangère, 1831–1962* (Paris: Fayard, 1994), p. 314.

41. Andrée Viollis, *Indochine SOS* (Paris: Gallimard, 1935), p. 69.

42. Raphaëlle Branche, *La Torture et l'armée pendant la guerre d'Algérie, 1954–1962*, pp. 137–46.

43. Ibid. p. 144.

44. Général Aussaresses, *Services spéciaux. Algérie, 1955–1957* (Paris: Perrin, 2001), p. 126.

45. Andrée Viollis, *Indochine SOS*, p. 23.

46. Jean-Marc Coicaud, *L'Introuvable Démocratie autoritaire. Les dictatures du Cône Sud: Uruguay, Chili, Argentine (1973–1982)* (Paris: L'Harmattan, 1996).

47. Paz Rojas B., *Pinochet face à la justice espagnole* (Paris: L'Harmattan, 1999).

48. Alain Touraine, *La Parole et le Sang. Politique et société en Amérique latine* (Paris: Odile Jacob, 1988), p. 384.
49. Alain Joxe, *Le Chili sous Allende* (Paris: Gallimard, 1974), p. 238.
50. In 1991, the Truth and Reconciliation Commission had accounted for 3,178 murders including 1,196 disappeared during the period from 1973 to 1990.
51. Olivier Dabène, *L'Amérique latine au XXe siècle* (Paris: Armand Colin, 1994), p. 135.
52. Antonia Garcia Castro, *'Où sont-ils?' Comprendre une intrigue. La permanence des disparus dans le champ politique chilien: enjeux mémoriels, enjeux de pouvoir (1973–2000)*, Sociology thesis, École des hautes études en sciences sociales, Paris, 2001.
53. The Dirección de Inteligencia National (DINA), that is to say the intelligence service, was set up in 1974. Its role was to enforce political repression which it did until 1977, when it was reorganised.
54. Antonia Garcia Castro, *'Oû sont-ils?'*, p. 51.
55. *Nunca Mas*, report of CONADEP, on the Internet at (*www.desaparecidos.org / arg / conadep / nuncamas*).
56. Rita Arditti, *Searching For Life. The Grandmothers of the Plaza de Mayo and the Disappeared Children of Argentina* (Berkeley: University of California Press, 1999).
57. Decree of 7 December 1941 given by Hitler stating that no explanation should be given about people who had been arrested and that no contact should be allowed between them and the outside world.
58. Antonia Garcia Castro, *'Oû sont-ils?'*, p. 8.
59. The OAS – Organisation de l'Armée Secrète – an insurrectional organisation formed in 1961 which committed acts of terrorism in France and Algeria. [Translator's note]
60. Victor Farias, *Los Nazis en Chile* (Barcelona: Seix Baral, 2000), p. 409.
61. Mario Ranalletti, *La Guerre d'Algérie et l'Argentine. Les influences de l'intégrisme catholique et des militaires français dans l'armée argentine (1955–1965)*, doctoral thesis, Paris, École des hautes études en sciences sociales, 2001.
62. Included in chapter V of *Nunca Mas*, report of CONADEP.
63. Marie-Monique Robin, *Escadrons de la mort, l'école française* (Paris: La Découverte, 2004), p. 340.

64. Sebastian Balfour, *Abrazo mortal. De la guerra colonial a la Guerra Civil en España y Marruecos (1909–1939)* (Barcelona: Ediciones Península, 2002).

65. Michael Richards, *Un tiempo de silencio. La guerra civil y la cultura de la represión en la España de Franco, 1936–1945* (Barcelona, Crítica, 1999), pp. 49–50.

66. Santos Juliá (ed.), *Víctimas de la Guerra Civil* (Madrid: Temas de Hoy, 1999); Francisco Espinosa, *La Columna de la muerte. El avance del ejército franquista de Sevilla a Badajoz* (Barcelona: Crítica, 2003).

67. Michael Richards, *Un tiempo de silencio*, pp. 39–40.

68. Josep Maria Solé I Sabaté, 'Las represiones', in Stanley Payne and Javier Tusell, *La Guerra civil. Una nueva visión del conflicto que dividio España* (Madrid: Temas de Hoy, 1996), pp. 585–634.

69. Michael Richards, *Un tiempo de silencio*, p. 29.

70. Yannick Ripa, 'Armes d'hommes contre femmes désarmées: de la dimension sexuée de la violence dans la guerre civile espagnole', in Cécile Dauphin and Arlette Farge, *De la violence et des femmes* (Paris: Albin Michel, 1997), pp. 135–6.

71. Maud Joly, *Histoire, mémoire et violence sexuée en Espagne, de la guerre civile au premier franquisme. Les tontes des femmes républicaines*, doctoral thesis, Institut d'études politiques de Strasbourg/Université Rennes 2-CRHISCO, 2001.

72. Michael Richards, *Un tiempo de silencio*, p. 29.

73. Emilio Silva y Santiago Macías, *Las fosas de Franco. Los republicanos que el dictador déjó en las cunetas* (Madrid: Ediciones Temas de Hoy, 2003).

74. Georges L. Mosse, *De la Grande Guerre au totalitarisme. La brutalisation des sociétés européennes* (Paris: Hachette, 1999), p. 201.

75. Christian Ingrao, *Les Intellectuels du SD, 1900–1945*, thesis, Université de Picardie, décembre 2001.

76. Christopher R. Browning, *Des Hommes ordinaires. Le 101e bataillon de réserve de la police allemande et la solution finale en Pologne* (Paris: Les Belles Lettres, 1994).

77. Christian Ingrao, 'Violence de guerre et violence génocide. Les pratiques d'agression des *Einsatzgruppen*', in Stéphane Audoin-Rouzeau, Annette Becker, Christian Ingrao and Henry Rousso (eds), *La Violence de guerre, 1914–1945. Approches comparées des deux conflits mondiaux* (Brussels & Paris: Complexe/IHTP-CNRS, 2002), pp. 219–41.

78. Ibid.
79. Filip Müller, *Trois ans dans une chambre à gaz d'Auschwitz. Le témoignage de l'un des seuls rescapés des commandos spéciaux* (Paris: Pygmalion, 1980).
80. Édouard Conte and Cornelia Essner, *La Quête de la race. Une anthropologie du nazisme* (Paris: Hachette, 1995), pp. 245–57.
81. *Journal official de la République française*, parliamentary debates, Senate, January 1916.
82. Raul Hilberg, *La Destruction des Juifs d'Europe* (Paris: Fayard, 1988 [1st edn 1985]).
83. Jean-Claude Pressac, *Les Crématoires d'Auschwitz. La machinerie du meurtre de masse* (Paris: CNRS, 1993).

5 Ways of bidding farewell

The biological fact of death which concerns every society has given rise to a range of cultural practices, enabling the living to take their leave of those no longer present. The purpose of these rites, analysed usually by anthropologists, is to help the bereaved accept death in the long term, to come to terms with the ultimate parting, and to sanction and channel the mourner's expression of grief. We have referred to the striking growth in the number of war dead from the second half of the nineteenth century. Have warring societies managed to go on observing traditional forms of final valediction, in spite of this increase?

As well as dealing in a benevolent or vengeful fashion with the corpses which war produced, the living have acted consciously in accordance with or in breach of accepted practices. Societies at war have striven to maintain their traditions, so far as conditions allowed. Age-old customs, instinctively followed, were revitalised by the very atmosphere of war, when patriotic fervour made them meaningful and real. But, because war represented a breach in the normal life of human beings on earth, a period during which upheavals and transgressions were no longer exceptional, populations under attack have also been inventive, behaved in new ways, conducted improvised funerals, and created new rituals.

As a general rule, funeral rituals take place in four stages: oblation, separation, integration and commemoration.[1]

During the ritual acts of oblation, the deceased is surrounded as if he were still alive. Depending upon local customs at different times, he is made ready for the journey to his final resting place, shown to his loved ones, placed in or brought to familiar surroundings. The symbolic purpose of these actions is to retain him for one final moment within the world of the living. In lending the body a semblance of life, the mourners make it easier to accept the irreparable transformation which has occurred.[2] The ultimate significance of the rituals surrounding separation, which include sustained or momentary contemplation of the body, is the acceptance of the dead person and of death. They eliminate any temptation to deny death and make it easier for those left behind to accept the fact that the person has gone. Through rituals of integration, the dead become part of memory, links in the chain of former generations. They join the hosts of those who have gone, lingering as vestiges in the hearts of the living. Finally, with its commemorative rituals, the community – whether that of just the family, a social group, the local community or the nation as a whole – recalls the circumstances in which people died and honours their memory.

The four stages occur in one form or another in all funeral rituals. They require knowledge, preparation, time and organisation, all of which are made difficult by war.

Traditions which are difficult to keep

An air of violence surrounded funerals in wartime on account of the omnipresence of death, the numbers of bodies, and the premature disappearance of a generation 'in the flower of youth'.

Within societies at war, soldiers and indeed the population as a whole grew unusually accustomed to death; and some will have had direct experience of living alongside dead bodies. This has resulted in particular kinds of behaviour, engendered by a range of mixed emotions, not often openly expressed in peacetime. Michael Herr frequently referred to such behaviour in his account of the Vietnam War: 'The living, the wounded and the dead travelled together in overloaded Chinook helicopters. Men thought nothing of stepping on half-covered bodies piled up in the cabin as they looked for a place to sit, or of joking about how weird those poor dead sods looked.'[3] As happened during various historical disasters, such as epidemics which lasted for some time, indifference intensified as people got used to the situation. They developed a hardened attitude, a lack of compassion towards the dead. On traditional battlefields, large numbers of bodies came to be seen as pestilential and burdensome rubbish, and vicious acts of revenge were sometimes perpetrated upon them. Elsewhere, away from the front, in odd pockets of land or of scrub where skirmishing was going on, in towns which had been bombed or to which troops had withdrawn, the dead encroached upon and hindered normal daily life. But routine and habit did not block out compassion for a fellow human being, whether he was a loved-one, a friend or ones alter ego, a fellow sufferer, a potential ally, an upright enemy.

Literature written after wars, and especially that produced following the 1914–18 War, contains countless descriptions of acts of compassion on the part of civilians and soldiers alike.[4] For example, Bougarel-Boudeville, the author of a patriotic novel full of military stereotypes published in 1920, described the funeral of a French prisoner of war in Germany. Many civilians attended it and German women wept at his graveside. The hero, Pierre, ponders on their unexpected behaviour: 'Why do they weep like this? Pierre wondered. Do these German women feel real compassion for our suffering? Do they experience the horror of it or are they only giving way to superficial emotions which conceal the hardness of their Teutonic hearts? Or are they weeping for their own men? Do they imagine them being treated by the French, as the French are treated in Germany? Or do they tell themselves they will be buried in hastily dug trenches on the battlefield by someone or other, so that they will never know where they lie?'[5]

Some of the mixed emotions felt by civilians in the face of violent death, which was now all around them, can be seen in this literary extract. The prisoner, that enemy bringer of death, was also an alter ego, carried off, so alone and far from home. And the weeping women, like the chorus in a tragedy, accompanied the stranger; they hoped too that a few tears of respect would be shed for their own dead in return. Although the body is that of an enemy, compassion triumphs over hatred, perhaps because the scene takes place far from the battlefield, during a lull, and the rites are performed by civilians, non-combatants.

The fact remains that, though death began to be distanced during the eighteenth century,[6] wars have been the scene of physical confrontation with dead bodies on a massive scale. From 1914 to 1918, the intimacy with death experienced at the front was progressively transmitted to the rear through the stories soldiers told, ceremonies expressing grateful thanks, and the repatriation of bodies. In a biographical account, a widow described her anguished experience thus: 'The gravedigger raised the shaky lid. Horrified, Emma and her nephew first saw a pair of enormous boots from which stuck out two thin white tibia, loosely bound in floppy puttees, strips of a once sky-blue greatcoat. Deathly pale, Emma looked away. Pierre, confronted for the first time with such an apparition, fainted. The gravedigger turned over the identity bracelet around the bones of the man's wrist. He was indeed Léon Marquizeaud of the 6th infantry regiment.'[7]

The discovery or rediscovery of the macabre was a brutal fact of life during wars of the industrial age. The whole of society came into contact with bodies in large numbers. What is more, they were disfigured, broken, strange, stared at long after they had passed away; or it was impossible to inspect them because they had disappeared or were sealed in lead-lined coffins. When people came face to face with death on a mass scale, it was difficult to perform acts of oblation. Taking as an example the scene just described, how could the protagonists, confronted by skeletal remains which bore little resemblance to a human form, respect the tradition of a farewell kiss which should have been given to someone who had just died? The child 'confronted for the first time with such an apparition' passed out. The phrase is ambiguous. Was it the first time he had seen a dead body?

That might have been possible, given his young age, but hardly likely insofar as life expectancy at the beginning of the twentieth century was sufficiently short for every child to have experienced the death of someone close at an early age. Was it not more likely the first time he had seen a body in such a decomposed state?

Was it the sheer scale, the numbers of dead, the physical injuries to bodies, caused by powerful weapons of war and the very nature of combat, which changed funeral practices, indeed brought about the creation of new ones? Rituals of respect and then of valediction for the person who had died, which had been observed since the end of the eighteenth century, involved the presence of a body and an act of vigil, and these could not possibly be performed in the same way during time of war. This led to simplifications, since those who grieved, comrades in arms in the first instance, later the families, did not have time to restore an expression of calm to a dead man's face or some semblance of humanity to his body before they took their leave of him for ever.

Lack of time, having to act with haste and urgency meant that ceremonies were conducted collectively, on an industrial scale, as if on a production line. Though such behaviour was unavoidable, there were certain compensations. Forms of farewell were retained which expressed basic feelings of social solidarity and of sympathy. We have described the determination shown in gathering up scattered body parts, which was so important to the opposing forces in the two World Wars, for the purposes of identifying the dead as accurately as possible in order to maintain public records. Actions of a less administrative kind were also carried out, which had more to do with feelings of obligation towards the dead. At Oradour-sur-Glane, after the massacre of 10 June 1944, 'human ashes' were carefully collected and placed in coffins. Likewise, half a century later, a Soviet mother whose son fell in Afghanistan commented: 'When a helicopter burns, they gather up the bits one at a time: they find an arm, a leg...'[8] This is how what can be referred to as 'improvised rites' developed; what was done in a hurry, furtively, to bid farewell on the spot to those who would disappear for ever.

Although societies at war discovered that death was an incontrovertible part of their existence, the living felt helpless when confronted with the injustice of its brutality. Torn between the dominant public sentiment of acquiescence towards war (whether wholehearted or forced) and their own personal bewilderment, they retained powerful feelings of ambivalence towards death in combat. Referred to as the ultimate possibility in war, death was nonetheless unbearable at a private and personal level. And this explains why speeches and sentiments referring to heroic death, to the enviable fate of those who sacrificed themselves for their country or for liberty, go hand in hand with an awareness that such sudden deaths represented wasted lives. Those who mourned had to find new ways of coming to terms privately with the idea of dying for one's country.

One can see how families in the First World War discovered their own ways of mourning following the death of sons, husbands and brothers.[9] Those who grieved did not, of course, forget to proclaim publicly the courage, gallantry and sense of duty of those who died. But such declarations could not hide the unbearable fact of their absence. Announcements of death, which were published in the press as early as August 1914, expressed ambivalence towards death in battle. They mingled expressions of patriotic pride and intense grief at their loss;[10] grief which was so intense that survivors spent the rest of their days remembering their loved ones. Inconsolable parents shut themselves away in their homes which they turned into shrines to their dead sons, a grief-stricken sister would endlessly write of a life full of promise for the brother so suddenly taken from her, and the lives of fiancées, wives and mothers were frozen in time. The gulf between public speeches of praise and the private suffering of the individual, between the importance of patriotic pomp and the powerlessness of individual gestures, explains in large measure why such acts of mourning went on so long, indeed why they would never end.

Finally, because of their powerful status within the community, and so far as it was possible, the war dead were given patriotic funerals either immediately or at a later date. In this respect, they did not really have their own independent identity. To the extent that the death of an individual was absorbed by the community, the gap between the public expression of grief and the way it was experienced and lived out at the private level became more marked. We have already seen how the authorities were led by public opinion into adopting certain measures with regard to the treatment of the dead. Also, the contradiction between personal suffering and public consolation explains why there was a gulf between improvised and arranged rites.

Towards the invention of new rituals

The forms, meaning and functions of improvised rites varied according to where they took place – literally on the battlefield itself or within the countries at war – with the body present or absent, and also according to how the individual was categorised – a soldier, a civilian caught up in the maelstrom, some sort of pariah. Furthermore, because of the circumstances, makeshift ways of providing an escort for bodies developed, for example around provisional graves, and these have already been discussed. Such ritual practices were strictly confined to times of war. They were gestures of oblation when that was possible, and especially of separation. All the rituals of integration and commemoration came later.

In the large majority of funeral ceremonies, rituals of oblation were suppressed, reduced to a minimum or substituted when that was possible by a last gesture, something which suddenly came to mind, the closing of eyes, the placing of a cloth, handkerchief or comparatively clean piece of material over the face, the slipping of a hand into the dead man's tunic to remove a letter which one knew would be there, a murmured lullaby, the straightening of a lock of hair.

Such gestures tend to be elusive in the variety of texts which exist: circulars, regulations, private letters, eyewitness accounts and literary narratives. At the moment of death, whatever the circumstances, mention of a silent message to the dying man, brief prayers and signs of the cross offered by the living punctuate descriptions of war.

Le Volontaire juif, a paper for war veterans seeking to keep alive the First World War spirit of 'sacred union', published an edifying example drawn from the 1914–18 War.[11] A small group of Jewish legionnaires was sent, during an operation, to bury the body of a German which had been abandoned near the French lines and had neither an identity tag nor papers. The men were struck by the sad loneliness of his death, enveloped as he was in nothing but a 'terrible smell'. Instinctively, they wanted to show some mark of respect before his body disappeared for ever into the earth. 'A prayer! There we were, five Jews... The dead man, or what remained of him, slithered on his back and slumped to the bottom of the grave. We pulled the piece of canvas back over him. Before filling in the hole, under a vast cold night sky, and between the two opposing armies watching us, our few muttered words of prayer rose into the air. There stood five French soldiers murmuring in the language of the Chaldeans that timeless plea, the prayer of sanctification, which every Jewish child recites at the burial of his parents.' As well as showing patriotic solidarity, the paper revealed how traditional rites were creatively adapted in an unforeseen situation. The prayer for the dead was spoken by five men rather than the ten prescribed by Jewish law. But above all, words of farewell spoken by a minority group (the Jewish prayer for the dead, or *kaddish*, to give it its new name) were used in exceptional circumstances, outside the framework of religious belief and irrespective of the nationality of the combatants.

Instructions issued in April 1913 by the head of the army medical service, perhaps anticipating a flood of victims, requested that the limbs of the deceased should be straightened if they had been 'affected by rigor mortis'. Similarly, the Belgian Red Cross, in a directive sent out in the autumn of 1943 about how mortuaries were to be organised in case of bombing, insisted that competent personnel should dress the most gaping wounds on corpses. The text also made clear that the washing of bodies, albeit only 'summary' and restricted to the face and hands, must be carried out.[12]

Furthermore, one can trace the evolution of attitudes towards those killed in war through changes which occurred in improvised written forms of farewell. On 10 August 1870, William, King of Prussia, wrote to Queen Augusta: 'I have just ridden across the battlefield of Sarrebrück and it was a dreadful spectacle. Our soldiers have placed wooden crosses made from branches on the communal graves and written the names of the officers. The inscription on one grave read: 30 Prussians and 75 French.'[13]

Since there were no individual graves and the dead were unidentified, the simplest form of homage was given with basic details of the number and nationality of those buried. Moreover, a minimum of care was shown when bodies, whether of friend or foe, were placed in such pits. So far as the 1914–18 War was concerned, the excavations in the vicinity of the trench where the bones of Alain-Fournier were exhumed, together with those of twenty other soldiers of the 288th infantry, offer an excellent illustration. Situated in woods at Saint-Rémy-la-Calonne, the grave contained the remains of infantrymen, ambushed on 22 September 1914 during heavy fighting and then buried by the Germans. In 1991, archaeological research revealed that the bodies had been laid out according to rank, officers first and then the ordinary soldiers, and with no signs of physical mistreatment or of systematic pillaging having taken place. Sufficient identification had been preserved, including twelve identity tags (the 1883 version) which meant that nineteen out of twenty-one could be named.[14] Similarly, near Arras, another military grave of the First World War which was excavated in 2001 contained the remains of around twenty British soldiers who died on 9 April 1917. Placed side by side at the bottom of the trench, they had been buried arm in arm. All of them came from the northern English port of Grimsby. The archaeologists explained this dance of death as a funeral ritual which the soldiers had carried out almost under fire: 'The bodies were aligned with their feet towards the front line and their heads turned towards the enemy indicating that war continued even after death. Above all, the linking of their arms signified friendship. They must have been buried immediately after the fighting before rigor mortis prevented them being arranged like this.'[15] Enough evidence was found at the bottom of the trench to identify individually these 'chums from Grimsby'.

There is ample evidence throughout this period of documents having been placed next to bodies which were hastily buried where they were. Whether written in a hurry or carefully inscribed, these details enabled subsequent identification to take place. Equally, they were marks of respect which sometimes contained the last wishes of an individual. Occasionally, such details were stuffed into a bottle and buried alongside the body by a comrade, slipped into the material used as a shroud, or simply left to chance in the turned-over earth. All showed how ritual forms of farewell, based more or less consciously on the cultural traditions of peacetime, were still being observed. The placing of memorials near the bodies of the dead by soldiers who formed digging parties should be viewed in the same light, as should the care they took in burying side by side in communal graves friends killed together during an engagement, and the few words they scribbled on crosses erected in no man's land and along the front line. Such and such 'of the 9th battery'; 'his friend from Saint-Brieuc'; another 'who will never forget him'.[16] Graves were also hurriedly dug by civilians who were being bombed. In September 1939, the inhabitants of Warsaw did so on open ground in their town squares, whilst they were being fired on by Nazi artillery. The hundreds of survivors of the nuclear explosion in Hiroshima who died during the days which immediately followed were 'buried here and there, around the hospital.'[17]

Away from the battlefields, similar gestures were made involving above all the laying of flowers, a practice which went on throughout the period in various circumstances and signifying different things. On All Saints' Day in 1914, French planes flew over the cemetery in Nancy and dropped flowers on the first monument to those killed in the war, perhaps inaugurating something later taken up by the authorities. Whatever the conflict, a number of propaganda messages referred to the fact that flowers were frequently placed on enemy graves, thereby demonstrating feelings of humanity towards their adversaries on the part of those caught up in the war. The fact that such comments appeared regularly was no proof of their veracity. Gestures of this nature were however made. That they were mentioned in the press during wartime shows how importantly they were viewed and that they were also seen as a form of tribute.

As well as the odd flower furtively left here and there, a spontaneous gesture in memory of either friend or foe, floral tributes were placed on graves as was normally done at funerals during peacetime. Such tributes added an extra dimension to the process of bidding farewell. But, during the First World War, in accordance with military regulations, no mark of respect could be placed on the graves of soldiers executed following court martial.[18] That did not prevent friends of the deceased covering them with flowers immediately after the burial, or ex-servicemen's associations and even pacifist organisations doing so in the years after the war. Flowers were at the very least an expression of farewell and, at the other end of the scale, an expression of disapproval at the execution and even of opposition to war. Be that as it may, the memory of those 'executed as an example' and whatever was done to commemorate them were not always veiled in secrecy. On the morning of 11 November 1998, for example, in the little village of Tauves (Puy-de-Dôme), a bunch of red roses was discreetly placed by persons unknown alongside the municipal wreath at the foot of the war memorial. Attached to it, written in a fine hand which might have been that of a teacher of the Third Republic, was the message: 'In honour of all 14–18 combatants, and in fond memory of Corporal Dauphin together with his friend, the brave soldier Brugière, and to all those sacrificed for the glory of their incompetent officers.' It was a simple bunch of red roses, a way of saying farewell once more, over eighty years later, and of denouncing an injustice.

In November 1940, 10,000 people in Brest placed bouquets on the grave of a British soldier which soon disappeared under a metre of flowers, according to the prefect. Clearly, in this case, the political significance of their action was more apparent than any personal gesture of farewell. However, when a death occurred, the immediate reaction was a gesture of this kind if a public expression of respect was also intended. This happened in Vire, during the summer of 1942, when the bodies of the crew of a bomber who died following a forced landing were buried, and the Germans allowed representatives of the prefecture and the municipality to attend. Perhaps they did so without any misgivings, seeking only to honour an adversary whom they respected. Perhaps permission was granted as part of their strategy of 'friendly' occupation. Whatever their thinking, they were confronted with a procession thought to number more than 2,000 people. The crowd was not allowed to enter the cemetery, however. But, in the days which followed, and despite the ban, the graves of these men disappeared beneath a sea of flowers.[19]

The same thing occurred in Villefranche-de-Rouergue in the autumn of 1943. Here, auxiliaries of the occupying army who had mutinied won the sympathy of the townsfolk. After their murder, they were buried in a shallow grave in a meadow just outside the little town. In the course of the following days, large quantities of flowers were surreptitiously placed at the burial site, and, under cover of darkness on All Saints' Day 1943, a number of people put bunches there. In displaying their feelings of compassion, the townsfolk were also expressing their opposition to the violent act of repression which had taken place.[20]

Traditional forms of mourning which became established over the century made the grave a focus of attention.

Viewed as a final resting place, it was both a monument erected to shelter the remains of the deceased for all eternity and the spot where mourners came to meditate. There, one was in the presence of the body and reminded of the person as well.[21] We have seen how the process which evolved in civil society also occurred within the armed forces. More and more, they tended to provide clearly marked, individual graves for their troops who died, difficult though it was to do so in the heat of major battles. What developed in these circumstances were more intimate funeral rites which sought to compensate for the shortcomings of collective rituals which were in the main unavoidably impersonal and anonymous.

The range of practices most commonly observed were those the purpose of which was to keep alive the memory of the dead, to embody them in writing or with photos. They embraced all types of literary expression that appeared in the aftermath of wars (clumsy testimonies or pieces contained in anthologies) in which words, pages and chapters were devoted to the memory of a single individual, a sort of counterbalance at a personal level to the anonymity of bones preserved in ossuaries. Those killed in action who had no final resting place were commemorated on paper within 'book-tombs', as Carine Trevisan called them. Whilst turning the pages which they wetted with their tears, those who mourned could meditate. In the face of death on a massive scale, writing, whether in the form of fiction, testimony, poem or book of remembrance, should be seen as 'a committal to the grave, allowing the severance of ties with the dead'.[22]

The act of reciting a roll call of the dead became more widespread in the course of the twentieth century. Resurrecting ancient customs, the practice was first observed within families or at private ceremonies conducted by associations of remembrance. After 1918, it was taken up during acts of public commemoration in local cemeteries or at the foot of memorials.

The written counterpart of these emotionally charged roll calls were the lists drawn up more widely after the

1914–18 War on war memorials and in books of commemoration of those whose bodies had been destroyed or broken. During the second half of the twentieth century, it was to become something of a cult, especially in the case of the Jews exterminated in Europe and the victims of the repressive measures adopted by the dictatorships in Chile and Argentina.[23] Almost complete lists of those who disappeared were published in martyrologies, yearbooks, as distinctive sections or annexes of specialist volumes, or engraved on memorials.

One of the dissident groups amongst the mothers who gathered in May Square has basically devoted itself to the commemoration of the disappeared. Its website takes the form of a memorial on which photos are pasted, and the screen image, with its black background, is called a 'commemorative wall'. It resurrects and depicts happy family scenes: images of classrooms, of first communions, of weddings, of going swimming at Mar del Plata; most of all it recalls the circumstances in which an individual disappeared and venerates that person as a hero. Commemorative shrines of this kind are becoming more common these days on the Internet. They are a way of giving a social dimension to private grief and of allowing the rest of the community and anyone else who feels concerned to share these people's suffering.

The invention of commemorative rituals follows therefore in the wake of contemporary technological developments in warfare. If the development of the international superhighway is one unexpected consequence, it is the measure of a phenomenon which has been growing over a number of decades: the interconnectedness in times of war of public and private ways of saying goodbye. Public expressions of farewell are all the more necessary since the immediate means of doing so are difficult, if not impossible, and also because the person who died is felt to have sacrificed himself for the sake of the community. Moreover, the strength of that communal farewell reinforces its equivalent private expression, without which mourning becomes impossible.

Impossible cremations

From the end of the eighteenth century, a movement towards cremation began to emerge in Europe which had an
influence on various groups of people (free-thinkers, intellectuals, agnostics and protestants, and both middle- and
working-class anti-clericals). It found public expression in
a demand for civil funeral ceremonies and secondarily for
the cremation of bodies. The World Fair in Vienna of 1873
gave these people the opportunity to show how the first cremation furnaces worked (the expression did not have the
sinister connotations it acquired after the Second World
War). The first association of crematorium specialists in
Europe was established on 29 April 1874.[24] In France too
the idea gained a following. A small group of radical sym-
pathisers even proposed a bill which would allow citizens
to choose between burial and cremation.[25] It came to nothing, because the initiative emanated from a relatively restricted circle of people and challenged Catholic doctrine.
In fact, cremation was officially condemned by the Church
in 1886, and the ban was only lifted in 1963. Nonetheless,
one year before the ban, the municipal council of Paris
had succeeded in permitting the cremation of remains –
unidentified or unclaimed – to take place in the inciner-
ator which had been built at the Père-Lachaise cemetery
and which was administered by the city. The measure was
limited to human remains which had come from university lecture theatres (foetuses and bodies used for teach-
ing purposes) and was defended on economic and health
grounds.

   This marked the beginning of administrative schemes for
the disposal of dead bodies in the unusual circumstances
in which individuals were less valued than was ordinarily
the case. Such schemes were also part of the process which
led to forms of farewell becoming more varied and more
personal. The groundswell of support for cremation, as well
as the right to choose the form of funeral one wanted, which
was granted on 29 October 1887, were an integral part of
this.

The whole business remained complicated throughout the twentieth century so far as those killed in wars were concerned. Firstly, cremation, as a way of disposing of the body, was infrequent in the West until the 1970s when it began to be used much more widely. Secondly, in wars in which identification became a matter of concern both for ordinary citizens and for the authorities, cremation was hard to accept. Finally, the shadow cast by the ideology and practices of the Nazis is fundamental to one's understanding of the slowness of the process of change which began in the last quarter of the nineteenth century. Even if, during the inter-war period, the Nazis were already officially recommending cremation, based on the German tradition, the memory of victims of the extermination camps being incinerated cancelled out all other considerations, at least for a while.[26]

But, as is true of all questions concerning funeral practices, broad issues can only be clarified in terms of specific cases. For example, mass cremations took place on both sides during the 1870–1 War. On the other hand, cremation in the aftermath of the Second World War seems to have been much less repugnant to the British than to other European nations.

However that may be, a reluctance to accept cremation predated the activities of the Nazis particularly in France. Compared with the rest of Europe, the movement in support of cremation which began in the 1880s developed much less widely there.[27] When, in the course of the first bloody battles of the Great War, the Germans introduced mass cremation, some French people, who were deeply shocked, saw it as proof of the barbarity of their opponents.[28] However, when the deputies in the National Assembly discussed the decontamination of battlefields on 18 June 1915, before voting on the bill concerning the cremation of unidentified bodies of French and Allied soldiers as well as those of Germans, scientific arguments were advanced in opposition to moral and political ones.

Lucien Dumont, who was the author of the bill and the Socialist Republican deputy for Indre and spokesman for

the Public Health Commission, was also a medical prac-
titioner. With other elected members and doctors, he expressed fears that both the water and the soil would be
polluted and that epidemics might occur, given the difficulties of decontaminating battlefields because of the large
number of bodies and the hot summer weather. From a
strictly hygienic point of view, human remains should be
dealt with rapidly and efficiently. Doctor Henry Thierry,
head of technical services in the Paris hygiene department,
outlined different methods of burning corpses. Straw and
petroleum had been thrown onto the bodies immediately
after the battle of the Marne, but they had only been super-
ficially scorched. Destroying them by burning in the open
air proved extremely difficult.

In May 1915, permission was granted to the Public
Health Commission for incineration trials to take place.
They were carried out using two pits at Heippes, in the
Meuse, on 14 June 1915 and supervised by Doctor Lemoine,
a chief army medical inspector and Professor of Hygiene at
Val-de-Grâce hospital. The body of a horse was placed in one
and the remains of two German soldiers in the other. The
latter had been buried in coffins in April and exhumed the
previous evening for the purposes of the experiment. Their
uniformed bodies were placed on a pyre, sprinkled with liq-
uid tar and then covered with another layer of wood.

In the eyes of those who carried it out, the test proved con-
clusive, since all that remained of the bodies after four and
a half hours was some ashes and a few lumps of spongy
tissue from the intestines, about the size of a fist. With
guarded optimism, the parliamentary commission stated
that experiments with the carcasses of horses showed that
the process became easier if the number of bodies was increased. Techniques had to be perfected, of course, and in
particular the level of the fire had to be raised to improve
combustion and allow the ash to be removed more easily.

Arguments of a rational kind such as these were challenged by people who relied on feelings and ethical points,
namely that one had to think of the soldiers and their families, afford them the comfort of the grave and the hope

that one day the remains of those who were missing would be identified. Alexandre Lefas of the Democratic Republican Union, the deputy for Ille-et-Vilaine, led this counter-attack. He ended his speech by reminding them that their enemy should also be treated humanely. 'Feelings of respect must be shown towards the enemy dead as well as to our own, for we as a people do not embrace a cult of strength which would lead us to insult our enemy, whether conquered, injured or dead.'[29]

Having been passed by the deputies, the proposal went before the Senate. Although those who drew up the bill and, apparently, the majority who voted for it in the Palais-Bourbon had no misgivings about cremation, one might have thought a different view would be taken in the Palais de Luxembourg. In fact, feelings ran high mainly amongst Catholics who believed interment in consecrated ground was the only proper way to mark the end of life on earth. Some of the senators were not opposed to cremation. Jean-François Félix Martin, for example, the Independent senator for Saône-et Loire, who put forward a counterproposal that unidentified bodies should be embalmed by injecting them with amyl alcohol, suggested that those bodies which remained unidentified after the war should be cremated. He was doubtless aware of strange ideas for getting rid of bodies being circulated at the time, such as that suggested by Raphaël Dubois, Professor of General Physiology at the University of Lyon, who supported the idea of embalming all unidentified bodies which would then be cremated at a later date.[30] Martin ended his speech with an oratorical flourish and to the applause of his colleagues. '[Once the war has ended] cremations will be . . . the obvious solution. They will not, of course, take place in ovens or furnaces but solemnly on pyres as in ancient times, acts of glorification in front of soldiers bearing arms, in the evening, on hilltops, where the sound of the cannon will burst forth once again in a gesture of supreme homage and final farewell.'[31]

But when the summer and the hot weather had passed and the fear of epidemics, which might have justified the project, had proved unfounded, and once all the bodies had been buried, there were really no physical or material reasons for the remains of soldiers killed in combat to be burnt as part of some official policy. The bill was rejected by the Senate on 27 January 1916. Notwithstanding Félix Martin's lyrical outburst, inspired by his view of the warrior's death as manly, this new form of farewell was not adopted and the tradition of Judeo-Christian burial was maintained for some time to come.

The religious dimension

The circumstances surrounding each new conflict led combatants and their families, the authorities and indeed the whole of civil society, to improvise ways of saying farewell and to invent new rituals which they assimilated and to which they gave an individual stamp. But, as a general rule, funerals were conducted according to the practices and traditions of the society at large, in the forefront of which were religious ceremonies. In accordance with monarchical traditions, the Church authorities in France accompanied armies throughout the nineteenth century, and particularly during the war of 1870–1, and saw to it that religious life was maintained at the front and in all theatres of war. Their pastoral activities were given a legal framework by the Republic in 1880, when they were integrated with medical personnel. Just as no great changes occurred in this respect with the changeover from the Second Empire to the Third Republic, so the separation of Church and State in 1905 did not really alter things either. Military chaplains – Catholics, Protestants and Jews – were from then on appointed by the army with the rank of captain. The creation of Moslem chaplains met with more resistance. Despite the fact that provision was made in 1914 for religious support to be made available, Moslem chaplains having the same status as those of other faiths were only introduced in February 1943 by General Giraud, and then only for the duration of the war.[32]

Throughout this whole period, chaplains took the view that dying for one's country was a way of dying for one's faith and so they gave regiments their blessing before they went into battle, introduced prayers specifically for soldiers, heard confidences and confessions from believers, and had long conversations to try to comfort the men during periods of calm. Though some were directly involved in the fighting, having been granted Papal dispensation which allowed them to kill, their principal role was to bring solace at the moment of death. They were busiest during engagements, staying with the dying under machine-gun fire whenever they could. When the battle was over, they organised funerals.

The involvement of all the different faiths alongside the armed services, which was already evident in the 1870–1 War, became more marked during the Great War.[33] It was barely ten years since the State had become secular. The stakes were high for the authorities who both wanted and needed to find ways of bidding farewell to those who were going off to die. With the support of the churches, their task was made much easier. But that support was not just a matter of course; as chaplains of the three main faiths, Catholic, Protestant and Jewish, sought to make clear how involved they were in the defence of the country during the whole conflict. Guided by their leaders, they gave their total and enthusiastic support to the Sacred Union.[34] The Church authorities, who responded to patriotic speeches and were accustomed to authoritarian arguments, were, in a word, 'guarantors' of the alliance between 'the sword and the aspergillum' so despised by anarchists, and practised the Sacred Union in the widest sense of that term throughout the Great War. Not content with concealing their mistrust of the Republic, which had become secularised to the point where matters spiritual were confined to the private sphere, the Church authorities were keen to adopt the precepts of the Sacred Union in their own sphere and to offer a hand of friendship to rival faiths. Their attitude had barely changed by the time of the Algerian War, in which some hundred and twenty priests, fifty pastors and twenty rabbis acted as military chaplains without challenging the position of either the army or the government.[35]

Photographs of ecumenical religious services at which
ministers of the different faiths officiated and also contemporary and subsequent statements exemplify the attitude they adopted. A number of private testimonies and
inspiring stories also bear it out. One, telling the story
of Rabbi Abraham Bloch who died of his wounds on 30
August 1914 having taken a crucifix to a dying Catholic
soldier, was above all meant to prove the patriotism and
spirit of sacrifice of Jewish citizens.[36] But, beyond any ideological purpose it might have had, this anecdote reveals
the importance of such gestures of help to the dying given
by army chaplains, and the same thing could be said of
Catholic priests who for their part respected the last rites
for Protestant, Jewish and Moslem soldiers who were fatally wounded.[37] As well as mutually shared actions and
words which had an ecumenical purpose, documents also
refer to a certain competitive spirit between pastors, priests
and rabbis seeking to comfort the dying with appropriate
prayers, the one carrying a bible, the other with a rosary
around his fingers. But it made no difference because, when
the final moments came, the most important thing for each
one of them was to bring comfort through religion.

Because it was the most public and ritualised form of
worship, the supreme moment of farewell from a religious
perspective was the service for the dead – the Catholic
mass – which was celebrated in the presence of people of
all faiths at impressive collective funeral ceremonies which
took place after major battles. Again, early on in the war,
this was not something which happened as a matter of
course. The action taken by the Jewish authorities, who
represented a religious minority which had experienced
certain difficulties in the recent past arising from the political and psychological circumstances surrounding the Dreyfus affair, illustrates well the changes which were taking
place. At the beginning of hostilities, the Chief Rabbi, Alfred Lévy, and Édouard de Rothschild, the President of the
Central Consistory, sought to defend the interests of Jews
who were fighting and to make sure their religion was represented at all national gatherings.[38] On 7 August 1914,

at a solemn service organised for the occasion, the Chief Rabbi gave his blessing to the French armed services and called upon all Jews in France to do everything they could to support their country in its ordeal. Fearing that there were not enough rabbis at the front, given the number of Jews who had been called up or who had volunteered, Alfred Lévy made several approaches to the Ministry of War suggesting there should be at least one chaplain for each corps, even if Jews were under-represented in certain units. In order to obtain additional postings, he argued that soldiers could not be allowed to die without the comfort of their religion.

The Sacred Union did however have its limitations. On several occasions, a particular minister of religion was not chosen by the dying and prayers were said in a spontaneous and improvised manner by the chaplain of one faith for soldiers, friend and foe alike, who clearly belonged to another. Abraham Bloch, the worthy rabbi who died taking a crucifix to a Catholic dying near to a mobile field hospital, referred to himself quite happily it seems as 'the Jewish priest'. The rabbinate was however concerned that the Catholic chaplaincy might be taking advantage of its numerical superiority and giving a Christian burial to Jewish soldiers. On the other hand, and to remain within an area of historical study which has been well covered, certain Jewish families expressed regret that soldiers of their own faith had not been buried with their Catholic comrades.

Just like its counterparts in other faiths and though divided between particularism and universalism, the Jewish Consistory wished above all to have its traditions respected. Indeed, the authorities of the different faiths were working towards the same end, if not together, in seeking to encourage the armed forces to organise services for the dead and to have appropriate religious symbols placed on graves. As we have already seen, the military authorities readily accepted that crosses should be placed on individual and mass graves of both identified and unidentified soldiers. Furthermore, once the principle of individual graves had been accepted, even though it was not consistently followed, these same authorities took it upon themselves early on in the war to have even the most insignificant graves marked with appropriate religious symbols. But this did not quell the fears of the leaders of minority religions. Following the first major assaults which took place in the spring and autumn of 1914, the rabbinate immediately challenged the automatic placing of crosses on graves.[39] As a result of various deals done with the Ministry of War, the High Command permitted Jewish chaplains to supervise the erection of funeral monuments and to replace Christian crosses whenever necessary with the Tablets of the Law. By October 1917, 3,500 Tablets, often edged with the tricolour, had been placed on battlefield graves close to the front.

The fact that bodies disappeared was another issue which had to be faced. The funeral ceremony for those who perished at sea was adapted for more general use; in civilian areas it was used in the absence of a body when a soldier had died far from home, under fire, having been deported, or in a medical unit; at the front it was used for those declared missing after a battle. A service was held, in some instances after a 'vigil in the absence of a body'.

The involvement of religious bodies in industrialised warfare led to them adopting practices which they elaborated as events unfolded, with the ultimate aim of bringing hope of a peaceful afterlife to those who lay dying. Thus, religious leaders were obliged to change and adapt their attitudes and rituals. In the tradition of the soldier-monk, priests became involved in the fighting. More importantly, chaplains did all they could to help soldiers die in peace, as far as that was possible. Risking their own lives, they made every effort to hear final confessions and to administer both extreme unction and the holy sacrament. Moreover, the Church was concerned about the fate of the huge number of soldiers who died without receiving the last sacraments. In a pamphlet which appeared in 1916, Father Dom Besse drew the attention of believers to the fact that: 'On the battlefield death comes suddenly. Often there are no death throes and the cut and thrust of war forces men to leave those who fall where they are. How can they all be helped when they are under constant bombardment?...Those killed in battle do not receive the comfort which the Church brings to the dying...How many die who have not commended their soul to God?...How many soldiers killed in battle are forgotten as they groan in the flames of purgatory? Reciting the service for the dead relieves the suffering of these unknown souls...Once comforted, their prayers will sustain their former comrades in arms.'[40]

Practical/theological adjustments were often far-reaching. In the Jewish religion, for example, bodies should be buried whole. Given the vast quantity of scattered remains, Jews had to accept that the only thing they could do was to pay their last respects without the complete body being there. In addition, widows could not remarry if the death of their first husband had not been officially established. From the time of the Great War until the end of the twentieth century, in an attempt to honour this law, religious leaders often tried to persuade couples to get divorced before husbands went off to war as a way of safeguarding the future. One can imagine how comforted believers might have been by such prescriptions and with what eagerness they would have sought to obey them!

An almost comic example such as this would certainly have created a gulf between religious leaders and their followers, rather than assuage the feelings of the latter. Though an extreme case, it nonetheless demonstrates how necessary it was for religious leaders to adapt in times of war.

Public funerals, official ceremonies

Funeral ceremonies, which might be described as social and ritualised expressions of farewell by the living to the dead, were moments of great intensity for societies at war, punctuating as they did trials of strength, bloody battles and bombing raids against civilian targets. For grieving families, as well as for their neighbours and fellow citizens, they offered some compensation and a way of overcoming their sense of loss at the absence of their loved ones and the fact they had been unable to say goodbye more directly. Public funerals allowed the dead to be brought back into the community of the living and, in this sense, had a political and patriotic function. As well as being occasions when sadness and grief could be openly expressed, they enabled those who took part to show their solidarity, their approval or their opposition to war. As happened when people bade farewell in the presence of the dead, these ceremonies took various different forms, reflecting a respect for tradition and at the same time adapting and bringing in new ways of expressing grief in time of war.

The authorities were always present in significantly larger numbers than private mourners at these funeral ceremonies, as if to show that as well as sending men to their death it was right for them to organise expressions of farewell. In this respect, the nation as a whole, represented by its public officials, was responsible for the funerals of those who were killed in or as a consequence of war. A new kind of ceremony for those who died for their country gradually emerged, beginning with the American and French Revolutions and becoming more established after the 1870–1 War, when a wounded nation came together to mourn those who had fallen defending their land. Setting aside religious and political differences, a different ritual was created embodying secular, State and nationalist values which represented a mixture of both a civil and a church funeral, civilian and military customs, a religious and a civic ceremony.

The chief characteristic of these French public war funerals was that they were arranged and financed by either municipal authorities or those of the prefecture. This came about as a result of both the law of 1904, which removed from the Church sole responsibility for funerals and gave it to local authorities instead, and the desire of the nation to honour those who had died for their country. Depending on the circumstances, mayors or prefects fixed both the date and the form of ceremony. They also drew up lists of those who were to be invited. Funerals were always organised in consultation with the military and Church authorities and usually – but not necessarily – with the families concerned. The authorities took charge of the arrangements, deciding on burial plots in the cemetery, having new graves dug or seeing that family vaults were properly prepared. They also authorised the transportation and preparation of the bodies and paid funeral directors for the provision of candle holders, coffins and the material used to drape them. It was also their responsibility to set up the platform for speeches and to arrange the chairs, having discussed who should sit where. Again, they decided on the hangings which were put up in religious buildings and public places and, from 1914 on, French flags became part of the decoration in Catholic and Protestant churches and in synagogues. Finally, the authorities arranged for sprays and wreaths of flowers to be provided with ribbons to indicate who they were from, for the funeral horses to be properly adorned and for cars and lorries to be hired as hearses.

Another feature of these funerals was that they were conducted for the most part, except in special cases, in accordance with the recognised Catholic burial service which had remained largely unchanged from the Council of Trent (1545–63) to Vatican II (1962–5). Here too a balance was struck between tradition and innovation. The most obvious change was the presence of emblems of the Republic in time of war: figures of authority, speeches, military and political symbols. The changes also included the provision of chapels of rest at the place where the person died, at the scene of a bombing for example, or when a body was brought back a long time after death, as happened when conscripts were repatriated from Algeria. Chapels of this kind replaced the normal practice of setting out for the funeral from where the person had lived. In adopting the rituals of the country's main religion, the Republic's demonstration of its respect for the dead was in keeping with forms and practices familiar to most of the population, in particular the everyday symbols of mourning. Thus, during the Great War, the chairs of elected representatives killed in battle were draped in black. For the Catholic Church, the solemnity of the funeral mass and absolution was intensified by the presence of officials. But above all, such ceremonies made up for the fact that other rites, and especially confession and extreme unction, had not been performed, which was largely what happened during great battles and when people were on the move in times of conflict. For minority faiths, such occasions gave them a greater sense of being part of the nation.

Political, military and religious leaders came together to organise ceremonies, though initially there was a certain amount of improvisation with each new conflict. They consulted about the decoration of church buildings and the routes which funerals would take, the music which was to be played and the performers, the sorts of speeches to be given, the kind of service and the seniority of the person who would conduct it. There is a wealth of material in the form of accounts, descriptions, photographs and films of the huge ceremonies which took place from the time of the 1870–1 War to that of the war in Algeria. They were always moving occasions, despite their grandiose and sometimes pompous aspects, given that the fervour with which people bade their farewells was all the more intense because the circumstances of the death were painful and obscure. However, less consensual opinions were often expressed at funerals such as these, reflecting a tradition which certainly predates the creation of the Republic.[41]

Given the particular circumstances which prevailed in France between 1940 and 1944, public funerals reflected the whole spectrum of such opinions. Mayors and prefects were given orders by the Vichy government requiring them to organise the mass funerals of the victims of Allied bombing raids with great care. So, they ensured that their representatives formed guards of honour, gave speeches and were named on written tributes attached to flowers. In this respect, they were maintaining an earlier tradition, as civilian victims were similarly honoured during the First World War. Other factors encouraged the regime to offer strict guidelines for the funerals of those killed by Allied bombs. It was a way of half voicing the perfidy of the British, the commiserations of the Germans and the solidarity of the French government.

The Allied bombing raid of 3 March 1942 on the Renault factory at Boulogne-Billancourt killed several hundred people. A huge funeral ceremony was organised in Paris on 8 March which lasted all day. Firstly, at ten in the morning, a solemn mass was celebrated in Notre-Dame in the presence of representatives of the French and German governments. When they left the cathedral, they went by car to the Place de la Concorde where a vast cenotaph had been erected in front of the bridge leading into the Tuileries Gardens. Around the cenotaph, which was draped in black, stood a line of Republican guards and policemen. The crowd, which had been summoned to attend by the radio and by newspapers, was held back by guards on horseback. Estimated at several tens of thousands of people, it waited whilst the officials around the cenotaph observed a minute's silence, listened to the last post and then Chopin's funeral march. This was followed by a silent procession during which flowers were laid. The last of the crowd did not drift away until the end of the afternoon. No incident was reported by the police who had been on duty since the previous day to prevent trouble. Despite a report published in all likelihood the same evening, an official of the prefecture of police made a contradictory statement the next day saying there had only been limited public interest in these huge ceremonies: 'Some suggested it was only a charade which would not bring back the dead. Others, seeing the French flag adorning the cenotaph, observed that it was good to see the tricolour again.'[42]

There were a number of complex reasons why repressive tactics on the part of the German and Vichy authorities were not always carried out. We have already mentioned their hesitancy and reluctance to become involved in funeral ceremonies, which was partly intuitive and could not really be explained on either political or rational grounds. It was easier to recognise and explain their desire to respect proper codes of behaviour so far as British military personnel were concerned. Early on, they had a political motive too in wanting to normalise relations between occupiers and occupied. The funerals of Allied air crew gave rise to large demonstrations in the occupied zone. In December 1940, 2,000 people attended the funeral of three British airmen at Lanester. Shouts of 'Long live England' erupted from the crowd. In July 1941, a thousand people filed past the coffin of an English seaman at Saint-Brieuc, after a collection had raised money for a marble tablet bearing the inscription 'He died for France'.[43]

Funerals were also occasions on which public and collective expressions of civil resistance could be displayed to occupying troops who appeared sometimes reluctant to challenge such behaviour. At Villeneuve-d'Ascq in April 1944, the National Front, a Resistance organisation close to the Communist Party, mobilised its supporters, so far as its clandestine nature would allow, for the funeral of eighty-six French hostages killed by German soldiers on the second of that month. A notice was fly-posted on the walls of the town: 'French men and women, we call upon you to stop work from 11.30 to midday on Wednesday, 5 April, to mourn and protest at the vile murder of the people of Ascq. As many as possible are asked to come to the funeral.' Reports say that between 10,000 and 35,000 people took part, either by following the cortège, standing with heads bowed as it passed by or in their place of work, and that the Germans in the town did not apparently react.[44]

As well as actual funerals, the commemoration and mourning of those who had died at an earlier date also encouraged expressions of resistance. Seventeenth of June 1941 marked the first anniversary of the German bombing raid on Rennes which preceded the occupation of the city. On that memorable day, between 3,000 and 4,000 people demonstrated outside the town's eastern cemetery where the victims were buried. Standing in front of the locked gates which were guarded by gendarmes, they sang the *Marseillaise*. The graves of British soldiers killed during the raid and buried there had also become the scene of semi-clandestine expressions of patriotic resistance. A

police report of 9 June 1941 made it clear that the authorities were having difficulty controlling the site.

'I am pleased to inform you that, in accordance with
your instructions, I delegated one of my officers to visit
the eastern cemetery at 18.30 today in order to remove all
messages prejudicial to public order placed on the graves of
British soldiers killed during the bombing raid of 17 June
1940. There follows a list of the objects which were removed
and placed under lock and key in the care of M. Orhan, the
superintendent of the cemetery. 161 bunches of mixed flowers (oxeye daisies, cornflowers, poppies) representing the
three French national colours, twenty or so marble plaques
bearing inscriptions such as: "To our allies", "Friends for
ever", "To our liberators", "To our friends", "Faith", "Hope",
"Our friends and allies of 1914–1918", two post cards with
the French and British flags intertwined, a banner inscribed "Honour and Motherland", a ceramic wreath with
a purple ribbon with the legend "Friends for ever", several
tricolour ribbons and a Cross of Lorraine.'[45] Just one week
before the unofficial commemoration took place, this account reveals a mixture of guilt and individual initiative
as they tried to do something which would not overstep
the mark, yet which was sufficiently coercive in accordance
with orders from above.

That these commemorative objects, with their symbolic,
patriotic value, were placed in the care of the cemetery
superintendent would seem to indicate that, in making a
distinction between the objects themselves and their significance, boundaries were set on the repressive measures
adopted. Grief could still be expressed with flowers, ribbons
and plaques under lock and key, as long as no gestures of
defiance were made in public. Feelings were respected but
at the same time their public expression was temporarily
stifled.

Acts of remembrance as a form of public protest which
were important at the beginning of the Occupation were
suppressed from 1942 onwards.[46] According to the police this was because funerals gave rise to very public
demonstrations of Gaullist, anglophile and anti-German

feelings. Specific measures were adopted preventing crowds from gathering near cemeteries. Yet, the repression of demonstrations mingling protest and remembrance in occupied France was not progressively intensified as the years passed. In particular, the funerals of French people killed in acts of reprisal by German troops at the end of the Occupation were belatedly allowed to take place though there was opposition from the occupying authorities. A requiem mass was held in Limoges cathedral on 21 June 1944 for 'the souls of the victims of Oradour-sur-Glane', in spite of threats from the German police and reluctance on the part of the regional prefect. The reason the inhabitants were able to organise a public ceremony of mourning was because two weeks previously SS troops of the *Das Reich* division had used the bodies as weapons.

In fact, the religious aspect of official war funerals was less important than the fusion of different elements in a collective ritual validated by the presence of individuals representing the nation. It would seem that purely civil ceremonies did not officially take place before the 1939–45 War. On the other hand, during this same period, there were families which declined to hold a religious service. Government officials therefore attended two ceremonies, the one religious (sometimes held simultaneously in both Protestant and Catholic churches), the other civil. And though there was some comfort to be derived from public ceremonies, certain people refused to take part, and a number of grieving families turned down an offer made by the authorities. For moral, political or ethical reasons, they preferred to be alone with their dead as they accompanied them to their final resting place, even though the cost of an official funeral would have been met.

How were funerals conducted both on the battlefield and away from it for those killed in war? Those who mourned sought ways of working through their grief by choosing improvised forms of ritual as well as established ones, by adopting age-old practices as well new ones, by accepting public ceremonies as well as private ones. The difficult but necessary task of coming to terms with the separation of the living and the dead was accomplished slowly and was marked by anniversaries and acts of commemoration.

Notes

1. Arnold Van Gennep, *Le Folklore français. Du berceau à la tombe* (Paris: Robert Laffont, 1998 [1st edn 1943]); Louis-Vincent Thomas, *Rites de mort. Pour la paix des vivants* (Paris: Fayard, 1986); Marie-Frédérique Bacqué (ed.), *Mourir aujourd'hui. Les nouveaux rites funéraires* (Paris: Odile Jacob, coll. 'Opus', 1997).
2. Emmanuelle Héran (ed.), *Le Dernier Portrait* (Paris: Réunion des Musées Nationaux, 2002), catalogue of the exhibition at the Musée d'Orsay devoted to masks and portraits of the dead in the nineteenth and twentieth centuries.
3. Michael Herr, *Putain de mort* (Paris: Éditions de l'Olivier, 1996), p. 32.
4. Rémy Cazals, Frédéric Rousseau, *14–18, le cri d'une génération* (Toulouse: Privat, 2001).
5. Bougarel-Boudeville, *Pierre Bartay prisonnier de guerre* (Tours: Mame et fils, 1920), p. 180.
6. According to the argument put forward by Philippe Ariès, *L' Homme devant la mort* (Paris: Seuil, 1975); taken up by Michel Vovelle, *La Mort et l'Occident de 1300 à nos jours* (Paris: Gallimard, 1983).
7. Lucie Marquizeaud, 'Emma', quoted by Olivier Faron, *Les Enfants du deuil. Orphelins et pupilles de la nation de la Première Guerre mondiale (1914–1918)* (Paris: La Découverte, 2001), p. 210.
8. Svetlana Alexievitch, *Les Cercueils de zinc* (Paris: Christian Bourgois, 1991), p. 182.
9. Stéphane Audoin-Rouzeau, *Cinq deuils de guerre, 1914–1918* (Paris: Noêsis, 2001).
10. Luc Capdevila and Danièle Voldman, 'Rituels funéraires de sociétés en guerre (1914–1945)', in Stépane Audoin-Rouzeau, Annette Becker, Christian Ingrao and Henry Rousso (eds), *La Violence de guerre, 1914–1945. Approches comparées des deux conflits mondiaux* (Brussels & Paris: Complexe/IHTP-CNRS, 2002), pp. 289–311.
11. *Le Volontaire juif*, avril 1931, no. 4, quoted by Philippe-E. Landau, *Les Juifs de France et la Grande Guerre. Un*

patriotisme républicain (1914–1941) (Paris: CNRS Éditions, 1999), p. 214.

12. *Revue internationale de la Croix-Rouge*, 298, octobre 1943, pp. 822–7.

13. Hans Soltau, *Volksbund Deutsche Kriegsgräberfürsorge. Service pour l'entretien des Sépultures Militaires Allemandes: ses origines et son action* (Kassel, 1987), p. 12.

14. *14–18 Aujourd'hui. Today. Heute*, no. 2, 1999, in particular Frédéric Adam, 'L'archéologie et la Grande Guerre', pp. 28–35.

15. A.D., 'Unis dans la mort comme au combat', *Sciences et Vie*, septembre 2001; Robert Belleret, 'L'étrange tombeau des "potes de Grimsby", martyrs de la guerre de 14–18', *Le Monde*, 11 novembre 2001.

16. Franc-Nohain and Paul Delay, *Histoire anecdotique de la guerre de 1914–1915* (Paris: P. Lethielleux, 1915), part 5, 'Les blessés, les morts', p. 105.

17. Docteur Marcel Junod (former delegate of the International Red Cross), *Le Troisième Combattant. De l'ypérite en Abyssinie (1936) à la bombe d'Hiroshima (1945)* (Paris: Payot, 1948), p. 252.

18. Nicolas Offenstadt, *Les Fusillés de la Grande Guerre et la mémoire collective (1914–1999)* (Paris: Odile Jacob, 1999), p. 59.

19. Jean Quellien, *Opinions et comportements politiques dans le Calvados sous l'Occupation allemande (1940–1944)*, two typed volumes, thesis to obtain the qualification to direct research, Université de Caen, 1997, pp. 118–20.

20. Mirko D. Grmek and Louise L. Lambrichs, *Les Révoltés de Villefranche. Mutinerie d'un bataillon de Waffen-SS, septembre 1943* (Paris: Seuil, 1998), pp. 47–8.

21. Carine Trevisan, *Les fables du deuil. La Grande Guerre: mort et écriture* (Paris: PUF, 2001).

22. Ibid. p. 199.

23. Serge Klarsfeld, *Le Mémorial de la déportation des Juifs de France* (Paris: 1978).

24. Paul Pasteur, 'Crémation militante en Autriche, 1880–1938', in Olivier Dumoulin and Françoise Thelamon, *Autour des morts. Mémoire et indentité* (Rouen: Publications de l'Université de Rouen, 2001), pp. 15–26; by the same author, 'Les débuts de la crémation moderne', *Le Mouvement social*, avril-juin 1997, pp. 59–80.

25. Jacqueline Lalouette, 'Les enterrements civils dans les premières décennies de la Troisième République', *Ethnologie française*, avril-juin 1983, pp. 111–28.

26. Paul Pasteur, 'Crémation militante en Autriche, 1880–1938'.

27. Jacqueline Lalouette, 'La Libre Pensée, l'Église et la crémation', *Le Mouvement social*, avril-juin 1997, pp. 81–91.

28. Thierry Hardier and Jean-François Jagielski, *Combattre et mourir pendant la Grande Guerre (1914–1925)* (Paris: Imago, 2001), p. 168.

29. Chambre des députés, *Journal des débats*, 18 juin 1915.

30. Thierry Hardier and Jean-François Jagielski, *Combattre et mourir pendant la Grande Guerre (1914–1925)*, pp. 154–5.

31. Sénat, *Journal des débats*, sitting of 27 January, 1916.

32. Xavier Boniface, *L' Aumônerie militaire française (1914–1962)* (Paris: Cerf, 2001).

33. Stéphane Tison, 'La violence et la foi. Discours de prêtres sur la guerre dans la Marne et la Sarthe, 1871–1939', *Annales de Bretagne et des Pays de l'Ouest*, 3, 2001, pp. 87–116.

34. Annette Becker, *La Guerre et la Foi. De la mort à la mémoire, 1914–1930* (Paris: Armand Colin, 1994). At the outbreak of the war, President Poincaré appealed for an 'union sacrée'. An all-party government was created and everyone came together in defence of the country. [Translator's note]

35. Xavier Boniface, *L'Aumônerie militaire française (1914–1962)*.

36. Franc-Nohain and Paul Delay, *Histoire anecdotique de la guerre de 1914–1915* (Paris: Lethielleux, 1915), volume 6, 'Les Aumôniers et les Ecclésiatiques aux Armées', pp. 55–7; Philippe-E. Landau, *Les Juifs de France et la Grande Guerre*.

37. Philippe-E. Landau, *Les Juifs de France et la Grande Guerre*, p. 23.

38. Ibid. p. 97.

39. Xavier Boniface, 'L'aumônerie militaire israélite pendant la Grande Guerre', *Archives juives. Revue d'histoire des Juifs de France*, 33/1, 2000, pp. 37–50.

40. R. P. Dom Besse, *La Prière pour les morts en temps de guerre* (Paris: Librairie de l'Art Catholique, 1916), pp. 123–5.

41. Emmanuel Fureix, 'Un rituel d'opposition sous la Restauration: les funérailles libérales à Paris (1820–1830)', *Genèses*, 46, mars 2002, pp. 77–100.

42. Report on the bombing of 3 March 1942, Archives de la préfecture de police de Paris, BA 1756.

43. Christian Bougeard, *Le Choc de la guerre dans le département des Côtes-du-Nord, 1939–1945* (La Guerche-de-Bretagne, Éditions Jean-Paul Gisserot, 1995).

44. Louis Jacob, *Crimes hitlériens. Ascq, Le Vercors* (Paris: Mellottée, 1946).

45. Report of the superintendant of police, head of security, to the central command, 9 June 1941, Archives municipales de Rennes 6H26; quoted in Grégory Tessier, *La Police municipale rennaise des années 1920 à 1941: entre continuités et ruptures*, master's degree thesis, Université de Rennes 2-CRHISCO, 2001, pp. 72–3.

46. Christian Bougeard, *Histoire de la Résistance en Bretagne* (La Guerche-de-Bretagne, Éditions Jean-Paul Gisserot, 1992).

6 Ritualised mourning in acts of commemoration

Although death is of primary concern to the immediate family and relations and is therefore a strictly private matter, mourning is bound to have a certain social dimension. This is all the more true for mourning which takes place in time of war, since warfare has come to involve whole populations, whether it is a civil war or a conflict between nations. Since the middle of the nineteenth century, new forms of ritual surrounding the dead have given rise to the structuring and shaping of every aspect of funeral rites. Thus, industrialised societies have gradually planned cemeteries and monuments, have set up associations to remember the dead and created liturgies to honour them; and all this has occurred within the context of more individualistic, democratic and secular forms of social organisation becoming established.

Changes in the ways wars were fought were also an integral part of this evolutionary process. Mass killing and the absence of bodies gave rise to commemorative rituals embracing everyone who had been killed and not just regular soldiers and their leaders. The purpose of such rituals was to perpetuate the memory of those who had lost their life as a member of a group or simply of the community in general. This ritualised behaviour, organised on a very large scale and expressed in various commemorative acts after each conflict, did however create certain tensions. It neither eliminated the difficulty of remembering collectively all those who had died nor the gulf between splendid acts of public homage to heroes and the suffering of those grieving in private.

From temporary war graves to national cemeteries

Commemorating the earth itself and the dead who have
nourished it with their blood is one way of affirming identity
in the aftermath of military conflict. It is the precursor of a
collective national memory. The creation and upkeep of war
cemeteries is a key element in the cult of the war dead.[1]
Between the second half of the nineteenth and the first
third of the twentieth century, Western states laid down the
principles and rules for honouring and remembering their
soldiers as they sought to protect their physical remains. It
was, however, more than a matter of merely considering a
shift from the communal burial grounds of an earlier age to
the individual grave of modern times. Something practical
had to be done in various stages. As a consequence, the use
of temporary graves was introduced in battle.

The location of temporary graves was as varied as the
scenes and the nature of the confrontations which occurred:
simple mounds of earth in gardens and public squares as in
Warsaw in 1939, burial sites where bodies were brought together, rows of bodies in roadside ditches as witnessed during the exodus of spring 1940 in France, plots in local village
cemeteries close to the front line. The vagaries of battle affected all improvised graves such as these. It was because
she realised how vulnerable these temporary graves were
that in 1917 Jane Catulle Mendès was desperate to discover
the body of her son, Primice, in the devastated landscape of
Champagne and to mark it with two bronze plaques, before
it was moved to its final resting place.[2]

Whilst the authorities were anticipating how, at a later
date, these brave soldiers would be revered in the national
consciousness, the bereaved sought above all to preserve
a final resting place for their loved ones. Thus the idea
was born that, following on from the temporary grave sites,
proper cemeteries should be created once peace returned
for all those who had been part of or attached to an army.
They truly were places where the remains of all those killed
in battle were brought together within a public space: not
only those who died under fire, but airmen and sailors as

well, doctors, chaplains, drummers and cooks. Those who succumbed subsequently in ambulances or hospitals at the rear as a result of their wounds are buried there too. War cemeteries are also the resting place of enemy soldiers who died in captivity, like the six Germans in the hospital at Arles in October and November 1918 whose date of burial in the town's cemetery is all that is known of them.[3]

Indeed, a wide range of people killed during the wars were brought together in these cemeteries; local soldiers of course, but also prisoners, others who died from disease, accident or exhaustion, volunteers and assorted foreigners who enlisted: the Indochinese and Senegalese, for example, who were in the French army during the First World War, Belgian, Russian, Czech and Croatian conscripts of the German army during World War Two, as well as volunteer labourers of the *Organisation Todt* (OT) in France. In addition, there were members of soldiers' families who had followed the armies, children, wives and mistresses – even babes in arms – who, unexpectedly, have their own tomb just inside the German war cemetery at Mont d'Huines in the department of Manche, where most of the soldiers of the Third Reich who died in western France were grouped together.[4] In Brest in 1943, the German authorities, having made clear that funeral ceremonies should vary depending on how the person had died, reminded everyone that all its nationals should be treated with respect. The officer responsible for graves gave the mayor of this town on the Finisterre coast the following instructions: 'Two grave diggers should be hired in addition to the existing personnel to carry out preparatory work before the burials take place and to assist the gardener B... with the meticulous upkeep of all German graves, including those of foreign workers who belonged to the OT.[5] The latter, together with Germans who committed suicide or who were shot, should be buried in the French cemetery at Kerfautras and not in the official war cemetery. They should, nonetheless, be grouped together in one designated area and not scattered around. Their graves (as opposed to the tombs of the heroic soldiers buried with honour in the official cemetery) should be decorated with a box hedge, a rose tree and a simple wooden cross.'[6] This last category comprised those considered dishonourable: soldiers who had been executed, shot by firing squad as an example to others, deserters, those who disobeyed orders, mutineers . . . and those who committed suicide. Several dozen belonging to the German army of occupation in France were buried in 1943 and 1944 both in the cemetery at Arles and in the cemetery of Saint-Jérôme in Marseille. A special plot, plot number 6, was set aside there for 'soldiers who had been executed or who had committed suicide and been buried without military honours'. This did not alter the fact that flowers were placed on their graves throughout the Occupation by the city of Marseille, as was done with all the others – in accordance with details set out in the armistice – and especially on the 'commemoration of heroes day', in March, which no doubt delighted the German authorities.[7]

We should perhaps remind ourselves that these large burial grounds were created out of physical necessity. However, their vital function as repositories of human remains was never of paramount importance, which explains why in the beginning they were thought of as temporary. Thus, the construction of war cemeteries prefigured the movement of bodies on a large scale, which mobilised the energies of armies, states and families throughout the various conflicts, and especially as wars ended. In order to pay homage to the dead in surroundings which were worthy of such ceremonies, exhumations were carried out, bodies were brought together and transported. This even included anonymous bones which were placed in caskets sector by sector, then collected together in large coffins in chapels of rest before being taken to vast ossuaries.

Though this was a huge task after the First World War, it was something which happened after all wars and involved those who died in all sorts of circumstances. In the 1920s, it did indeed affect all the countries who had been involved in the conflict. The numerous small military cemeteries which had been created in the mountains of northern Italy were demolished and the human remains were exhumed and transported to large ossuaries in the valleys. Even if the British insisted that their dead remained where they died in battle, they nonetheless had them moved to a final resting place in cemeteries which were often smaller than those of other nations involved and included soldiers who came from every corner of their Empire. The Americans organised the repatriation of 45,588 bodies across the Atlantic – 764 being sent to their country of origin in Europe – and in addition had five large cemeteries built in France for the remaining third of the American troops who died during the Great War and who were destined to remain close to the front line.[8] Congress agreed that two hundred and fifty dollars be allocated for the remains of each individual soldier.

It was indeed in the aftermath of war that those involved in the funeral business were especially busy, with work also going to a whole number of related trades. As well as funeral directors, who were suspected of getting rich whilst the nation grieved, other associated tradespeople such as monumental masons, earthwork contractors, carpenters, nurserymen and gardeners were in great demand, as were those in the building sector and in public works.[9]

The 240 German cemeteries built in France after 1871, 1918 and 1945 for the million who were killed in the three wars are illustrative of the changes taking place.[10] Those who died, in turn victors and vanquished, were beneficiaries of an organisation established by the Treaty of Frankfurt and also by the German and French laws of 1872 and 1873. In France, the State introduced compulsory purchase orders on the grounds of public need. Having compensated communities or individuals who owned the land which was needed, they handed it over to the Germans for their use. Though they were granted on a concessionary basis, these parcels of land remained under the administrative authority of the host nation. Whatever the outcome of the fighting, the peace process involved the upkeep of cemeteries which began during the 1880s. From that time onwards, German war graves, whether mass graves in the

fields of the Moselle or individual tombs surrounded by railings within local cemeteries in the Marne, formed part of
the landscape of funeral monuments in France.

After 1918, these familiar German graves were particularly prominent in the north and east of the country. The
growing numbers of the dead and the increased importance
of both individual and collective homage, and of course the
defeat, meant that rows of black crosses were an increasingly striking presence in the countryside.

During the French campaign in the spring of 1940,
cemeteries were modelled on those created between 1914
and 1918. Experience too was important. In the north, at
Dunkirk and Calais in particular, the army made use of
those which already existed and which had been well looked
after as a result of administrative procedures established
under the Treaty of Versailles. Elsewhere, in Charente,
Eure and Calvados, temporary cemeteries were created as
and when they were needed. During the Occupation and
until June 1944, German burials were divided between military plots in garrison towns, temporary graves in the municipal cemeteries of small communities and First World
War cemeteries. In the south, prefects sent circulars to local
authorities telling them to follow 'the same procedures as
those adopted after 1870 and 1914', which meant that plots
were to be provided for the burial of Germans and cemeteries enlarged if they were too small. Amongst others, Istres,
Miramas and Saint-Chamas in the Bouches-du-Rhône had
to be extended.[11] Municipal authorities demanded that
these tasks be classified as requisitions, considering them
too onerous a burden on their finances which had worsened
under the terms of the armistice of June 1940. It was for the
French State to shoulder the burden. The demands of municipal councils were not always heeded, but despite their
recriminations the work seems always to have been carried
out, graves kept up, flowers placed on them, paths weeded,
and so on.[12]

From the time of the Allied landings in Normandy, and
given that battles took place once more between troops on
the move, German cemeteries were created for the most

part in temporary American and British ones. Once the French State had been re-established, the secretariat of the Veterans' Association paid the burial expenses of enemy troops whereas the Ministry of the Interior paid those of paramilitaries belonging to the French Milice.[13]

The status of British military cemeteries in occupied France also changed during the course of the Second World War. In 1939, Great Britain officially owned its cemeteries on French soil. As ex-allies of France in the 1914–18 War, and still enemies of the Germans, they administered them through the Imperial War Graves Commission. The war itself and the reversal of its alliances rendered this state of affairs null and void so far as France was concerned, and thus the status of British cemeteries was revised. Those looking after them were taken prisoner by the Wehrmacht and the Vichy regime took over the responsibilities of the Imperial War Graves Commission. In accordance with established procedures, British graves were granted the same indemnity as permanent French ones, with all war cemeteries being the responsibility of the Reich as agreed under the terms of the armistice. In June 1941, in response to a request by the Imperial War Graves Commission, the International Committee of the Red Cross inspected English and Canadian cemeteries in occupied France in the presence of the German Red Cross and army personnel. They informed the British that proper care was being taken of their graves. According to the French Red Cross, there were simply 'less flowers than when British caretakers were present',[14] due to the circumstances.

The nature and upkeep of war cemeteries has varied according to national traditions and practices.[15] As a consequence, there are more trees and flowers such as begonias, poppies and pansies in British and German than in French ones. The shape of headstones, the inscriptions, the colour of crosses, the way the plants are arranged, the upkeep of the grass and gravel paths also differ. Flowers were banned in German cemeteries during the inter-war period, initially for reasons of cost. It was a way too of not distracting attention from the heroism and tragic end of those who died in battle. While the British, Americans and French all supported uniformity in their national cemeteries, they also insisted on a single grave for each individual. German cemeteries, on the other hand, were built with the initial intention of merging the individual with the group by listing them collectively on memorials.

With the exception of military plots in small local cemeteries, which are more restrained and have the more intimate feel associated with ordinary graves, national cemeteries in the age of mass wars are vast and the graves themselves standardised. Despite the care taken with their construction, exemplified by those in north and west France, they stretch out in a landscape far removed from the day-to-day lives of those who mourn. Visits by families and veterans began immediately after the war of 1870–1.[16] Although tourist visits to military cemeteries and battlefields became institutionalised after the Great War[17] and increased at the end of the twentieth century as a result of the combined effect of commemorative events and people's interest in their heritage, a chilly air of solitude lingers over these lines of stones. So that an intense atmosphere of contemplation or less personal feelings of grief might prevail in these national cities of the dead, their upkeep was of the utmost importance if they were to remain places of recollection and commemoration.

Associations for the remembrance of the dead

Linking the public and the private sphere, and bringing together veterans, families and states, associations dedicated to remembering the dead have played a major role in the evolution of funeral rites. In particular, they have contributed to the move away from improvised rites to more codified forms of remembrance.

The first associations dedicated to rituals of national commemoration of the dead developed in the United States during the early years of the nineteenth century. Various groups sought to erect monuments to the memory of major figures who had been active in the American Revolution.[18]

In 1856, a group of women set up the Mount Vernon Ladies' Association of the Union and bought George Washington's house as a place of meditation and remembrance. At the same time, another association of women was engaged in an effort to raise funds and erect a monument to him. Women therefore played an important role, which was not the case with later European associations. The memorial activities to which they devoted a great deal of energy gave women a semi-public position, and they did not miss the chance of becoming involved in civic affairs. However, women's associations were less influential than those created by male veterans.

The principal association of Union veterans, the Grand Army of the Republic (GAR), was founded in 1866. From its inception, it dedicated itself to the upkeep of the graves of those who fell during the war and played a key role in the organisation of ceremonies of remembrance associated with them. It devised a service composed of prayers, hymns, patriotic songs and funereal music. Above all, it sought to have established a day on which those who died in the war would be officially commemorated. At the same time, though in the other camp and not strictly speaking a veterans' association, the Ku Klux Klan resembled in some measure the GAR. Initially, the members of the Klan described themselves as the ghosts of dead Confederate soldiers. The GAR had similarly begun as a secret society.[19] Its initiation rite involved remembering those who died in the war. The initiate entered a room blindfolded and knelt down. When the blindfold was removed, he found himself standing before a coffin draped in the American flag, bearing the name of a single victim of the great battle of Andersonville, on which was placed a copy of the Bible. This ceremony was not restricted to a circle of initiates for long. It came to involve both families and the nation as a whole.

Nevertheless, the mystical presence at memorial ceremonies of those killed in action alongside those who had survived lasted into the twentieth century amongst veterans who had a quasi-religious attitude to war and were still living it out in their imagination. A good example would be the popular Nazi *Horst Wessel* song, far removed in time and space from the American Civil War. In this war song, as the Storm Troopers marched along in serried ranks, they are accompanied every step of the way by the spirit of their dead comrades who have fallen in battle.[20] These verses summoned up the invisible presence of the dead in support of their comrades under fire, something which often happened during the First World War, as in the memorable lines published at the instigation of Maurice Barrès 'Arise dead comrades!'[21] He persuaded adjutant Jacques Péricard to revise the report he had sent to the press in April 1915 about a counter-attack in the trenches by a handful of injured poilus.[22] The revised version published by Payot in 1918 read as follows: 'Arise dead comrades! A sign of madness? No. Because the dead responded. They said: We will follow you. And rising up in answer to my call, their spirit imbued my spirit, so that it became ball of fire, a wide river of molten metal...'[23]

To return to the United States following the Civil War, those who had been orphaned placed flowers on graves in 1868 and responded to the roll call of names of the dead during one of the earliest ceremonies held at the Arlington cemetery. Thus, they prefigured what would happen during the great European ceremonies of remembrance. In 1899 as a result of various initiatives, several associations which honoured the memory of Civil War veterans came together to form a General Federation of the Union, while in the southern states people began to gather on Memorial Day as fixed by the victors in the north. The following year, Congress began the acquisition of battlefields to transform them into places of commemoration.

After the First World War, memorial associations were set up modelled on those created in the Civil War, except that Union and Confederate dead were jointly honoured as the nation was now one. Alongside the main First World War veterans' association, the American Legion, another association, the American Field of Honor, campaigned for the creation of cemeteries on the other side of the Atlantic. They said they would help families bury their dead close to the front. Those who found it hard to leave the remains of their loved ones so far from home were given assistance by the association to have them repatriated to a national military cemetery or to an ordinary family grave.

Without giving details of the countless American associations which existed, we would simply say that while establishing ritualised forms of commemoration which included the whole panoply of memorials (tombs, ossuaries, cenotaphs and cemeteries) they linked funerals with acts of remembrance and patriotic ceremonies.

Given the importance of war graves in helping us to remember, things developed along similar lines in Europe where national organisations were concerned initially with the upkeep of cemeteries. As in the United States, ritualised forms of mourning at national ceremonies were initiated by these associations. The associations themselves were entirely public bodies in Great Britain, private organisations in Germany and State-aided private bodies in France. In the Southern Cone, on the other hand, there were only embryonic groupings at the end of the nineteenth century. Veterans' associations which commemorated wars and those who died in them existed in Argentina, such as the Association of Soldiers who fought in Paraguay.[24] But in Paraguay itself, veterans of the war of the Triple Alliance, who lacked any organisation, were not registered and helped by the republic until 1896, almost thirty years after their defeat.[25] They were then used for their own ends by nationalist movements in the first decade of the twentieth century.[26] Certain patrician elites instituted a commemoration of the dead to create a sense of national identity in the 1900s.

In France, the largest of these organisations – Souvenir Français (the National Association of French Remembrance) – was set up in 1887 by an Alsatian, Xavier Niessen, who had chosen to retain his French nationality after 1871. Like its predecessors in the United States, its aim was to help the different groups of veterans formed after the defeat to organise ceremonies commemorating the dead of 1870–1 by putting up monuments in cemeteries, at battle sites or in their local communities, and to ensure above all that the graves of those who died for their country were looked after. The statutes of this organisation declared: 'The object of Souvenir Français is: 1) to maintain, both in France and abroad, the graves of French soldiers and sailors who died for their country and to guarantee the preservation of those graves; 2) to perpetuate the memory of men who brought honour to their country with their noble deeds... It has only one aim: To pay dutiful homage to those who died winning glory or defending their country.'[27] It was a private body, legally authorised to carry out its activities by a ministerial order of 29 August 1887, and was organised on a national basis with a management committee in Paris and local sections throughout the country. Before the First World War, Souvenir Français, with thirty years of experience in the field, helped to define how the dead were commemorated. For the first time, the dead would be accorded some individuality by having their names engraved on plaques and monuments.[28] The Church, the State and families would be brought together for funerals and the inauguration of monuments, and cemeteries would be maintained. After 1918, the only major change was the growing role of the State in the organisation of funerals and cemeteries and in the creation of magnificent forms of liturgy.

Except for much greater involvement on the part of the State, none of these practices had changed by the beginning of the twenty-first century, as demonstrated by the activities of Souvenir Français at Avranches in the department of Manche.[29] Following the restoration of the monument to those who died in all wars from 1870–1 on, undertaken under its auspices in 1956, it was again responsible for the ceremonies in 2001 commemorating the centenary of the first monument.

Created in 1919, the German People's Association for the Upkeep of War Graves (*Volksbund Deutshe Kriegsgräberfürsorge*, or VDK) grew out of the various associations formed during the war from the autumn of 1918 onwards. It was a federation of very diverse bodies, when viewed in terms of its denominational, geographical, sociological and political make-up, and was an entirely private organisation, as the German State, defeated and disorganised, gave no help at the time with the upkeep of war graves.[30] The VDK, which wanted to be a federal body with pacifist and ecumenical aspirations, could not however escape the twists and turns of its nation's history. After a difficult start with Germany in a state of revolution, it was able to do some good work in the second half of the 1920s, helped by the growing stability of the Weimar Republic and urgent demands from the families of soldiers who had been killed. From 1933 on, it was subjected to more and more pressure by the Nazi regime to change its message of peaceful reconciliation to one which encouraged the glorification both of those who died as heroes for the fatherland and of German power. Like its French and British counterparts, the VDK had also supported the creation of a day of national mourning for the dead. As a result of Nazi coercion, it became the day for the commemoration of heroes, that same day which the municipal council of Marseille willingly respected during the Occupation of France.

The VDK answered a deep social need. So much so that, following Nazification between 1933 and 1945, it reestablished its original ideology in 1946 and undertook once more the upkeep of cemeteries and commemorated the victims of the two World Wars both at home and abroad. It rebecame an entirely private organisation dependent on voluntary subscriptions, as originally constituted, though with the advent of welfare state obligation the Federal German Republic has become its principal generous donor.

Our rapid survey of large commemorative associations does not include the host of smaller groups which have grown up or the range of their activities. Concerned always with the social dimension of commemoration and wanting to foster mutual aid, some have sought to perpetuate the pain of grief, such as the National Association of the Sons of the Dead and the Association of French War Orphans founded in 1927 or the National Association of the Families of the Martyrs of Oradour created in the winter of 1944–5. Others have adopted a more educational role and are less concerned with ritual remembrance, such as the National Committee for the Commemoration of Verdun, established in 1926. In the town which remains symbolic of the conflagration of the Great War, it contributed during the 1950s to the construction of a memorial the main purpose of which was pedagogical and formative, thus indicating how attitudes had evolved.

Creating a commemorative environment

From the end of the nineteenth century, spaces devoted to commemoration were organised around emblematic structures such as graves, ossuaries, cemeteries, cenotaphs. These shaped the way acts of remembrance were conducted in two or three stages (which varied according to their exact nature and location) very like funeral ceremonies; they involved the Church, the war memorial, soldiers' graves, the laying of sprays of flowers and wreaths, meditation, a procession, and a formal dinner with which the ceremony closed.

The scale of death and the ways people died during the First World War resulted in a whole array of different memorials across the length and breadth of the country. Apart from a dozen or so municipalities in France, most of the 36,000 local communities erected a war memorial during the 1920s, since the majority of municipal cemeteries had witnessed the burial of local people between 1921 and 1923.[31] Because huge numbers of soldiers were never found, Western societies created a tomb for an unknown soldier and acts of remembrance around it.[32] These tombs were subsequently opened after each war. In France, this took place at the end of the Second World War, the war in Algeria, and belatedly after the war in Indo-China; in America after the Second World War and the wars in Korea and Vietnam. Canada also decided, late in the day at the end of the 1990s, to repatriate the remains of an unknown Canadian soldier who died during the Great War and whose body had remained in Europe.

Given that the American army now systematically identifies bodies by their DNA, it is unlikely that the remains of unknown soldiers will be placed in the Arlington National Cemetery to commemorate the dead of future wars. But the place of the unknown soldier at the heart of acts of remembrance following the First World War was illustrative not simply of technical changes in warfare and in ways the dead were remembered, it revealed too a much more profound transformation in the way the war dead were viewed.

This was also true of ossuaries. In France until 1914, they were the regulation burial place for ordinary soldiers. At the end of the 1870–1 War, the first monuments were erected in honour of the unknown dead buried in mass graves beneath them, such as the cross at the camp of Conlie in 1873 and the Champagné column which was put up near Le Mans (Sarthe) in 1875. Until the First World War, ossuaries, where assorted bones could be seen, glorified those who died heroically in war by putting them on display.[33] This was the case at Bazeilles (Sedan), where skulls, tibias and humerus were heaped together with marching boots in underground chambers on both sides of a passageway. Until 1914, German bones could be seen lying opposite French ones. Following the invasion of France, the German authorities discovered these 'trophies' and decided the German bones should be buried.[34] At a much later date, a similar affirmation of military glory was in evidence at the ossuary worthy of the pharaohs which Franco had built between 1940 and 1956 by thousands of Republican prisoners near the Escorial, the *Valle de los Caidos*. In it, the remains of Nationalist soldiers killed in the war were to be preserved, and it was to be Franco's own tomb when he died.[35] A concrete cross fifty metres tall stood over the basilica built into the mountainside. Though the whole construction was dedicated to the memory of those killed on the winning side in the Civil War, it also consecrated the triumph of Franco's crusade.

But the monumental ossuaries built in France after the Great War were to serve another purpose. Firstly, they provided a resting place for unidentified remains and a graveside for the families of those who had disappeared. Indeed, the monuments within which these remains were placed were real tombs even though they contained the bones of many men, for they brought together the bones of unknown soldiers just as mass graves did. Attempts were made to compensate for the anonymity of death on a mass scale by the care taken in constructing such buildings. The history of the different edifices constructed around Verdun allows us to trace the way monuments evolved as part of the commemorative process.[36] The first building project undertaken by the municipality began in 1917, but the monument itself celebrating victory was not inaugurated until 1929. Though it was a satisfactory response to national feelings of patriotism, little attention was paid to the commemoration of the dead. To satisfy this need, a second monument called the 'Trench of Bayonets' was quickly built and inaugurated in 1920. It was the creation of André Ventre, an architect in the Department of Historic Buildings who was very involved in reconstruction work. A concrete slab resting on enormous columns, it resembled a gigantic tomb and recreated the legend of soldiers 'buried upright, perhaps still alive, their bayonets fixed in their rifles'.[37] Once more, the notion of collective sacrifice took precedence over that of individual loss. Because countless bodies were still being discovered in the region, which was visited by the curious as well as grieving relatives seeking remains, a wave of public opinion emerged fostered by the Catholic Church and veterans' associations in support of a communal mausoleum suitable for more private meditation. Though seen as vital, the proposal did not altogether meet with the approval of the municipality which was still licking its wounds and had already made a financial contribution towards the other monuments.

In the winter of 1918–19, the Bishop of Verdun consecrated a chapel inside a wooden hut, which differed little from the other temporary huts built all over these devastated parts of the country. On the open space in front of the building, flanked by two cannons, a submissive statue of the Virgin Mary, her finger held to her lips, greeted pilgrims. Perhaps the hope was that those who approached would restrain their cries of horror as they entered a house of prayer which had become a gigantic repository for all the bones found in the region. The building of the definitive ossuary was entrusted to Léon Azéma, also heavily involved in reconstruction work, and it was conceived as an ecumenical religious and funeral monument. The outline plan specified that, alongside the Catholic shrine, three buildings for Protestants, Jews and Moslems were to be erected. Although the first stone was laid in 1920, the whole structure was not completed until 1932; this was because of the high cost of the work and also because little public money was available. But already for a decade, the ossuary had been a place of constant pilgrimage as individual widows, orphans, families and friends or parties made up of memorial associations and veterans visited it.

As well as communal graves, then, there were the tombs of the unknown soldier which were real graves for real, albeit unknown, men. Thirteen years after the inauguration of the tomb of the unknown soldier of the Great War at the Arc de Triomphe, General Weygand recalled the sentiments which lay behind the creation of this memorial shrine: 'It offered a place of honour to an unknown soldier who would be "the Son of all those Mothers who never found their own Sons"... and was a tomb where the families [of those who disappeared] could pray... The idea of honouring the humblest and least well-known of our heroes in an unknown soldier immediately struck a chord with the public.'[38] Their specific function was to provide a resting place for someone whose identity could not be known. Were he to be identified, he would have to be replaced. Yet in affording recognition to individuals though they remained unknown, these tombs were memorials in their own right. More than ossuaries, the tombs of unknown soldiers strengthened the rituals of mourning through large-scale national acts of remembrance.

In Rome, the tomb of the unknown soldier was placed beneath the Altar of the Nation, situated at the heart of the great Il Vittoriano monument commemorating the unification of Italy and dedicated to King Victor-Emmanuel II.[39] The ceremony took place on 4 November 1921, the day on which victory was celebrated and when the body of an unknown soldier was brought into the city. When it arrived, as if from a funeral parlour, a solemn mass was held at the church of *Santa Maria degli Angeli* (Our Lady of the Angels). When the service ended, a procession formed to go to the Altar of the Nation at the Il Vittoriano monument. There the burial took place, as it would have done at an ordinary cemetery, in the presence of a great gathering composed of the royal family, representatives of political, religious and military bodies, veterans and bereaved families. The nature of the ceremony did not alter until the collapse of fascism, apart from changes due to the evolution of the political situation in Italy.

In London, the unknown soldier is buried alongside kings and queens in Westminster Abbey. In the centre of the Pantheon in Asunción, the tomb of the unknown soldier of the Chaco War is flanked by two of the greatest presidents of the modern Paraguayan Republic (Bernardino Caballero who presided over the rebuilding of the country after the war of the Triple Alliance, and Eusebio Ayala, who governed the country during the Chaco War). These three tombs are encircled, like a treasure, by the funeral urns of nineteenth-century leaders and those of the two great military figures in these wars, General Diáz in the war of the Triple Alliance and General Estigarribia in the Chaco War.

The tomb of the unknown soldier at the Arc de Triomphe, having become the 'Altar of the Nation', was in 1929 the brief resting place of the remains of Marshal Foch before they were taken to Notre-Dame de Paris. Subsequently, tombs to unknown soldiers provided a link between those who disappeared in a succession of wars and were more than simply national altars. Whereas the remains of unknown soldiers of the two World Wars as well as of the Korean and Vietnam Wars were buried at the Arlington Memorial, in France it was different. Only the unknown soldier of the 1914–18 War was buried at the Arc de Triomphe. The unknown soldier of the 1939–45 War was buried in 1950 in the crypt of the lantern tower at the church of Notre-Dame-de-Lorette, as were the ashes of unknown deportees in 1955 and the remains of unknown soldiers from North Africa in 1977 and Indochina in 1980.

The various types of monument to the dead represent the final forms of support for the whole ritualised process of commemoration. Unlike ossuaries and the tombs of unknown soldiers, monuments from the Great War on, with one or two exceptions,[40] were not real tombs, though they had a predominantly commemorative function and often served as cenotaphs. The sites of all monuments were places for the open expression of mourning and for meditation, and the rituals which accompanied their inauguration took the form of religious ceremonies.

The trend which began at the end of the nineteenth and lasted throughout the following century reflected in large measure the significance of monuments as physical objects which encouraged the act of remembrance. In France, monuments began to be built after the 1870–1 War, during which many soldiers were buried anonymously in mass graves or placed in ossuaries. The construction of tombs and the erecting of monuments in departments and districts which had sent significant numbers of soldiers and *gardes mobiles* (militia) were ways of honouring those who disappeared. These were the first memorials to ordinary soldiers and *gardes mobiles* and were built in the main some time after the events and as a result of private initiatives, such as that of local branches of Souvenir Français.[41]

The monument in the region of Elboeuf, where bloody fighting took place in the last days of December 1870 and the early part of January 1871, is another illustration of the way in which public and private, secular and religious, patriotic and more personal interests became involved in these new forms of commemorative enterprises.[42] A fund was set up in September 1872 to erect a monument in memory of all those who had fallen there, *gardes mobiles* and *francs-tireurs* (irregulars) who came from several departments (Ardèche, Landes, Loire-Inférieure, Charente-Inférieure, Calvados, Eure-et-Loir, Seine, Eure, Seine-et-Oise), as well as gendarmes, customs officers and sailors. The inauguration ceremony took place in the presence of representatives of the military, political and religious authorities – an admiral, a deputy, and a cardinal-archbishop who blessed the monument. An estimated crowd of 20,000 was present at this belated non-funeral, which took the place of the ceremonies which could not be held at the time of death.

After the First World War, the underlying principles governing ceremonies which centred on memorials to the dead did not change though the scale of them did. For example, the separation of Church and State did not mean that ceremonies became truly secular. Though it was still possible for headstones and graves to incorporate religious emblems under the laws of separation, they were forbidden on memorials. It was all a question of definition. How did one determine whether a monument was a gravestone or a memorial? Structures erected in cemeteries were considered to be gravestones, whereas those put up in public squares, outside town halls, churches or schools were not allowed to have a cross or other religious symbols. The policy, outlined in a circular sent out by the Ministry of the Interior in 1919, was in fundamental opposition to the practices and wishes of a public which was profoundly Catholic. It was overturned in a judgement made by the Council of State on 4 July 1924. These changes of attitude meant that there were some memorials without crosses, particularly in rural communities which had erected them early on and in accordance with the law of 1919, alongside others built at a later date.

The difficulty of disentangling the civic aspect from the religious was particularly marked in the case of the monument in the Père-Lachaise cemetery in Paris.[43] When the war ended, the city as a whole had no monument to the dead, though one had been hurriedly built in each arrondissement. A plan was presented to the city council to fill this gap. The idea was to build it at Père-Lachaise, which had become the focal point of all public funeral ceremonies in the city since it was opened in 1804. The arguments of councillors against the project illustrate the gradual development of the ritualised expression of grief in acts of remembrance. In their eyes, cemeteries were places for the dead, only to be visited by families paying their respects.

They should not become the focus for civic and public ceremonies.

The difficulty in fact arose from the way in which the
ritualised expression of grief in acts of remembrance was
evolving. Unlike monuments built after the war of 1870–1,
those erected for the 1914–18 War grew out of a collaboration between citizens, local communities and the State. The
law of 25 October 1919 concerning the 'commemoration and
veneration of those who died for France during the Great
War' established the principle of State aid to communities
for everything they did to honour the heroes who died for
their country. The decision as to whether the commemorative function of what was built was more important than its
role as a tombstone was not simply left to the initiative of
private individuals. In most cases, municipalities did however involve local people in the decision-making process,
just as they accepted the help of the ecclesiastical authorities.

In the 1920s, therefore, French Jews were actively involved in the campaign to construct monuments and put up
commemorative plaques.[44] Every community sent a list of
those missing to Albert Manuel, the secretary of the Consistory in Paris, whose job it was to gather all the information and draw up a golden book of all Jews who died
for their country. By 1921, Dijon, Épinal, Rouen, Saint-
Étienne, and Vitry-le François had already honoured the
dead in their synagogues. Tablets of black marble, sometimes ornamented with the tricolour and quotations from
the prophets, were put up. The names of dead soldiers were
inscribed in gold letters. But Paris had not yet paid its
homage. The Consistory of the capital decided that a similar plaque should be unveiled at the great synagogue in the
Rue de la Victoire. Families considered this modest homage
somewhat inadequate. They campaigned for the erection of
a proper monument, and won the argument. And though
the actual representation of a soldier or grieving relative
was not acceptable in such a setting, realism was not ruled
out, as a helmet, a rifle, a flag, and the Tablets of the Law
were all sculpted in stone.

There were so many monuments to those who died in the Great War, which was what the general public wanted, that no difficulties arose when they were used again after the Second World War and subsequent colonial conflicts. New names were added to them, and not just those of military personnel. The general viewpoint was, however, that only those 'who died for France' with a gun in their hands should be added. That was the case for Resistance fighters 'who died for France'. Civilian victims, on the other hand, notably hostages executed by the Germans, were not listed. Thus, any monument commemorating those killed in the Second World War drew distinctions based on the way they died. Resistance fighters, hostages, deportees, those in the armed forces and the victims of bombing raids were not treated in the same way and were honoured, in most cases, on different monuments.[45]

However, despite this, until the mid-1960s, most monuments retained their function as places for civic, patriotic and more private remembrance. In the majority of cases, their architecture was that associated with war graves and cemeteries: plaques on which names were inscribed, obelisks, sometimes military enclosures. There was also the monument commemorating the Bir-Hakeim Maquis, built rather belatedly a few kilometres from the cirque of Mourèze (in the Hérault), which looked exactly like a military cemetery with the same number of individual white crosses as the number of partisans killed. The essential purpose of all these monuments was to preserve for ever the name of each person in the village or community who had died.

A change occurred in the middle of the 1960s, at the same time as feelings about death were evolving along with forms of mourning and of remembrance.

The history of memorials to the Nazi crimes at Auschwitz and Dachau shows us how one particular group shaped the development of collective commemoration.[46] At the very beginning of the 1950s, on the initiative of several associations of deportees and adopting procedures which were in vogue at the time, two international architectural competitions for the building of monuments were launched.

The idea was to express through a monumental work of art particularly painful feelings of grief over what happened in the war. After several years of discussion about the details of the projects, the two competitions were actually launched in 1957 and 1958, and the buildings inaugurated in 1967 and 1968 respectively. The competition for the memorial at Auschwitz was the first in a long series which has continued until the present day and they always give rise to controversy because the issues involved are so complex. In the final years of the twentieth century, the competition for a memorial to European Jews who were victims of the Holocaust, which was launched in Berlin in 1990, brought into the open most of the principal questions raised: Can the horror be transfigured through art? Which victims should be honoured? What importance should be given to the commemorative, religious, political and ideological aspects of such memorials?

For a long time, questions such as these have lain behind all discussion about commemoration, exacerbated by the unique characteristics of the genocide of the Jews. Just as some people in the 1920s wanted the cathedral of Rheims, which was being rebuilt at the time, to remain in its ruined state as a testimony to the barbarity of those who destroyed it, so the Polish government declared in 1947 that the two ruined camps of Auschwitz-Birkenau should remain as they were. The justification which accompanied their declaration caused the outcry. In the government's view, the ruined site should serve as a 'memorial to the martyrs of the Polish nation and to other peoples'. Although, just two years after Hitler's downfall, Jewish sensibility concerning a memorial was not as developed as it was to become in the 1970s, the statement itself was difficult to accept; as was the plan in 1990 to have a Carmelite house at the entrance to the camp.

The debate over Dachau was equally intense. The camp was used initially as a prison for captured SS troops. Then, when the buildings had been cleaned up, they provided temporary accommodation for refugees from Eastern Europe, before they were finally destroyed in 1965. Despite the fact that they were used continuously, the first attempt to create a memorial proved premature. A collection of photographs was put together and an exhibition held at the camp just before the Nuremberg Trials opened in November 1945. It was the first of many would-be solutions adopted in response to different proposals for memorials, none of which produced a consensus. While international pressure grew for the federal government to look after the graves of Nazi war victims – which were in fact mass graves – competing funeral ceremonies were held imbued with the atmosphere of the Cold War. Discussions about a monument were still going on in 1956, more than ten years after the camp was liberated, because those involved had such divergent interests. In 1960, on the initiative of the Catholic hierarchy, a chapel was built to the north of the camp, followed in 1967 by a Protestant one and a Jewish memorial.

Though the role of the churches was less pronounced as society became secularised in the course of the twentieth century, they nonetheless played as crucial a part in acts of remembrance as in actual funerals. In this respect civic religion and religion itself were intertwined and all beliefs merged. So, before each country in turn chose an official day on which to commemorate its war dead, 1 November, All Souls' Day, became the generally accepted date with ceremonies taking place in cemeteries at which priests officiated. The anniversary of the ceasefire in the First World War, 11 November, was also chosen because of its proximity to All Souls' Day. However, big ceremonies with large numbers of veterans present tended to merge with patriotic parades and were not entirely compatible with more private feelings of grief.

Towards private forms of ritual

Just as the way corpses were treated reflected the demands and expectations of families so the social development of a public memory of war came about as a result of negotiations between public authorities, those who had experience of battle and the rest of society. Some wanted to educate people or to convey a political message; most simply wanted their dead not to be forgotten. The history of the commemoration of the dead which has shaped all forms of remembrance is the history of people's relationship with death and war. It has to do with the spread of democracy, the growth of individualism and indeed the idea of community within Western societies. Thus, in acts of commemoration there has been a move away from the cult of national heroes to a recognition of the sacrifice made by ordinary individuals and, in the course of the twentieth century, to the inclusion within the collective memory of all members of society: women as well as soldiers, minorities as well as the majority.[47] The process has resulted in twin developments: on the one hand, specific identifiable groups have been included in acts of remembrance such as cultural minorities (those from the colonies, gypsies, Harkis in France,[48] American-Indians, Afro-Americans, members of immigrant groups in the United States, etc.) and social minorities (foreigners in transit, homosexuals, etc.); on the other hand, all conflicts and all groups have been merged within a single expression of grief.

In the 'golden book' of Plougastel-Daoulas, *Les Victimes des guerres du XXe siècle*, the city's collective traumas resulting from three wars have been brought together. The wars involved are those of 1914–18, 1939–45 and the war which took place in Algeria.[49] The Foreword written by the mayor responsible for the production of the book makes clear what his intentions were in this act of commemoration: 'Two hundred pages against barbarity. Two hundred pages which preserve four hundred names from anonymity and which ensure they will live on in the memory of this community. From the marble inscription on the memorial inaugurated in 1994, we move from a long list of names to the human reality of young lives pitilessly cut down in different wars.' Each name in the book is followed by a few lines of biographical details as well as the individual's dates of birth and death, and sometimes by a few words as to how they died, some photos or a photomontage of their life. The 'golden book', which declares itself to be a work of commemoration, adds that no mention is made of those

who 'survived illness or their wounds (with untold suffering) nor of those disabled in the Great War who are remembered by their families and the older citizens of Plougastel.'
There is a note of regret in the fact that they are not mentioned. The whole population cannot escape the effects of
war. Merely to recite the names of the young people who
died for their country is an inadequate expression of the
community's recognition.

The wish to achieve a state of quiet reflection in remembering as individuals those killed in war has influenced
the creation of new forms of collective memory.[50] Since the
1960s, the general public has abandoned acts of remembrance in Europe, as in the United States where Memorial
Day has become an occasion for going shopping or having
a picnic.[51] Furthermore, apart from significant moments of
public emotion, political commentators have sought to establish meaningful links between the living and the dead
as individuals. With the siting of memorials in public parks
where we experience a desire to meditate, as on the Internet
and in 'golden books', we now find faces alongside names.
Increasingly, the stories of people's lives, which are moving in their very ordinariness, illuminate these portraits
and resonate with those who leaf through a book, click on
a screen or quietly reflect in the Peace Park in Hiroshima,
at Yad Vashem in Jerusalem or at the Vietnam memorial
in Washington. The collective memory of war has become a
private scrapbook devoted to shattered lives. Just as those
who mourned gave a social dimension to their grief in order
to share it through writing, by becoming militant, or by having a small memorial dedicated to the loved one they had
lost,[52] so now the wider community finds that its collective
memory of wars is that of individuals and the tragedies
which befell them.

Notes

1. George L. Mosse, *De la Grande Guerre au totalitarisme.
   La Brutalisation des sociétés européennes* (Paris: Hachette-
   littératures, 1999).

2. Stéphane Audoin-Rouzeau, 'Corps perdus, corps retrouvés. Trois exemples de deuils de guerre', *Annales. Histoire, Sciences sociales*, janvier-février 2000, pp. 47–71.
3. Dossier 'Cimetières et tombes allemandes (1870–1945)', Archives départementales des Bouches-du-Rhône, 76 W 426.
4. Ariarig Sauvage, *L'Ennemi enterré chez soi. Sépultures militaires allemandes et culte funéraire sur le sol français, de 1870 à nos jours*, Master's thesis, CRHISCO-Université Rennes 2, 2001, p. 59.
5. Underlined in the text.
6. Kreiskommandantur 623, letter no. 2881/43, Brest, 20 July 1943, Archives départementales d'Ille-et-Vilaine fonds Fréville, 52J174.
7. Dossier 'Cimetières et tombes allemandes (1870–1945)', Archives départementales des Bouches-du-Rhône, 76 W 426.
8. Mark Meigs, 'La mort et ses enjeux: l'utilisation des corps des soldats américains lors de la Première Guerre mondiale', *Guerres mondiales et conflits contemporains*, 175, juillet 1994, pp. 135–46.
9. Béatrix Pau-Heyries, 'Le marché des cercueils (1918–1924)', *Revue Historique des Armées*, 3, 2001, pp. 65–80.
10. Ariarig Sauvage, *L'Ennemi enterré chez soi*, p. 50.
11. Dossier 'Cimetières et tombes allemandes (1870–1945)', Archives départementales des Bouches-du-Rhône, 76 W 426.
12. 'Réquisitions/Entretien des tombes de soldats allemands (1940–1944)', Archives départementales d'Ille-et-Vilaine, 170 W 785, 170 W 817, 170 W 851.
13. Ministry of Public Finance, telegram of 25 January 1945 to regional commissioners of the Republic and to prefects, circular no. 18.
14. *Revue internationale de la Croix-Rouge*, 276, 23e année, décembre 1941, pp. 1004–1005.
15. Annette Becker, *Les Monuments aux morts. Mémoire de la Grande Guerre* (Paris: Errance, 1988).
16. Paul-Noël Armand, 'Léon Besnardeau a inventé la carte postale commémorative', *La Province du Maine*, 17, 1991.
17. Collection of *Guides illustrés Michelin des Champs de bataille, 1914–1918*, Clermont-Ferrand, Michelin et Cie, 1919 and subsequent years; Suzanne Brandt, 'Le voyage aux champs de bataille', in Jean-Jacques Becker (ed.), *Guerre et cultures, 1914–1918* (Paris: Armand Colin, 1994), pp. 411–16.

18. G. Kurt Piehler, *Remembering War. The American Way* (Washington, DC & London: Smithsonian Institution Press, 1995).
19. Ibid. pp. 62–3.
20. George L. Mosse, 'Souvenir de la guerre et place du monumentalisme dans l'identité culturelle du national-socialisme', in Jean-Jacques Becker (ed.), *Guerre et cultures 1914–1918*, p. 284.
21. Jean-Norton Cru, *Du témoignage* (Paris: Alia, 1997[1st edn 1930]), pp. 70–6.
22. Jean-Norton Cru, *Témoins. Essai d'analyse et de critique des souvenirs de combattants édités en français de 1915 à 1928* (Nancy: Presses Universitaires de Nancy, 1993[1st edn 1929]), pp. 378–83.
23. Jacques Péricard, *Debout les morts! Souvenirs et impressions d'un soldat de la Grande Guerre. Pâques rouges* (Paris: Payot, 1918), p. 168.
24. National Library of Asunción, F317, 1891. In the military library of Asunción, the Gill and Zeballos collections contain numerous memoirs of Argentinian veterans.
25. Dossiers of authenticated and unauthenticated veterans and records (1896 and beyond), Ministry of Defence, Asunción.
26. Military museum of Asunción, Gill and Zeballos collections, dossier 90, F40, 'Demonstration in support of war veterans, 1920'. Cf. Arsenio López Decoud (and others), *La República del Paraguay. Un siglo de vida national 1811–1911* (Buenos Aires: Talleres Gráficos de la Companía General de Fósforos, 1911), p. 245, Andrès Barbero Museum, Asunción, H. 1116.
27. Le Souvenir Français, national society for the upkeep of graves of soldiers and sailors who died for their country, *Rapports de l'assemblée générale du 24 mai 1896*, Paris.
28. Unlike those of the First World War, monuments to those who died in the 1870–1 War do not include all the soldiers from the local community who fell in battle. They register the categories of soldiers involved, recording in a subjective manner only certain attributes of the various units: mobile, regulars, irregulars, Papal guards; they also include soldiers killed in wars during the Second Empire and in colonial expeditions, etc.
29. Armelle Carnet, *Les Origines de la mémoire de guerre à Avranches: le monument du Souvenir français*, Master's thesis, CRHISCO-Université Rennes 2, 2000.

30. Hans Soltau, *Volksbund Deutsche Kriegsgräberfürsorge. Service pour l'entretien des sépultures militaires allemandes: ses origines et son action* (Kassel, 1987).

31. One will recall the extraordinary case of the small commune of Nampty (Somme), near Amiens, which, though on the front line during the First World War, lost no-one in the 1870–1 War or during the 1914–18 War, the 1939–45 War or the Algerian War. In Nampty, according to Michel Curie, 'they commemorate neither 11 November nor 8 May. But believers, especially those whose grandparents lived in the village, show special devotion to the statue of Notre-Dame-des-Vertus', in Michel Curie, 'Deux villages sans morts ni monuments', *Le Monde*, 5 novembre 1998, p. 15.

32. War memorials have been studied extensively by historians of war and of remembrance, especially in relation to the First World War. Without going into details concerning these analyses, we recall the solemn and public acts of remembrance which such memorials fostered, revealed in the pioneering work of Antoine Prost, *Les Anciens Combattants et la société française, 1914–1939* (Paris Presses de la Fondation Nationale des Sciences Politiques, 1977). Also, 'Les monuments aux morts de la Première Guerre mondiale', in a special issue of *Guerres mondiales et conflits contemporains*, 167, juillet 1992, and in particular Antoine Prost, 'Mémoires locales, mémoires nationales: les monuments de 1914–1918 en France', pp. 41–50.

33. Annette Becker, 'Monuments aux morts après la guerre de Sécession et la guerre de 1870–1871: un legs de la guerre nationale?', *Guerres mondiales et conflits contemporains*, 167, 1992, pp. 23–40.

34. Ibid. p. 29.

35. Michael Richards, *Un tiempo de silencio. La guerra civil y la cultura de la represión en la España de Franco, 1936–1945* (Barcelona: Crítica, 1999), pp. 77–8.

36. Antoine Prost, 'Verdun', in Pierre Nora (ed.), *Les Lieux de mémoire* (Paris: Gallimard, 1984), vol.2, *La Nation*, pp. 111–41.

37. Jean-Norton Cru states that this legend developed after the war as a result of tourists visiting the front who suggested there was something 'supernatural' about a row of bayonets sticking out of the earth beneath which bodies were buried. During the war, in fact, bodies were frequently buried after

battle in sections of unused trenches. Rifles were placed in the ground to mark the graves. Jean-Norton Cru, *Du témoignage*, pp. 76–8.

38. Général Weygand, *Le 11 novembre* (Paris: Flammarion, 1932), pp. 131–2.

39. Catherine Brice, *Monumentalité publique et politique à Rome. Le Vittoriano* (Rome: École française de Rome, 1998).

40. One thinks of the war memorial at Laurens (Hérault) erected in the cemetery. Even today, it remains the 'true' monument for the villagers. See the Conclusion.

41. Antoine Prost, 'Les monuments aux morts. Culte républicain? culte civique? culte patriotique?', in Pierre Nora (ed.), *Les Lieux de mémoire*, vol. 1, *La République*, pp. 195–225.

42. Karine Hamel, 'Disparition d'une mémoire. Les morts de la Guerre de 1870–1871 en Seine-Inférieure', in Olivier Dumoulin and Françoise Thelamon, *Autour des morts. Mémoire et identité* (Rouen: Publications de l'Université de Rouen, 2001), pp. 263–78.

43. Danielle Tartakowsky, *Nous irons chanter sur vos tombes. Le Père-Lachaise, XIXe-XXe siècle* (Paris: Aubier, 1999).

44. Philippe-E. Landau, *Les Juifs de France et la Grande Guerre. Un patriotisme républicain (1914–1941)* (Paris: CNRS Éditions, 1999).

45. Serge Barcellini and Annette Wieviorka, *Passant, souviens-toi! Les lieux du souvenir de la Seconde Guerre mondiale en France* (Paris: Plon, 1995).

46. Aymone Nicolas, *L'Union internationale des architectes et les concours internationaux d'architecture et d'urbanisme (1949–1969). Desseins d'architecture et de politique*, History of Art thesis, Université Paris I, 2002, pp. 282–99.

47. Although, for example, it was decided in the United States in 1948 that the graves of unidentified soldiers would be marked by a cross: they were therefore unidentified Christian soldiers!

48. Indigenous North African soldiers who served alongside their metropolitan French counterparts. [Translator's note]

49. Plougastel-Daoulas, *Livre d'or. Les victimes des guerres du XXe siècle. 'Les chemins de la mémoire'* (Plougastel: Le Comité de Rédaction, 1999).

50. For example 'the wall of faces', the monument honouring veterans of the Korean War, unveiled in 1995 in the Washington

National Memorial Park. Inscribed on the wall in the place of the names of the veterans are 24,000 photographs; see André Gunthert, 'Le mur des images du Washington Hall', *Vingtième siècle. Revue d'histoire*, 51, 1996, pp. 155–7.

51. Institut d'histoire du temps présent, *La Mémoire des Français. 40 ans de commémoration de la Seconde Guerre mondiale* (Paris: CNRS, 1986); Gérard Namer, *La Commémoration en France, de 1945 à nos jours* (Paris: L'Harmattan, 1987); Jay Winter and Emmanuel Sivan (eds), *War and Remembrance in the Twentieth Century* (Cambridge: Cambridge University Press, 1999).

52. Stéphane Audoin-Rouzeau, *Cinq deuils de guerre, 1914–1918* (Paris: Noêsis, 2001).

Epilogue: The presence of dead bodies

The photographed shadows of those killed at the epicentre of the explosion in Hiroshima have in their own way survived modern war in which bodies are pulverised.[1] The anonymous bodies heaped up in the camps before being buried in huge mass graves, the atomised inhabitants of Japanese cities, those who were seized and then disappeared in Chile and all the other unknown victims of wars which were supposed to produce 'zero deaths' lie in the virtual mausoleums of our present-day conflicts; conflicts which have led to the technical, political and cultural disappearance of bodies.

We were introduced to these new types of war dead in the twentieth century with the inauguration of tombs of unknown soldiers at the beginning of the 1920s in Europe and the United States. The century ended with another unknown soldier. Michael J. Blassie, a pilot, came down north of Saigon on 11 May 1972 and was declared missing. His family, convinced he was the unknown soldier of the Vietnam War buried at the Arlington National Cemetery, obtained permission from the Pentagon on 13 May 1998 to have a DNA test done on his bones. Having been identified as those of Lieutenant Blassie, a decision was taken to return his remains to his family so that he could be buried next to his father at Saint Louis in Missouri.[2]

What happened to the remains of the unknown soldier of the Vietnam War encapsulates the paradox of those killed in wars in the West during the twentieth century. We have witnessed a highlighting of the individual in the age of the masses; the combing of intelligence sources to establish the identity of bodies when enormous amounts of energy were being expended on better ways of getting rid of them; the request of parents to see, touch and preserve the tiniest fragment of their loved one like a relic at a moment in history when the dead are set apart from the world of the living; ever more elaborate funeral ceremonies and expressions of grief over war in societies where secularisation and the desire for immortality tend to deny death and to reduce funerals to their bare essentials in times of peace.

At Laurens in the Haut-Hérault, a very unusual memorial was erected after the First World War: namely a tomb. Around thirty young men of the area had died fighting for their country. In 1923, when sixteen bodies were handed back to families who had requested it, it was decided not to bury them in family graves as happened most frequently in such cases, but to keep them together for ever.[3] They were placed in a communal grave, on which stood a monument surrounded by railings just like an 1870 war grave. But in this case, parents personalised it. Portrait photographs of those buried were attached to metal or marble plaques and were inscribed: 'Here lies' and 'Eternal regrets'. The plaques were fixed to the iron railings of the enclosure or placed at the foot of the obelisk. Eighty years after it was erected, this half-private, half-public grave, which has both a military and a civil function, and where patriotism is a part of both private pain and public grief, is still decorated with flowers by the municipality and the descendants of those commemorated. And the façade of the primary school still bears the first memorial to those from the village who died. Placed at the entrance to the building, it was meant to be seen by the young schoolchildren. When they arrived at school each day, they would read the following inscription: 'Children, do not forget. They died for you', which created a personal daily link between the generations.[4]

The photos from the 1920s hung on the railings of the war memorial in Laurens prefigure the numbered funeral sites on the Internet of those who disappeared during the campaign of repression in Argentina and the fleeting television images of those pulverised in the World Trade Center. Like the ancient world, where sarcophaguses of the dead were placed at the roadside just outside the city so that passers-by would learn about the life of the person who had died, Western society continues to honour its war dead with ceremonies of public mourning.

In societies where life expectancy continues to increase and where premature death has become unacceptable, and in a culture where dying seems an archaic fate, a vestigial fact of human existence which we would like to control, the practice of war, which civilisations find inescapable – though war itself now seeks to avert death – confronts us with the tragedy and the physical reality of dead bodies. War interrupts, temporarily though persistently, the slow process which began during the century of the Enlightenment whereby the dead have been removed from the world of the living. From the revolutionary wars in Europe and America up to the Second World War, and beyond, albeit sporadically, the bodies of the dead have been a constant presence for the living; and those who escaped death have gathered round those bodies the better to hate them, to care for them, to love them... This is what the Soviets did in 1942 with the remains of Zoya Kosmodemianskaya, known as Tania, a fighter who was executed by German soldiers on 5 December 1941 at Petrívchewo, to the west of Moscow.[5] A propaganda leaflet telling of her suffering has on its cover a picture of her half-naked body, revealing a frozen breast. It was her final portrait. Indeed, the practice of showing a final portrait continued in France until the beginning of the 1950s.[6] But the elevation to heroic status of this particular fighter was based in part on the eroticisation of her body.

How strange things are at the beginning of the third millennium. In the near future, American military personnel will probably be equipped with electronic discs which will store details of their identity and therefore of their genetic code. At the same time as DNA tests now enable us to identify scientifically those killed in war, though they may have been buried for years, military technology has the capacity to completely pulverise the bodies of those it hurls into its deadly vortex. Will the tombs of unknown soldiers soon be replaced by those of unknown civilians who have disappeared?

Notes

1. Docteur Shuntaro Hida, *Little boy. Récit des jours d'Hiroshima* (Paris: Quintette, 1984).
2. Laurent Zecchini, 'Le soldat inconnu de la guerre du Viêt-nam porte désormais un nom', *Le Monde*, 2 juillet 1998.
3. Decisions of the municipal council, 24 November 1921, 18 May 1922, 26 December 1923. Registre des délibérations du conseil municipal de Laurens (1912–1959), Archives municipales de Laurens (Hérault).
4. Decision of the municipal council, 21 February 1919; ibid.
5. Jacques Lorraine, *Tania la partisane*, Alger, imp. Baconnier, censure no. 11 953 (around 1943–1944). The story is known because of this propaganda leaflet containing numerous illustrations of her execution. It was published in Algiers by France combattante at the end of the Second World War.
6. Emmanuelle Héran (ed.), *Le Dernier Portrait* (Paris: Réunion des musées Nationaux, 2002), catalogue of an exhibition at the Musée d'Orsay devoted to final portraits and death masks of the 19th and 20th centuries.

Bibliography

Wars

Alexievitch, Svetlana, *Les Cercueils de zinc* (Paris: Christian Bourgeois, 1991).

Audoin-Rouzeau, Stéphane, *1870. La France dans la guerre* (Paris: Armand Colin, 1989).

Audoin-Rouzeau, Stéphane, and Annette Becker, *14–18. Retrouver la guerre* (Paris: Gallimard, 2000).

Audoin-Rouzeau, Stéphane, Annette Becker, Christian Ingrao and Henry Rousso (eds), *La Violence de guerre, 1914–1945* (Brussels: Complexe, 2002).

Barnabé, Patrice, 'Guerre et mortalité au début de la guerre de Cent ans: l'exemple des combattants gascons (1337–1367)', *Annales du Midi, revue de la France méridionale*, 235, 2001, pp. 273–305.

Becker, Jean-Jacques, Jay M. Winter, Gerd Krumeich, Annette Becker and Stéphane Audoin-Rouzeau (eds), *Guerre et cultures, 1914–1918* (Paris: Armand Colin, 1994).

Bodin, Michel, *Les Africains dans la guerre d'Indochine, 1947–1954* (Paris: L'Harmattan, 2000).

Boniface, Xavier, *L'Aumônerie militaire française (1914–1962)* (Paris: Cerf, 2001).

Bouthillon, Fabrice, 'Mythes guerriers, guerres mythiques', *Commentaire*, 92, winter 2000–2001, pp. 912–16.

Branche, Raphaëlle, *La Torture et l'armée pendant la guerre d'Algérie, 1954–1962* (Paris: Gallimard, 2001).

Chesnais, Jean-Claude, *Les Morts violentes en France depuis 1826* (Paris: PUF, 1976)

Clastres, Pierre, *Archéologie de la violence. La guerre dans les sociétés primitives* (Marseille: Éditions de l'Aube, 1997).

Corvisier, André, *Les Hommes, la Guerre et la Mort* (Paris: Économica, 1985).

Corvisier, André, *La Guerre. Essais historiques* (Paris: PUF, 1995).

David, Dominique, 'La guerre dans le siècle', *Politique étrangère*, 3–4, autumn–winter 2000, pp. 645–58.

Dreyfus-Armand, Geneviève, and Laurent Gervereau (eds), *Voir, ne pas voir la guerre* (Paris: Somogy, 2001).

Destexhe, Alain, *Rwanda. Essai sur le génocide* (Brussels: Complexe, 1994).

Dumézil, Georges, *Heurs et malheurs du guerrier* (Paris: Flammarion, 1985).

Edgerton, Robert B., *Death or Glory. Legacy of the Crimean War* (Boulder, CO: Westview Press, 1999).

Élie, Jérôme, 'Victimes des guerres civiles le dilemme de l'évaluation doit-il grever l'analyse?', *Relations internationales*, 105, spring 2001, pp. 109–121.

Fernandez, Danièlle, 'L'opinion publique américaine et la question des "Missing in Action"', in Jean-Michel Lacroix and Jean Cazemajou (eds), *La Guerre du Viêt-nam et l'opinion publique américaine (1961–1973)* (Paris: Presses de la Sorbonne Nouvelle, 1991), pp. 133–40.

Gibson, James W., *Warrior Dreams. Paramilitary Culture in Post-Vietnam America* (New York: Hill & Wang, 1994).

Goldstein, Joshua S., *War and Gender. How Gender Shapes the War System and Vice Versa* (Cambridge: Cambridge University Press, 2001).

Guilaine, Jean, and Jean Zammit, *Le Sentier de la guerre. Visages de la violence préhistorique* (Paris: Seuil, 2001).

Hilberg, Raul, *La Destruction des Juifs d'Europe* (Paris: Fayard, 1985).

Horne, John, and Alan Kramer, *German Atrocities, 1914. A History of Denial* (New Haven: Yale University Press, 2001).

Jauffret, Jean-Charles, *Soldats en Algérie, 1954–1962. Expériences contrastées des hommes du contingent* (Paris: Autrement, 2000).

Jeffords, Suzan, *Hard Bodies. Hollywood Masculinity in the Reagan Era* (New Brunswick & New Jersey: Rutgers University Press, 1994).

Keegan, John, *A History of Warfare* (New York: Knopf [London: Hutchison], 1993); [*Histoire de la guerre, du néolithique à la guerre du Golfe* (Paris: Dagorno, 1996)].

Keeley, Lawrence H., *War Before Civilization. The Myth of the Peaceful Savage* (Oxford: Oxford University Press, 1996).

Krouck, Corinne, *Les Combattants français de la guerre de 1870–1871 et l'écriture de soi: contribution à une histoire des sensibilités*, thesis, Université Paris I, 2001.

Landau, Philippe, *Les Juifs de France et la Grande Guerre*, doctorate supervised by Michelle Perrot and Pierre Vidal-Naquet, Université Paris VII, 1993.

Levillain, Philippe, and Rainer Riemenschneider (eds), *La Guerre de 1870–71 et ses conséquences* (Bonn: Bouvier, 1990).

Martin, Andrew, *Receptions of War. Vietnam in American Culture* (Norman: University of Oklahoma Press, 1993).

Mauss-Copeaux, Claire, *Appelés en Algérie. La parole confisquée* (Paris: Hachette, 1998).

Ministère de la Guerre, 'L'éducation brusquée d'un Nord-Africain. Le soldat nord-africain et les campagnes d'Europe', *Études*, February 1947, pp. 181–99.

Mosse, George L., *De la Grande guerre au totalitarisme. La brutalisation des sociétés européennes* (Paris: Hachette, 1999).

Nières, Claude, *Faire la guerre. La guerre dans le monde, de la préhistoire à nos jours* (Toulouse: Privat, 2001).

Payne, Stanley, and Javier Tusell, *La Guerra civil. Una nueva visión del conflicto que dividio España* (Madrid: Temas de Hoy, 1996).

Pecaut, Daniel, 'De la banalité de la violence à la terreur: le cas colombien', *Cultures et conflits*, 24, 1996.

Prost, Antoine, *Les Anciens Combattants et la société française, 1914–1939*, 3 volumes (Paris: Presses de la Fondation nationale des sciences politiques, 1977).

Puiseux, Hélène, *Les Figures de la guerre. Représentations et sensibilités, 1839–1996* (Paris: Gallimard, 1997).

Richards, Michael, *Un Tiempo de silencio. La guerra civil y la cultura de la represión en la España de Franco, 1936–1945* (Barcelona: Crítica, 1999).

Roth, François, *La Guerre de 70* (Paris: Fayard, 1990)

Vernant, Jean-Pierre, *Problèmes de la guerre en Grèce ancienne* (Paris: EHESS, 1999).

Death

Ariès, Philippe, *Contribution à l'étude du culte des morts à l'époque contemporaine*, Rapport à l'académie des sciences morales et politiques, 1966.

Ariès, Philippe, 'La mort inversée. Le changement des attitudes devant la mort dans les sociétés occidentales', *Archives européennes de sociologie*, VIII, 1967.

Ariès, Philippe, *Essai sur l'histoire de la mort en Occident, du Moyen-Âge à nos jours* (Paris: Seuil, 1975).

Ariès, Philippe, *L'Homme devant la mort* (Paris: Seuil, 1985).

Baudrillard, Jean, *L'Échange symbolique et la mort* (Paris: Gallimard, 1976).

Bertherat, Bruno, 'La morgue de Paris', *Sociétés et représentations*, June 1998, pp. 273–93.

Chiffoleau, Jacques, *La Comptabilité de l'au-delà. Les hommes, la mort et la religion dans la région d'Avignon à la fin du Moyen Âge (vers 1320–vers 1480)* (Rome: Mélanges de l'École française de Rome, 1980).

Chrétien, Vincent, *Ceux de 14–18. La violence et la mort de guerre représentées par la presse illustrée, la littérature enfantine et la caricature*, Université Rennes 2/CRHISCO, 2000.

Croix, Alain, and Fañch Roudaut, *Les Bretons, la Mort et Dieu, de 1600 à nos jours* (Paris: Messidor, 1984).

De Baecque, Antoine, *La Gloire et l'Effroi. Sept morts sous la Terreur* (Paris: Grasset, 1997).

Dechaux, Jean-Hugues, *Le Souvenir des morts. Essai sur le lien de filiation* (Paris: PUF, 1997).

Dewitte, Philippe, 'La dette du sang', *Hommes et migrations*, 1148, November 1991, pp. 8–11.

Douzou, Laurent, 'Les morts de la Résistance', in Olivier Dumoulin and Françoise Thelamon (eds), *Autour des morts. Mémoire et identité* (Rouen: Presses Universitaires de Rouen, 2001), pp. 409–17.

Faas, Horst, and Tim Page, *Requiem par les photographes morts au Viêt-nam et en Indochine* (Paris: Marval, 1998).

Freud, Sigmund, 'Considérations actuelles sur la guerre et sur la mort', *Essais de psychanalyse* (Paris: Payot, coll. 'Petite Bibliothèque Payot', 2001).

Gorer, Geoffrey, *Ni pleurs ni couronnes* (Paris: EPEL, 1995).

Guillaume, Pierre, 'Le cadavre dans les hospices bordelais au XIXᵉ siècle', *Annales du Midi, revue de la France méridionale*, 235, 2001, pp. 327–37.

Héran, Emmanuelle (ed.), *Le Dernier portrait* (Paris: Réunion des Musées Nationaux, 2002).

Hintermeyer, Pascal, *Politiques de la mort* (Paris: Payot, 1981).

Hoffenberg, Peter H., 'Landscape, Memory and the Australian War Experience, 1915–1918', *Journal of Contemporary History*, 36, 2001, pp. 111–31.

Hulin, Michel, *La Face cachée du temps. L'imaginaire de l'au-delà* (Paris: Fayard, 1985).

Jourdan, Didier, *Le Droit et la Mort. Le principe républicain de la liberté funéraire à l'épreuve du temps*, thesis, Université Montpellier 1, June 1989.

Kantorowicz, Ernst H., *Mourir pour la patrie* (Paris: PUF, 1984).

Kelly, George Armstrong, *Mortal Politics in Eighteenth Century France. Réflexions historiques* (Waterloo: Canada, 1986).

Lebrun, François, *Les Hommes et la mort en Anjou* (Paris: Flammarion, 1975).

Meigs, Mark, 'La mort et ses enjeux. L'utilisation des corps des soldats américains lors de la Première Guerre mondiale', *Guerres mondiales et conflits contemporains*, 175, 1994, pp. 135–46.

Mengozzi, Dino, *La Morte e l'immortale. La morte laica da Garibaldi a Costa* (Rome: Piero Lacaita, 2000).

Morin, Edgar, *L'Homme et la mort dans l'histoire* (Paris: Corréa, 1951).

Morin, Edgar, *L'Homme et la Mort* (Paris: Seuil, 1977).

Robert, Jean-Louis, and Jay Winter, 'Un aspect ignoré de la démographie urbaine de la Grande Guerre: le drame des vieux à Berlin, Londres et Paris', *Annales de Démographie Historique*, 1993, pp. 303–29.

Schmitt, Jean-Claude, *Les Revenants, les vivants et les morts dans la société médiévale* (Paris: Gallimard, 1994).

Schwartz, Vanessa R., *Spectacular Realities. Early Mass Culture in Fin-de-Siècle Paris* (Berkeley: University of California Press, 1998).

Tenenti, Alberto, *La Vie et la mort à travers l'art du XVe siècle* (Paris: Serge Fleury, 1983).

Thomas, Louis-Vincent, *Anthropologie de la mort* (Paris: Payot, 1976).

Thomas, Louis-Vincent, *La Mort africaine* (Paris: Payot, 1982).

Urbain, Jean-Didier, *L'Archipel des morts. Le sentiment de la mort et les dérives de la mémoire dans les cimetières d'Occident* (Paris: Payot, coll. 'Petite Bibliothèque Payot', 1998).

Vovelle, Michel, 'Encore la mort, un peu plus qu'une mode?', *Annales ESC*, 1982.

Vovelle, Michel, *La Mort et l'Occident, de 1300 à nos jours* (Paris: Gallimard, 1983).

Cemeteries

Auzelle, Robert, *Dernières demeures* (Paris: R. Auzelle, 1965).

Bilici, Faruk, 'Les cimetières musulmans en France', *Les traditions funéraires dans le monde arabo-musulman*, colloquium organised by l'Institut français des études anatoliennes, Istanbul, October 1991.

Bloquert-Lefevre, M.-S., *Les Sépultures militaires sur le territoire national, 1914–1918* (Paris: Institut Catholique de Paris/ Université Paris IV, 1992).

Clarke, Hugh V., *A Life for Every Sleeper. A Pictorial Record of the Burma-Thailand Railway* (Sydney: Allen & Unwin, 1986).

Deutsche Kriegsgräber. Am Rande der Strassen. Frankreich, Belgien, Luxemburg und Niederlande, (Kassel: Volksbund Deutsche Kriegsgräberfürsorge E.V., 1997).

Eltin, Richard A., *The Architecture of Death. The Transformation of the Cemetery in Eighteenth-Century Paris* (London: 1984 and 1987).

Fay, Émile, *Les Cimetières et la police des sépultures,* thesis, Faculté de droit, Paris, 1900.

Grive-Santini, Catherine, *Guide des cimetières militaires en France* (Paris: Le Cherche-Midi, 1999).

Le Normand-Romain, Antoinette, 'La guerre vue à travers la sépulture funéraire', in Philippe Levillain and Rainer Riemenschneider (eds), *La Guerre de 1870–71 et ses conséquences* (Bonn: Bouvier, 1990), pp. 494–505.

Longworth, Philip, *The Unending Vigil. A History of the Commonwealth War Grave Commission 1917–1967* (London: 1967).

Sauvage, Ariarig, *L'Ennemi enterré chez soi. Sépultures militaires allemandes et culte funéraire sur le sol français, de 1870 à nos jours*, thesis for Masters degree, Université Rennes 2/CRHISCO, 2001.

Soltau, Hans, *Service pour l'entretien des sépultures militaires allemandes. Ses origines et son action* (Kassel: Volksbund Deutsche Kriegsgräberfürsorge E.V., 1987).

Tartakowsky, Danielle, *Nous irons chanter sur vos tombes. Le Père-Lachaise, XIXe–XXe siècle* (Paris: Aubier, 1999).

Urbain, Jean-Didier, 'Les cimetières d'Occident. Des sociétés de conservation', *Études*, August–September 1982, 357/2–3.

Rites and Liturgies

Andrieux, Françoise, 'L'image de la mort dans les liturgies des églises protestantes', *Archives des sciences sociales des religions*, 39, January–June 1975.

Bacqué, Marie-Frédérique (ed.), *Mourir aujourd'hui. Les nouveaux rites funéraires* (Paris: Odile Jacob, coll. 'Opus', 1997).

Chaïb, Yassine, *L'Émigré et la Mort. La mort musulmane en France* (Aix-en-Provence: Édisud, 2000).

Goldberg, Sylvie Anne, *Les deux rives du Yabbok. La maladie et la mort dans le judaïsme ashkénaze* (Paris: Cerf, 1989).

Hidiroglou, Patricia, *Rites funéraires et pratiques de deuil chez les Juifs en France, XIXe–XXe siècle* (Paris: Les Belles Lettres, 1999).

Jauffret, Jean-Charles, 'La question du transfert des corps, 1915–1934', *Traces de 14–18* (Carcassonne: Les Audois, 1997), pp. 133–46.

Losonczy, Anne-Marie, 'Le saint et le citoyen au bord des tombes. Sanctification populaire de morts dans les cimetières urbains colombiens', *Religiologiques*, 18, Autumn 1998.

Pau-Heyries, Béatrix, 'Le marché des cercueils (1918–1924)', *Revue Historique des Armées. Mélanges*, 3, 2001, pp. 65–80.

Péruchon, Marion, *Rites de mort, rites de vie. Les pratiques rituelles et leur pouvoir, une approche transculturelle* (Paris: ESF, 1997).

Pourcher, Yves, 'La fouille des champs d'honneur. La sépulture des soldats de 14–18', *Terrain*, 20, 1993, pp. 37–56.

Pulby, Joseph, *Le Monopole des pompes funèbres*, thesis, Faculté de droit de Paris, 1904.

Saindon, Marcelle, *Cérémonies funéraires et postfunéraires en Inde. La tradition derrière les rites* (Québec: Presses de l'Université de Laval, 2000).

Thomas, Louis-Vincent, *Rites de mort pour la paix des vivants* (Paris: Fayard, 1985).

Tobie, Nathan, *Rituels de deuil* (Grenoble: La Pensée Sauvage, 1995).

Van Gennep, Arnold, *Les Rites de passage* (Paris: Picard, 1981 [1st edn, 1909]).

Mourning

Audoin-Rouzeau, Stéphane, *Cinq deuils de guerre, 1914–1918* (Paris: Noêsis, 2001).

Barcellini, Serge, 'La gestion du deuil par l'État français au lendemain de la Seconde Guerre mondiale', in Francine-Dominique Liechtenhan (ed.), *Europe 1946, entre le deuil et l'espoir* (Brussels: Complexe, 1996), pp. 121–40.

Loraux, Nicole, *Les Mères en deuil* (Paris: Seuil, 1990).

Loraux, Nicole, *La Voix endeuillée. Essai sur la tragédie grecque* (Paris: Gallimard, 1999).

Thébaud, Françoise, 'La guerre et le deuil chez les femmes françaises', in Jean-Jacques Becker *et al.*, *Guerre et cultures, 1914–1918* (Paris: Armand Colin, 1994), pp. 103–10.

Trevisan Carine, *Les Fables du deuil. La Grande Guerre: mort et écriture* (Paris: PUF, 2001).

Commemoration

Barcellini, Serge, 'Sur deux journées nationales commémorant la déportation et les persécutions des "Années noires" ', *Vingtième siècle. Revue d'histoire*, 45, 1995, pp. 75–98.

Dalisson, Rémi, 'La célébration du 11 novembre, ou l'enjeu de la mémoire combattante dans l'entre-deux-guerres (1918–1939)', *Guerres mondiales et conflits contemporains*, 192, 1998, pp. 5–23.

Dolot, Général, *Les Tombes militaires et le Souvenir français en Tunisie (1881–1923)* (Tunis: 1930).

Fratissier, Michel, 'À l'origine de la panthéonisation de Jean Moulin', in Jean Sagnes (ed.), *Jean Moulin et son temps (1899–1943)* (Perpignan: Presses Universitaires de Perpignan, 2000), pp. 145–54.

Institut d'histoire du temps présent, *La mémoire des Français. 40 ans de commémorations de la Seconde Guerre mondiale* (Paris: CNRS, 1986).

Le Bail, Benjamin, *La Mémoire de l'occupation allemande à Jersey*, thesis for Masters degree, Université Rennes 2/CRHISCO, 2001.

Namer, Gérard, *La Commémoration en France, de 1945 à nos jours* (Paris: L'Harmattan, 1987).

Nora, Pierre (ed.), *Les Lieux de mémoire* (Paris: Gallimard, 1984–1992), 7 volumes.

Piehler, Kurt G., *Remembering War. The American Way* (Washington, DC & London: Smithsonian Institution Press, 1995).

Tison, Stéphane, 'La violence et la foi. Discours de prêtres sur la guerre dans la Marne et la Sarthe, 1871–1939', in *Annales de Bretagne et des Pays de l'Ouest*, vol. 108, 3, September 2001, pp. 87–116.

Weygand, Général, *Le 11 novembre* (Paris: Flammarion, 1932).

Winter, Jay, *Sites of Memory, Sites of Mourning. The Great War in European Cultural History* (Cambridge: Cambridge University Press, 1995).

Winter, Jay, and Emmanuel Sivan (eds), *War and Remembrance in the Twentieth Century* (Cambridge: Cambridge University Press, 1999).

Ypersele, Laurence van, and Axel Tixhon, 'Célébrations de novembre 1918 au royaume de Belgique', *Vingtième siècle. Revue d'histoire*, 67, July–September 2000, pp. 61–78.

Monuments

Amato, Alain, *Les Monuments en exil* (Paris: Éditions de l'Alanthrope, 1979).

Armand, Paul-Noël, 'Léon Besnardeau a inventé la carte postale commémorative', *La Province du Maine*, 17, 1991.

Barcellini, Serge, and Annette Wieviorka, *Passant, souviens-toi! Les lieux du souvenir de la Seconde Guerre mondiale en France* (Paris: Plon, 1995).

Becker, Annette, *Les Monuments aux morts, mémoire de la Grande Guerre* (Paris: Éditions Errance, 1988).

Becker, Annette, 'Les monuments aux morts après la guerre de Sécession et la guerre de 1870–1871. Un legs de la guerre nationaliste', *Guerres mondiales et conflits contemporains*, 167, 1992, pp. 23–40.

Bodet, Georges (ed.), *Miroirs de l'histoire. Les monuments aux morts de l'Anjou* (Angers: ECA3, 1999).

Boniface, Xavier, 'L'aumônerie militaire israélite pendant la Grande Guerre', *Archives juives. Revue d'histoire des Juifs de France*, 33/1, March 2000.

Brice, Catherine, *Monumentalité publique et politique à Rome, le Vittoriano* (Rome: École française de Rome, 1998).

Hervé, Pierrick, *Le Deuil, la Patrie. Construire la mémoire communale de la Grande Guerre, l'exemple du département de la Vienne*, thesis, Université de Poitiers, 1998.

Hervé, Pierrick, 'La mémoire communale de la Grande Guerre: l'exemple du département de la Vienne', *Guerres mondiales et conflits contemporains*, 192, 1998, pp. 45–59.

Landau, Philippe, 'Le monument de Douaumont (1938): l'appel à la fraternité dans une France tourmentée', *Archives juives*, 28/1, 1995, pp. 86–90.

'Les monuments aux morts de la Première Guerre mondiale', special issue of *Guerres mondiales et conflits contemporains*, 167, July 1992.

Moisan, Hervé, *Sentinelles de pierre. Les monuments aux morts de la Guerre de 1914–1918 dans la Nièvre* (Saint-Pourçain-sur-Sioule: Bleu Autour, 1999).

Prost, Antoine, 'Les monuments aux morts, culte républicain? culte civique? culte patriotique?', in Pierre Nora (ed.), *Les Lieux de mémoire, I, La République* (Paris: Gallimard, 1984).

Sauber, Marianne, 'Traces fragiles. Les plaques commémoratives dans les rues de Paris', *Annales ESC*, 3, 1993, pp. 715–28.

Tillier, Bertrand, 'Le monument aux martyrs d'Oradour-sur-Glane par Fenosa', *Vingtième siècle. Revue d'histoire*, 55, 1997, pp. 43–57.

Index